COMPULSIVE BEAUTY

OCTOBER BOOKS

Annette Michelson, Rosalind Krauss, Yve-Alain Bois, Benjamin Buchloh, Hal Foster, Denis Hollier, and John Rajchman, editors

Compulsive Beauty

Hal Foster

an OCTOBER book

The MIT Press
Cambridge, Massachusetts
London, England

Third printing, 1997
First MIT Press paperback edition, 1995

This book was set in Bembo by DEKR Corporation and was printed and bound in the United States of America.

Library of Congress Cataloging-in-Publication Data

Foster, Hal.
  Compulsive beauty / Hal Foster.
    p.   cm.
  "An October book."
  Includes bibliographical references and index.
  ISBN 0-262-06160-0 (HB), 0-262-56081-X (PB)
  1. Surrealism.   2. Erotic art.   3. Psychoanalysis and art.
  I. Title.
  N6494.S8F66   1993
  709'.04'063—dc20

                                                    93-19023
                                                        CIP

For Elizabeth Foss Foster

Contents

Interpretive delirium begins only when man, ill-prepared, is taken by a sudden fear in the *forest of symbols*.

—André Breton, *L'Amour fou* (1937)

Max Ernst, *The Swan Is Very Peaceful,* 1920.

In 1916 André Breton was an assistant in a neuropsychiatric clinic at Saint-Dizier. There he tended a soldier who believed that the war was a fake, with the wounded made up cosmetically and the dead on loan from medical schools. The soldier intrigued the young Breton: here was a figure shocked into another reality that was also somehow a critique of this reality. But Breton never developed the implications of this origin story of surrealism, and the usual accounts of the movement do not mention it. For these accounts present surrealism as Breton wanted it to be seen, as a movement of love and liberation, and this story speaks rather of traumatic shock, deadly desire, compulsive repetition. My essay is an attempt to see surrealism from this other side, in a way that might comprehend such a crazy scene. In this respect it is the origin story of my text as well.[1]

✤ ✤

Over the last decade surrealism has returned with a vengeance, the subject of many exhibitions, symposia, books, and articles. Lest I merely add another line to the list, I want to begin my essay with a reflection on the past repression and present recovery of this movement. For not so long ago surrealism was played down in Anglo-American accounts of modernism (if not in French ones). In effect it was lost twice to such art history: repressed in abstractionist histories founded on cubism (where it appears, if at all, as a morbid interregnum before abstract expressionism), it was also displaced in neo-avant-garde accounts focused on dada and Russian constructivism (where it appears, if at all, as a decadent version of vanguardist attempts to integrate art and life).

In Anglo-American formalism surrealism was considered a deviant art movement: improperly visual and impertinently literary, relatively inattentive to the imperatives of form and mostly indifferent to the laws of genre, a paradoxical avant-garde concerned with infantile states and outmoded forms, not properly modernist at all.[2] For neo-avant-garde artists who challenged this hegemonic model three decades ago, its very deviance might have made surrealism an attractive object: as an *impensé* of cubocentric art history, it might have exposed the ideological limitations of this narrative. But such was not the case. Since this formalist model of modernism was staked on the autonomy of modern art as separate from social practice and grounded in visual experience, its antagonist, the neo-avant-garde account of modernism, stressed the two movements, dada and constructivism, that appeared most opposed to this visualist autonomy—that sought to destroy the separate institution of art in an anarchic attack on its formal conventions, as did dada, or to transform it according to the materialist practices of a revolutionary society, as did constructivism.[3] Again surrealism was lost in the shuffle. To the neo-avant-gardists who challenged the formalist account in the 1950s and 1960s, it too appeared corrupt: technically kitschy, philosophically subjectivist, hypocritically elitist. Hence when artists involved in pop and minimalism turned away from the likes of Picasso and Matisse, they turned to such figures as Duchamp and Rodchenko, not to precedents like Ernst and Giacometti.[4]

Obviously times have changed. The formalist ideal of optical purity has long since fallen, and the avant-gardist critique of categorical art is fatigued, at least in practices that limit "institution" to exhibition space and "art" to traditional media. A space for surrealism has opened up: an *impensé* within the old narrative, it has become a privileged point for the contemporary critique of this narrative. And yet for the most part art history has filled this new space with the same old stuff.[5] Despite its redefining of the image, surrealism is still often reduced to painting; and despite its confounding of reference and intention, surrealism is still often folded into discourses of iconography and style. One reason for this art-historical failure is a neglect of the other principal precondition for the return of surrealism as an object of study: the dual demands of contemporary art and theory.

Again, in the 1960s and 1970s minimal and conceptual artists concerned with the phenomenological effects and the institutional frames of art turned to dada and constructivism for support. However, in the 1970s and 1980s these concerns developed beyond such historical tropisms: on the one hand, into a critique of media images and institutional apparatuses, and, on the other, into an analysis of the sexual determination of subjectivity and the social construction of identity—an analysis first prompted by feminist critiques and then developed by gay and lesbian ones. Although the surrealists were hardly critical of heterosexism, they were concerned with the imbrication of the sexual in the visual, of the unconscious in the real; indeed, they introduced this problematic into modern art in a programmatic way. Feminist and gay and lesbian critiques have compelled such questions to be asked anew, particularly in a psychoanalytic frame, and to do so historically was to turn to surrealism among other sites.[6] Similarly, as a blind spot in the Anglo-American view of modernism, surrealism became a retroactive point of reference for postmodernist art, especially of its critique of representation. In the 1980s this critique was often advanced through allegorical appropriations, especially of media images. Like the troubling of identity by sexuality, this troubling of reality via the simulacrum was also undertaken by surrealism, and to be involved in this problematic was to become interested in this art.[7]

Although I only touch on these contemporary concerns here, they are immanent to my approach, and this leads to another incentive to rethink

———

surrealism today. Especially when extended to such figures as Duchamp and Bataille, surrealism is a site of an agonistic modernism within official modernism—again, a crucial reference for a critical postmodernism. Today, however, this particular battle appears won (the greater war is another matter), and if formalist modernism is not the totalistic Blue Meany it was often made out to be, Duchamp, Bataille and company are no longer the *bêtes noires* they once were.[8] And yet this countermodernist status is not the only surrealist claim to critical value now. For surrealism is also the nodal point of the three fundamental discourses of modernity—psychoanalysis, cultural Marxism, and ethnology—all of which inform surrealism as it in turn develops them. Indeed, the great elaborations of these discourses are initiated in its milieu. It was there that Jacques Lacan first developed the Freudian concept of narcissism into the famous model of the mirror stage, i.e., of the emergence of the subject in an imaginary situation of (mis)recognition, of identification, alienation, and aggressivity.[9] (Along the way I will also suggest the deferred action of surrealism on Lacanian conceptions of desire and the symptom, trauma and repetition, paranoia and the gaze.) It was there too that Walter Benjamin and Ernst Bloch first developed the Marxian notion of the uneven development of productive modes and social relations into a cultural politics of the outmoded and the nonsynchronous—of a critical reinscription of old images and structures of feeling in the present. Finally, it was there that Georges Bataille, Roger Caillois, and Michel Leiris first developed Maussian accounts of the ambivalence of gift exchange and the collectivity of *la fête* into a radical critique of the equivalence of commodity exchange and the egotism of bourgeois self-interest. These elaborations are important to much postwar art and theory—which points again to the genealogical connections between surrealism and recent practice, even as it also suggests a triangulated set of concepts with which to map surrealism. Contemporary criticism has treated such concepts, to be sure, but not in concert.[10] As a result, no general theory of surrealism has emerged that does not rehearse its partisan descriptions or impose alien ideas upon it. This essay attempts to address some of these wants.

Heretofore art history has framed surrealism in terms of traditional categories (with "objects" sometimes substituted for "sculpture") and/or surrealist self-definitions (e.g., automatism, dream interpretation), despite the fact that the principal figures of the movement often questioned both types of terms. For example, in the early years the surrealists devoted little theoretical reflection to painting; in the 1924 "Manifesto of Surrealism" Breton addressed it only as an afterthought, in a footnoted list of mostly historical painters deemed surrealist *avant la lettre*. And when they did consider painting it was often in order to argue for other practices in its stead as more psychically incisive and/or socially disruptive; such is the case with the 1930 Aragon manifesto "La Peinture au défi" (Challenge to Painting) and the 1936 Ernst treatise "Au-delà de la peinture" (Beyond Painting), the titles of which alone point to such predilections.[11] Later, of course, Breton did present an account of surrealism in terms of painting—as an art suspended between automatist gesture and oneiric depiction.[12] But this model was also advanced to recruit artists and to gain support, and it is partly due to the institutional bias of art history and art museum alike that it has remained the dominant definition.

Lost in this dominance are not only alternative practices (e.g., the more anthropological concerns of Bataille, Leiris, and others; the more political activities of Pierre Naville, René Crevel, and others) but also contemporary critiques of this definition. After all, Breton developed his formula in defense against critiques of surrealist painting—*critiques made in the name of surrealism,* i.e., in the name of a radical exploration of the unconscious rather than an aesthetic treatment of it. In the first issue of the first surrealist journal *La Révolution surréaliste,* Max Morise wrote that "stream of thought cannot be viewed statically" and that "secondary attention necessarily distorts an image"—in other words, that automatism was extrinsic to visual art and that the dream was compromised by pictorial ratiocination. His judgment was clear: "The images are surrealist, but not their expression."[13] Two issues later Pierre Naville was more contemptuous of the Bretonian formula of surrealist painting. Though residually futurist, the argument of this early surrealist convert to the Communist Party was also socially historical: that painting is at once too mediated to express the unconscious and not mediated enough to capture the technological spectacle of twentieth-century life. At the very moment that Russian constructivists declared the anachronism of bourgeois painting in the new collectivist order of the communist East, Naville suggested its obsolescence in the new spectacular order of the capitalist West:

> I have no tastes except distaste. Masters, master crooks, smear your canvases. Everyone knows there is no *surrealist painting*. Neither the marks of a pencil abandoned to the accident of gesture, nor the image retracing the forms of the dream, nor imaginative fantasies, of course, can be described.
>
> But there are *spectacles*. . . . The cinema, not because it is life, but the marvelous, the grouping of chance elements. The street, kiosks, automobiles, screeching doors, lamps bursting the sky. Photographs. . . .[14]

Despite its enthusiasm for spectacle, this polemic is also proto-situationist, and surrealist precedents did inspire situationist practices of *dérive* and *détournement*.[15] More important here is the early recognition that no given categories, aesthetic *or* surrealist, could comprehend surrealism conceptually—could account for its heterogeneous practices or address its quintessential concerns with psychic conflict and social contradiction.

Another model is still needed, and I propose one here. In my reading automatism is not the only key, nor the dream the royal road, to the unconscious of surrealism.[16] I want to locate a problematic in surrealism that exceeds its self-understanding, and in this regard neither the stylistic analysis that still dominates art history, nor the social history that has done much to transform the discipline, will suffice. However, neither can this problematic be derived apart from surrealism and then projected back upon it, as sometimes occurs in semiotic analyses.[17] If there is a concept that comprehends surrealism, it must be contemporary with it, immanent to its field; and it is partly the historicity of this concept that concerns me here.

I believe this concept to be *the uncanny,* that is to say, a concern with events in which repressed material returns in ways that disrupt unitary identity, aesthetic norms, and social order. In my argument the surrealists not only are drawn to the return of the repressed but also seek to redirect this return to critical ends. Thus I will claim that the uncanny is crucial to particular surrealist oeuvres as well as to general surrealist notions (e.g., the marvelous, convulsive beauty, and objective chance). In this respect the concept of the uncanny is not merely contemporaneous with surrealism, developed by Freud from concerns shared by the movement, but also indicative of many of its activities. Moreover, it resonates with the aforementioned notions, Marxian and ethnological, that inform surrealism, particularly its interest in the outmoded and "the primitive."[18]

My essay is thus theoretical. This does not automatically render it ahistorical, for again the concepts I bring to bear on surrealism, derived from Freud and Marx and inflected by Lacan and Benjamin, are active in its milieu.[19] My essay is also thus textual. But I do not regard the uncanny as a mere iconography of surrealism: it cannot be seen in this object or that text; it must be read there, not imposed from above but (as it were) extracted from below, often in the face of surrealist resistance. This textual emphasis is not meant to deprecate the art (its formulaic versions are fairer game). On the contrary, it is to take surrealism as seriously as possible: not as a sundry collection of idiosyncratic visions but as a related set of complex practices, one that develops its own ambiguous conceptions of aesthetics, politics, and history through difficult involvements in desire and sexuality, the unconscious and the drives. In short, surrealism for me is less an object to be subjected to theory than a theoretical object productive of its own critical concepts.

Now if the experience of the uncanny is not foreign to the surrealists, the concept of the uncanny is not familiar.[20] When they do intuit it, they often resist it, as its ramifications run counter to the surrealist faith in love and liberation. Nonetheless, they remain drawn to its manifestations, indeed to any reappearance of repressed material. This is the basis of surrealist connections between symbols and symptoms, beauty and hysteria, critical interpretations and paranoid projections. It is also the link that connects the early experiments in automatic writing, dream recitals, and mediumistic sessions to the later involvements in hysteria, fetishism, and paranoia.

Therein lies the efficacy of the uncanny as a principle of order that clarifies the disorder of surrealism. Yet I do not mean to recoup surrealism for any system, psychoanalytic or aesthetic. Rather, I hope to deontologize it as I defamiliarize it: to ask *how* is the surreal rather than *what* is surrealism. It is for this reason that I juxtapose it with the uncanny. No doubt this reading will appear sometimes obscure and tendentious, sometimes obvious and tautological. On the one hand, the uncanny is nowhere directly thought in surrealism; it remains mostly in its unconscious. On the other hand, it is everywhere treated in surrealism; it is all but proposed, in the most famous definition of surrealism, as its very "point":

> Everything tends to make us believe that there exists a certain point of the mind at which life and death, the real and the imagined, past and future, the communicable and the incommunicable, high and low, cease to be perceived as contradictions. Now, search as one may one will never find any other motivating force in the activities of the Surrealists than the hope of finding and fixing this point.[21]

The paradox of surrealism, the ambivalence of its most important practi-tioners, is this: even as they work to find this point they do not want to be pierced by it, for the real and the imagined, the past and the future only come together in the experience of the uncanny, and its stake is death.

❦ ❦

To read surrealism in terms of the uncanny is to regard it obliquely: no one object of inquiry, no simple line of argument, will suffice. Hence I deal with an anamorphic array of practices and texts in the belief that the return of the repressed not only structures the central oeuvres of surrealism but also surfaces in its marginal sites. (I hope my map will be of use in other regions of the surrealist forest of symbols too, e.g., film.)

In order to argue a connection between the surreal and the uncanny, the encounter of surrealism with psychoanalysis must first be sketched. This is done in chapter 1, where I also rehearse the difficult development of the theories of the uncanny and the death drive in Freud. In my account the surrealists are led toward these principles by their own research, and the result is an intense ambivalence.

Chapter 2 considers the surrealist categories of the marvelous, convul-sive beauty, and objective chance in terms of the uncanny—as anxious crossings of contrary states, as hysterical confusings of different identities. Here a reading of two Breton novels reveals that the two primary forms of objective chance, the unique encounter and the found object, are not objec-tive, unique, or found in any simple sense. Rather, they are uncanny, and this to the degree that they invoke past and/or fantasmatic traumas.

In chapter 2, I propose a reading of the surrealist object as a failed refinding of a lost object. In chapter 3, with the art of Giorgio de Chirico, Max Ernst, and Alberto Giacometti in mind, I suggest an account of the surrealist image as a repetitive collaging of a primal fantasy. The risks for these artists are high: even as they deploy psychosexual disturbance—to disrupt conventional pictorial space (de Chirico), artistic identity (Ernst),

and object relations (Giacometti)—so too are they threatened by it. And yet
the rewards are also great, for they are led to new types of artistic practice
("metaphysical" painting, collage techniques, and "symbolic" objects respectively), indeed to a new conception of art: the image as an enigmatic
trace of a traumatic experience and/or fantasy, ambiguous in its curative
and destructive effects.

In chapter 4 I propose as a *summa* of surrealism a body of work often
shunted to its margins: the tableaux of *poupées* (dolls) by Hans Bellmer.
These erotic and traumatic scenes point to difficult intricacies of sadism and
masochism, of desire, defusion, and death. Such concerns are at the core of
surrealism, and at this core it splits into its Bretonian and Bataillean factions.
The *poupées* will help us to define this split; they will also point us to a
critical connection between surrealism and fascism.

If in chapters 2 and 3 I argue that surrealism works over the traumas
of individual experience, in chapters 5 and 6 I suggest that surrealism also
treats the shocks of capitalist society. Chapter 5 develops in a social register
the uncanny confusion between animate and inanimate states discussed in a
psychic register in chapter 2. Here I read such surrealist figures as the
automaton and the mannequin in terms of a traumatic becoming machine
and/or commodity of the body. In this way the surrealists open up a social-
historical dimension of the uncanny.

This dimension is explored further in chapter 6, which considers in
collective terms the uncanny return of past states discussed in subjective
terms in chapter 3. Here I argue that surrealism works through historical as
well as psychic repression, and that it does so primarily through a recovery
of outmoded spaces. In this way a question that haunts my text comes into
focus: can the disruptions of the uncanny be consciously, indeed critically,
deployed—and in a social-historical frame?

Finally, in chapter 7 I propose that surrealism is governed by two
psychic states above all: on the one hand, a fantasy of maternal plenitude,
of an auratic, pre-Oedipal space-time before any loss or division; on the
other hand, a fantasy of paternal punishment, of an anxious, Oedipal space-

time where "man, ill-prepared, is taken by a sudden fear in the *forest of symbols.*"[22] Here, for all its claims to erotic liberation, the heterosexist determinations of this movement are clear—though I also suggest that they are not as fixed as they first appear. In a brief conclusion I return to some of these more problematic points.

⁌ ⁍

It is a pleasure to thank friends who have incited this text in different ways. For over a decade Rosalind Krauss has worked to rethink surrealism, and to do so in an expanded frame, most recently in *The Optical Unconscious.* Although we often take different directions, I make my way in parallax with hers. I am also grateful to Susan Buck-Morss, whose work on Walter Benjamin and Theodor Adorno has clarified certain aspects of surrealism for me. For more indirect assistance I want to thank my friends Thatcher Bailey, Charles Wright, and Alla Efimova; all my colleagues at *October* and *Zone,* but especially Benjamin Buchloh, Jonathan Crary, Michel Feher, and Denis Hollier; as well as Anthony Vidler, who worked on his *Architectural Uncanny* as I worked on my surrealist version. Thanks also to Roger Conover, Matthew Abbate, and Yasuyo Iguchi at the MIT Press. I am grateful to the Department of Art History at the University of Michigan for the opportunity to present an initial draft of the book as a seminar series in April 1990. Its final writing was supported by a Paul Mellon Fellowship from the Center for Advanced Study in the Visual Arts.

For support of other kinds I once again thank my executive director-producer, Sandy Tait, and my counterparts in Oedipal crime, Thomas, Tait, and Thatcher Foster. Finally, however, an essay with a topic like mine can be dedicated to one person alone. In "The Uncanny" Freud dwells for a moment on the figure of the mother. "There is a humorous saying," he writes, "'Love is homesickness.'"[23] So it is for me too.

Ithaca, Summer 1992

COMPULSIVE BEAUTY

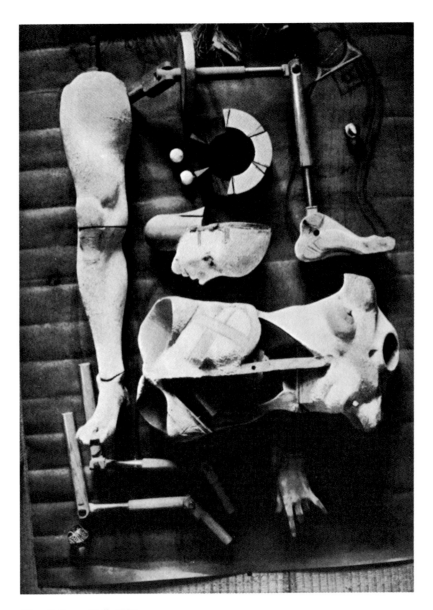

Hans Bellmer, *Doll*, 1934.

Beyond the Pleasure Principle?

In the first year of World War I, 18-year-old André Breton was a medical student. In 1916 he assisted Raoul Leroy, a former assistant to Jean-Marie Charcot, the famous choreographer of hysteria, at the neuropsychiatric clinic of the Second Army at Saint-Dizier. In 1917 he interned under Joseph Babinski, another former student of Charcot, at the neurological center at La Pitié; and later in 1917 he worked as a *médecin auxiliaire* at Val-de-Grâce, where he met Louis Aragon, also a medical student. Treatment at these institutions included free association and dream interpretation, the very techniques that inspired the automatist devices of early surrealism. Just as significant, however, is that Breton first intuited the existence of a psychic (sur)reality on the basis of the *délires aigus* of the soldiers under care there— i.e., symptoms of shock, of traumatic neurosis, of scenes of death compulsively restaged. It was partly on such evidence and precisely at this time that Freud developed the notion of compulsive repetition essential to the theories of the uncanny and the death drive.

Thus it was in a medical milieu that the young surrealists were exposed to (proto)psychoanalytical categories. This is ironic for a few reasons. First, this milieu was as hostile to psychoanalysis as it was to surrealism. Second, surrealism was predicated on the *extra*medical use of such categories, which were both proclaimed as aesthetic (e.g., hysteria as "the greatest poetic discovery of the nineteenth century")[1] and adapted as critical (e.g., the paranoid-critical method). These two ironies lead to a third: crucial though surrealism was to the French reception of Freud, it did not embrace him easily; the relationship was vexed, especially for Breton.[2]

Breton first knew psychoanalysis only through summaries. Not until 1922 could he begin to read Freud in translation, and even then the works important to my account appeared rather late (e.g., *Essais de psychanalyse*, which included "Beyond the Pleasure Principle" and "The Ego and the Id," in 1927, and *Essais de psychanalyse appliqué*, which included "The Uncanny," in 1933).[3] There was a personal clash: Freud disappointed Breton when they met in Vienna in 1921, and in 1932 Breton piqued Freud when Breton accused him of self-censorship in *The Interpretation of Dreams*.[4] And then there were theoretical differences. First, they differed on the value of hypnosis: whereas surrealism began with hypnotic sessions, psychoanalysis commenced with the abandonment of hypnosis, or so Freud often insisted.[5] So, too, they disagreed on the nature of dreams: while Breton saw them as portents of desire, Freud read them as ambiguous fulfillments of conflictual wishes. For Breton dreams and reality were *vases communicants,* and surrealism was pledged to this mystical communication; for Freud the two were in a relation of distorted displacement, and the very antirationality of surrealism on this score made it suspect.[6] Finally, they differed on questions of art, both on specifics (Freud was conservative in taste) and on essentials. Freud regarded art as a process of sublimation, not a project of desublimation, as a negotiation of instinctual renunciation, not a transgression of cultural prohibition. Breton is not his complete opposite here, but he did oscillate between these poles: drawn to sublimation but leery of its passive aspect, drawn to transgression but leery of its destructive aspect.[7] This list of differences could be extended; suffice it to say that surrealism does not merely illustrate psychoanalysis, or even serve it loyally. The relation of the two is a magnetic field of strong attractions and subtle repulsions.

Part of the problem was that the surrealists received psychoanalysis in a context dominated by the psychiatry of Jean-Marie Charcot and Pierre Janet, the first a teacher of Freud (with whom he had to break in order to found psychoanalysis), the second a rival (with whom he quarreled about precedent), not to mention the psychiatry of Emil Kraepelin (who was openly hostile to Freud). This Janetian orientation was also tactical for Breton, for it allowed him to privilege automatist techniques far more than did Freud, who, though he practiced free association, did so in part to be rid of hypnosis and always in the service of interpretation. In this way Breton developed a conception of the unconscious at a remove from Freudian models of conflictual forces, a conception of a *champ magnétique* of associations registered through automatist means, an unconscious based on originary unity rather than primal repression. Indeed, in the "Manifesto" (1924) Breton defines surrealism "once and for all" in Janetian terms as "psychic automatism," and, again, early surrealism was given over to automatist texts and hypnotic sessions.[8]

However, the difficulties with Freud were nothing compared to the conflicts with Janet and company. For Janet psychic phenomena were "dissociated," without symbolic value, a matter of mental disorder, not of artistic vision. This normative stance was attacked by the surrealists, who railed against the psychiatric discipline first in "Lettre aux médecins-clefs des asiles de fous" (1925) and then in *Nadja* (1928), where Breton charged that "madmen are *made* there."[9] Janet, along with Paul Abély and G. G. de Clérambault (a teacher of Lacan), counterattacked: Janet dismissed the surrealists as "obsessives" and Clérambault as *procédistes* (i.e., mannerists committed to formulas that only masqueraded as freedoms). This delighted Breton, who preserved these peevish responses as an epigraphic foil to his "Second Manifesto of Surrealism" (1930).[10]

This debate about psychiatry is important, but more pertinent here are the divergent valuations given automatism. Even as Janet and company stressed automatism they feared it might produce a "disintegration of personality."[11] Thus in order to affirm automatism Breton had to transvalue it,

3

viewed as it was negatively as a psychological threat by the French school and indifferently as a technical means by Freud. Perhaps its nugatory status appealed to Breton; by its appropriation he could affront both the scientism of French psychiatry and the rationalism of Freud.[12] In any case, contra Freud Breton made automatism central to surrealism, and contra the French school he recoded it: far from a dissociation of personality, automatism was seen to reassociate such diverse dichotomies as perception and representation, madness and reason (for Janet such "synthesis" could only be conscious). Thus the importance of psychic automatism to Bretonian surrealism: shifted away from strictly therapeutic uses and purely mystical associations, revalued as synthetic end rather than dissociative means, it permitted a conception of the unconscious based less on division than on reconciliation, less on dark primordial and perverse infantile contents à la Freud than on "*one original faculty* of which the eidetic image gives us an idea of which one still finds a trace among primitives and children."[13] Just as importantly, automatism appeared to access this idyllic space, or at least to record its liberatory images: "Surrealism begins from that point."[14]

And yet this charmed conception of the unconscious was soon challenged, not only extrinsically by Freudian models but also intrinsically in automatist practice. Although automatism was embraced because it seemed to offer a reconciliatory, even Hegelian conception of the unconscious, its logic pushed the surrealists toward recognitions in line with the late Freudian theory of a primal struggle between life and death drives—or so I want to suggest. In any case, the very insistence on a primal unity to be attained through the unconscious suggests an intimation of the exact contrary: that psychic life is founded on repression and riven by conflict.

Of course, Breton and company framed the question of automatism very differently. For them the problem was one of authenticity, i.e., of the threat posed by calculation and correction to the pure presence of the automatist psyche.[15] But this formulation missed the more fundamental problem—that automatism might not be liberatory at all, not because it voided the controls of the (super)ego (such was its express purpose) but because it decentered the subject too radically in relation to the unconscious. In short, the question of the constraints of the conscious mind obscured the more important question of the constraints of the *unconscious* mind. In many ways the fact that Bretonian surrealism confused decentering with liberation, psychic disturbance with social revolt, made for the aporia around which it swirled. This aporia was often manifested as an ambivalence: on the one hand, the surrealists desired this decentering (as Breton proclaimed in 1920 and Ernst reaffirmed in 1936, surrealism was pledged against "the principle of identity");[16] on the other hand, they feared this decentering, and automatist practice exposed its risks most dramatically. For automatism revealed a compulsive mechanism that threatened a literal *désagrégation* of the subject, and in doing so it pointed to a different unconscious from the one projected by Bretonian surrealism—an unconscious not unitary or liberatory at all but primally conflicted, instinctually repetitive.

The surrealists were not oblivious to this aspect of automatism. In the *époque des sommeils* death was an obsessive theme (the hypnotic sessions were terminated when an entranced Robert Desnos stalked a less-than-enthralled Paul Eluard with a kitchen knife), and in *Surrealism and Painting* Breton relates the psychic state achieved through automatism to nirvana.[17] This state is also described as "mechanical," and in the first text in *La Révolution surréaliste* 1 automatism is figured by automatons: "Already, automatons multiply and dream."[18] This association suggests the full ambiguity of surrealist automatism: a "magical dictation" that renders one a mechanical automaton, a recording machine, an uncanny being because ambiguously sentient, neither animate nor inanimate, double and other in one.[19] One is possessed marvelously but mechanically, like the eighteenth-century automaton cherished by the surrealists, the *Young Writer* of Pierre Jacquet-Droz, who scratched the same words again and again—a "marvelous" figure perhaps, but driven rather than free.

What is this compulsive mechanism at work in automatism? To what principle does it attest? "All is written," Breton proclaimed as the automatist motto.[20] He meant this statement metaphysically (not deconstructively), but

Pierre Jacquet-Droz, *Young Writer*, c. 1770.

it can be read in another way too: "all is written" in the sense that inscribed in each of us is our end, our death.[21] Like the major Bretonian categories that issued from it (the marvelous, convulsive beauty, objective chance), surrealist automatism speaks of psychic mechanisms of compulsive repetition and death drive—speaks of them in the register of the uncanny.[22] It is to this notion that I want to turn.

⁙ ⁙

As is well known, the uncanny for Freud involves the return of a familiar phenomenon (image or object, person or event) made strange by repression. This return of the repressed renders the subject anxious and the phenomenon ambiguous, and this anxious ambiguity produces the primary effects of the uncanny: (1) an indistinction between the real and the imagined, which is the basic aim of surrealism as defined in both manifestoes of Breton; (2) a confusion between the animate and the inanimate, as exemplified in wax figures, dolls, mannequins, and automatons, all crucial images in the surrealist repertoire; and (3) a usurpation of the referent by the sign or of physical reality by psychic reality, and here again the surreal is often experienced, especially by Breton and Dalí, as an eclipse of the referential by the symbolic, or as an enthrallment of a subject to a sign or a symptom, and its effect is often that of the uncanny: anxiety. "The most remarkable coincidences of desire and fulfilment, the most mysterious recurrence of similar experiences in a particular place or on a particular date, the most deceptive sights and suspicious noises."[23] This sounds like the marvelous according to the surrealists; it is in fact the uncanny according to Freud.

Freud traces the estrangement of the familiar that is essential to the uncanny in the very etymology of the German term: *unheimlich* (uncanny) derives from *heimlich* (homelike), to which several senses of the word return.[24] Freud asks us to think this origin both literally and fantasmatically; here he comments on the uncanniness of female genitals for male subjects:

This *unheimlich* place, however, is the entrance to the former *heim* of all human beings, to the place where everyone dwelt once upon a time and in the beginning. There is a humorous saying: "Love is homesickness"; and whenever a man dreams of a place or a country and says to himself, still in the dream, "this place is familiar to me, I have been there before," we may interpret the place as being his mother's genitals or her body. In this case, too, the *unheimlich* is what was once *heimisch,* homelike, familiar; the prefix "un" is the token of repression.[25]

This uncanny homesickness is evoked in important apprehensions of the surreal, as is the primal fantasy of intrauterine existence. Indeed, all the primal fantasies according to Freud (seduction, castration, the primal scene or the witnessing of parental sex, as well as intrauterine existence) are active in surrealist reflections concerning subjectivity and art. And whenever we encounter such reflections certain questions will recur: are these fantasies defined in terms of heterosexual masculinity? Are the uncanny and the surreal as well? How does sexual difference, difference vis-à-vis castration, impact upon this apprehension?

Primal fantasies involve infantile and/or primordial states, which are also active in the uncanny: "An uncanny experience occurs either when repressed infantile complexes have been revived by some impression, or when the primitive beliefs we have surmounted seem once more to be confirmed."[26] Among such "primitive" beliefs Freud notes "animistic mental activity" and "omipotence of thought," magic and witchcraft, the evil eye and the double—several of which were also entertained by the surrealists.[27] Some assumed doubles (e.g., the "Loplop" persona of Max Ernst), while others examined the evil eye either specifically in anthropological terms or generally in psychoanalytical terms—in terms, that is, of the gaze.[28] These two avatars of the uncanny, both of which obsessed the surrealists, suggest why the uncanny produces anxiety, for the evil eye represents the gaze as a castrative threat, while the double, according to Freud, represents a once protective figure transformed by repression into a "ghastly harbinger of death."[29] For Freud the evocation of these two repressed states, castration and death, epitomizes the uncanny.[30] Yet for a long time (at least the six years since *Totem and Taboo* [1913]) he could not grasp the principle at work in these strange returns of the repressed, the dynamic of these repetitions. Obviously it was not that of pleasure (at least as heretofore conceived), to which the psyche had appeared to be pledged. Whatever it was, it held the key not only to the uncanny but to a new conception of desire and sexuality, the unconscious and the drives.

Freud only completed "The Uncanny" in May 1919, a month or two after he drafted *Beyond the Pleasure Principle;* it was this text that provided the catalytic concept for the essay. There exists, Freud now argued, an instinctual compulsion to repeat, to return to a prior state, "a principle powerful enough to overrule the pleasure principle"; and it is this compulsion that renders certain phenomena "daemonic": "whatever reminds us of this inner repetition-compulsion is perceived as uncanny."[31] If we are to grasp the surreal in terms of the uncanny, we must be acquainted with its theoretical basis, i.e., with the final Freudian model of a struggle between life and death drives as intuited in "The Uncanny" and articulated in *Beyond the Pleasure Principle* and related texts. Significantly, Freud conceived this "beyond" of the pleasure principle on the basis of evidence that, though heterogeneous, is hardly extrinsic to the experiences and/or interests of the primary surrealists: the play of infants at the point of language, the traumatic neuroses of World War I veterans, and the compulsive repetition (as opposed to the concerted recollection) of repressed material in analytic treatment. I will focus on the first two instances (as does Freud in *Beyond the Pleasure Principle*); the third type of repetition will be discussed in chapter 2.[32]

The specific play that intrigued Freud was the famous *fort/da* game devised by his eighteen-month-old grandson with a string attached to a spool. In order actively to master rather than passively to suffer the periodic disappearances of his mother, the little boy represented the event symbolically: he would throw away the spool, repudiate it (*fort!* gone!), only to recover it with the string, each time with delight (*da!* there!). Freud interpreted the game, which points to the psychic basis in repetition of all representation, as an ingenious way for the infant to compensate for the deprivation of the mother, "the instinctual renunciation" demanded by civilization.[33] Yet this reading did not explain the compulsive repetition of the game: why would the little boy symbolically repeat an event, the disappearance of the mother, that was precisely not pleasant?

An answer came by way of a distant quarter in which Freud worked about the same time: the traumatic neuroses of war veterans fixated on events of fright or shock. The dreams of the soldiers reenacted the traumatic events, and this contradicted the simple idea of the dream as wish fulfillment. The war dreams, Freud eventually speculated, were belated attempts to "prepare" the subject to master the shock of the event, to develop the protective anxiety "whose omission was the cause of the traumatic neurosis."[34] After the fact, with his "protective shield" already breached by excessive stimuli, the soldier subject could only futilely repeat a useless preparation.[35] In this tragic display Freud also saw evidence of a compulsion to repeat, of a principle which overrode that of pleasure.

Compelled by this principle Freud rewrote his theory of the drives. A drive, Freud now held, is "an urge inherent in organic life to restore an earlier state of things," and as the inorganic precedes the organic, "the aim of all life," he concluded in a famous phrase, "is death."[36] In this model the essence of the drive is its conservative nature, its homeostatic goal; death becomes immanent to life, and life a "detour" to death. A new opposition emerges: no longer self-preservative (ego) drives versus sexual drives, but the life drive (which now subsumes the other two) versus the death drive, Eros versus Thanatos. "The aim of [the first] is to establish even greater unities and to preserve them thus—in short, to bind together; the aim of [the second] is, on the contrary, to undo connections and so to destroy things."[37] Yet, as with the first opposition, this one is never pure. The two drives appear only in combination, with the death drive "tinged with eroticism."[38] And the subject is always caught between these two forces, in a state of relative (de)fusion.

This theory is notoriously complicated, not to say contradictory. On the one hand, the repetitions of the infant, the shock victim, and the analysand are attempts respectively to overcome loss, to defend against shock (exogenous or external), to deal with trauma (endogenous or internal); in this regard they appear pledged to the binding or fusion of the subject. On the other hand, these repetitions may also be compulsive; as such they appear pledged to the undoing or defusion of the subject. So when does repetition serve binding and life, and when defusion and death? Moreover, when, in the search of the lost object, is repetition driven by desire, and when by death? If all drives are ultimately conservative, can that of life finally be opposed to that of death? As the formula "an urge inherent in organic life" suggests, the death drive may not be *beyond* the pleasure principle but rather anterior to it: dissolution comes *before* binding—at the level of the cell as well of the ego. In this sense the death drive may be the foundation rather than the exception of the pleasure principle, which may indeed "serve" it.[39] Could it be that this theory, like its object the drive, works to *suspend* such contradictions, that this is its very function?[40] In any case, these complications in Freud also appear in surrealism. In fact, I want to suggest, it is precisely at these points of greatest difficulty—where pleasure and death principles appear to serve one another, where sexual and destructive drives appear identical—that surrealism is at once achieved and undone.

All of this is counterintuitive, to say the least. The death drive theory seems anathema to the surrealist affirmation of love, liberation, and revolution, at least as conventionally thought. And yet if the surreal is bound up with the uncanny, then so too is it bound up with the death drive. In short, just as surrealist automatism suggests not liberation but compulsion, so surrealism in general may celebrate desire only, in the register of the uncanny, to proclaim death. According to this hypothesis, the thrust of surrealism goes against its own ambition. Typically surrealism (automatist, oneiric, or otherwise) is said to contest the reality principle in a celebration of the pleasure principle, to flaunt the self-preservative drives in an embrace of the sexual drives. This is true as far as it goes, which is simply not far enough, for in this celebration the surrealists may be led to a point where "the pleasure principle seems to serve the death instincts,"[41] where self-preservative and sexual drives appear overcoded by a greater destructive force.

A brief outline of the development of the death drive theory will begin to illuminate this deconstructive hypothesis; here I will note only the Freud texts that discuss sadism and masochism, as both terms are crucial not only to his new theory but also to surrealist practice. Several texts announce or develop the insights of "The Uncanny" and *Beyond the Pleasure Principle*. In *Instincts and Their Vicissitudes* (1915), published four years before "The Uncanny" but not translated into French until 1940, the economic conception of the drives is already sketched ("the final goal of every instinct" is to abolish "the condition of stimulation"),[42] and yet the model of self-preservative drives versus sexual drives is still in place. More importantly, sadism is held to be primary and not, as in the death drive theory, masochism. However, on this point Freud is ambiguous, even contradictory, and the possibility of a primary masochism is at least allowed. For in this text Freud first proposed the concept of "drive reversal" by which the aim of the drive moves between active and passive modes, and that of "turning round" by which the subject can become the object of the drive.[43] As I will suggest in chapter 3, such concepts are implicit in surrealist theories of artistic subjectivity.

In "A Child Is Being Beaten," published in German and translated into French in the same years as "The Uncanny" (1919 and 1933 respectively), the primacy of sadism is even more in doubt. Here Freud considers the masochistic fantasy of a little girl patient—that it is she who is beaten by the father—as prior to the distanced version of "a child is being beaten." Finally, in "The Economic Problem of Masochism" (1924), published five years after "The Uncanny" but translated five years earlier (1928), masochism is deemed original and sadism secondary, and the death drive is said to move from the one to the other. In protection of the subject this destructive drive is directed toward the world, where it confronts objects as so many things to master, so many tests of power. When this aggressive relation is sexual it is sadistic; otherwise the destructive drive remains bound within the subject, a condition Freud calls "original erotogenic masochism."[44]

Since the death drive is "tinged with eroticism," pleasure may be felt in destruction and desire aroused by death. Again, this commonality of the sexual and the destructive was intimated by the surrealists; in the form of sadism it fascinated them.[45] Such sadism cannot be excused, but neither should it be dismissed, for Freud not only derives it from masochism as a projection of the death drive, but also situates it at the origin of sexuality. And it is fundamental to surrealism, perhaps evident in its very mandate, in painting, collage, and assemblages alike, to destroy the object as such.[46] Typically directed at figures of woman, this sadism is often compounded with a "punishment" exacted for her putative castration—more precisely, for her projected representation of this state, of its threat to the patriarchal subject.[47] In this respect surrealist images must be subjected to feminist critique.[48] However, it should be remembered that these are representations (whose performativity is open to debate); that they are often ambiguously reflexive about male fantasies, not merely expressive of them; and that the subject positions of these fantasies are more slippery than they first seem. It should also be recalled that underneath this sadism lies a masochism, extreme in certain works (e.g., the *poupées* of Hans Bellmer) but operative throughout surrealism.

Were the surrealists aware of this Freudian model? There are no references to the pertinent texts in surrealist writing before 1929, and only a few thereafter. This silence is not only due to the fact that *Beyond the Pleasure Principle* was not translated until 1927 and "The Uncanny" only in 1933; a resistance is also involved. The death drive theory is a very disputed aspect of Freudian thought. However sympathetic it is to psychoanalysis, surrealism cannot be expected to comprehend a theory of repetition and death, pledged as it is to the service of liberation and love. Or can it?

I noted that death was an obsessive theme in the *époque des sommeils;* the surrealists were also fascinated by suicide.[49] The first surrealist *enquête,* in *La Révolution surréaliste* 2 (January 15, 1925), addresses this subject directly:

> Inquiry: one lives, one dies. What is the role of will in all this? It seems that one kills oneself as one dreams. It is not a moral question that we pose: IS SUICIDE A SOLUTION?[50]

The implication here is that volition plays a minimal role in the mechanisms of life and death, which are "beyond" morality, good and evil, just as the death drive is "beyond" the pleasure principle. This qualification renders the question ambiguous: in what sense is suicide a solution, and a solution to what? Is it a willful act that solves, i.e., concludes, the ennui of life? Or does it bespeak an involuntary mechanism that solves, i.e., completes, the drive to death? In his reply Breton simply quotes Théodore Jouffroy: "Suicide is a badly conceived word; the one who kills is not identical to the one who is killed." For Breton, it seems, suicide does not define the subject so much as it decenters him or her. In short, death is a dissociative principle, not a surrealist one, and it must be opposed to surrealist love—that is to say, it must be distanced from it.

Almost five years later, in *La Révolution surréaliste* 12 (December 15, 1929), Jean Frois-Wittmann, the only French psychoanalyst of the first generation to write for the primary surrealist journals, published a text titled "Les Mobiles inconscients de suicide." Suicide, Frois-Wittmann argues, is prompted not only by melancholy, the inability to surrender a lost love object, but also by the death drive, *"l'appel du néant,"* to which theory he

---

refers.[51] Apart from this citation in a surrealist context, the essay is important because it suggests that the death drive is active not only in sexual desire (as in *la petite mort*) but also in intoxication and reverie, all states to which the surrealists aspired. Significantly, however, Frois-Wittmann resists the ramifications of the theory. In a text published four years later in *Minotaure* 3–4 (December 14, 1933) he places modern art under the aegis of the pleasure principle as if in defense of the "beyond" of this principle. I say "in defense" because Frois-Wittmann argues an "affinity" among modern art (primarily surrealism), psychoanalysis, and "the proletarian movement,"[52] and in order to argue this point he must suspend the defusion posited by the death drive theory, for clearly it impedes any project of affinity, let alone of revolution. Crucial though psychoanalysis was to surrealism, this aspect had to be resisted and/or recoded—not only for the liberatory model of the unconscious (let alone the supreme status of love) to be upheld, but also for the political commitment to revolution (let alone the social cohesion of the group) to be sustained.[53] In this regard perhaps Frois-Wittmann not only introduced the death drive theory to the Bretonian surrealists but also posed its difficult problematic for them.

In any case, Bretonian surrealists were aware of the theory by late 1929 at least. The preface to the program of the first showing of the 1930 Buñuel-Dalí film *L'Age d'or*, written by Breton but signed collectively, includes a section titled "The Sexual Instinct and the Death Instinct."[54] Here Breton engages the concept of the death drive, but only in surrealist terms, and the result is a symptomatic contradiction. On the one hand, he embraces the theory in order to transvalue it, to place it in the service of revolution ("to urge the oppressed to satisfy their hunger for destruction and . . . to cater to the masochism of the oppressor").[55] On the other hand, lest it undercut the surrealist premise in love, he defends against the theory, concludes contra Freud that Eros, not death, is "the farthest, the slowest, the nearest, the most entreating voice." In short, Breton first conflates the Freudian drives and then reverses them in value. The death drive, though apparently assimilated, is actually elided, and Eros is restored not only as primary but also as liberatory:

> The day will soon come when we realize that, in spite of the wear and tear of life that bites like acid into our flesh, the very cornerstone of that violent liberation which reaches out for a better life in the heart of the technological age that corrupts our cities is LOVE.

Again, the Bretonian insistence on love appears compensatory, as if in defense against its other term of destruction. The same is true of the Bretonian insistence on resolution, the Hegelian reconciliation of such dualisms as waking and dreaming, life and death: this too appears as a compensatory defense not only against the splitting of the subject but also against the dominance of defusion. Such reconciliation is the raison d'être of Bretonian surrealism: automatism is to resolve the opposition of perception and representation; objective chance, the opposition of determinism and freedom; *amour fou*, the opposition of male and female; and so on.[56] Breton refers all these oppositions to the splitting wrought by the Cartesian discourse of rational man. But is the splitting that surrealism seeks to overcome that of the Cartesian cogito—or that of the Freudian psyche? Is it truly in the service of psychoanalysis, of its most difficult insights regarding split subjectivity and destructive drives?[57]

"Freud is Hegelian in me," Breton once remarked,[58] and clearly his surrealism is humanist. (Its first collective statement reads: "Il faut aboutir à une nouvelle déclaration des droits de l'homme.")[59] The surrealists did not need the 1844 manuscripts of the young Marx to ascribe to his problematic of present alienation and future liberation: they too tended to presuppose a human nature that, suppressed, could be freed, and they too wanted to see this nature in terms of an Eros not haunted by its destructive other. In

Bretonian surrealism this "early Marxian" account of the human subject comes into tension with the "late Freudian" one: as the first was officially embraced, the second was variously intuited, engaged, warded away.[60] At some moments Breton and company work to *separate* desire and death, to oppose the first to the second—only to find in times of desire the presence of death. At other moments they work to *reconcile* desire and death (as in the two "Manifesto" definitions of surreality), to qualify the second with the first—only to sense that this point of reconciliation is the very *punctum* of the uncanny, i.e., the point where desire and death interpenetrate in a way that brooks no affirmative reconciliation.[61]

In this way if surrealism does indeed serve psychoanalysis, it is a service rendered ambivalently, sometimes inadvertently—as when surrealism seeks liberation only to enact repetition, or when it proclaims desire only to bespeak death. In my account, then, certain surrealist practices intuit the uncanny discoveries of psychoanalysis, sometimes to resist them, sometimes to work through them, sometimes even to exploit them: i.e., to use the uncanniness of the return of the repressed, the compulsion to repeat, the immanence of death for disruptive purposes—to produce out of this psychic ambivalence a provocative ambiguity in artistic practice and cultural politics alike.

Man Ray, *Fixed-Explosive,* 1934.

2

_____

COMPULSIVE BEAUTY

If automatism points to an unconscious less liberatory than compulsive, this is all the more true of the marvelous, the concept that superseded automatism as the basic principle of Bretonian surrealism. Advanced by Breton, the marvelous has two cognates: convulsive beauty and objective chance, the first announced in *Nadja* (1928), the second developed in *Les Vases communicants* (1932), and both refined in *L'Amour fou* (1937).[1]

As a medieval term the marvelous signaled a rupture in the natural order, one, unlike the miraculous, not necessarily divine in origin.[2] This challenge to rational causality is essential to the medievalist aspect of surrealism, its fascination with magic and alchemy, with mad love and analogical thought. It is also fundamental to its spiritualist aspect, its attraction to mediumistic practices and gothic tales (e.g., Mathew Gregory Lewis, Ann Radcliffe, Edward Young) where the marvelous is again in play.[3] These enthusiasms suggest the project to which the surrealist marvelous is implicitly pledged: the reenchantment of a disenchanted world, of a capitalist society made ruthlessly rational.[4] They also suggest the ambiguity of this project, for in all three manifestations of the marvelous—medieval, gothic, and surrealist—it is not clear whether it is an external or internal event, of otherworldly, secular, or psychic agency.

However, the primary purpose of the surrealist marvelous is clear: the "negation" of the real, or at least of its philosophical equation with the rational. If "reality," Aragon writes in 1924, "is the apparent absence of contradiction," a construct that effaces conflict, then "the marvelous is the eruption of contradiction in the real," an eruption that exposes this construct as such.[5] Like Breton throughout his life, Aragon refers the marvelous to love. However, six years later in "La Peinture au défi" he is more expressly political: the marvelous is a "dialectical urgency" in which one "bourgeois" reality is subverted, and another revolutionary world advanced. Here the marvelous appears responsive to historical contradiction, which, Aragon implies, might be evoked through aesthetic "displacement."[6] This intuition underwrites his support of surrealist collage; it also resonates with the Benjaminian emphasis on "profane illumination" in surrealism, its "materialistic, anthropological inspiration."[7]

For Breton, on the other hand, the marvelous is more personal than political. In his 1920 essay on the early collages of Ernst, a text that develops the nascent aesthetic of surrealist dislocation, Breton stresses the subjective effects of the marvelous, its disorientation of "memory," its disruption of "identity."[8] However, he soon qualifies this marvelous aesthetic in order to accommodate painting (whose facture cannot decenter the subject, artist or viewer, as can the dislocations of collage). More importantly here, he defends against its psychic ramifications. Ever Hegelian in his definitions of the surreal, Breton sees the marvelous in terms of resolution rather than contradiction: "What is admirable about the fantastic," he writes in the "Manifesto," "is that there is no longer anything fantastic: there is only the real."[9] For Breton, unlike for Aragon, contradiction is a problem to overcome poetically more than a profane illumination to exploit critically.

Given the paradox of a state at once otherworldly, secular, and psychic, how are we to understand the surrealist marvelous? In all its variants, I will argue, the marvelous *is* the uncanny—but projected, at least in part, away from the unconscious and repressed material toward the world and future revelation.[10] (It is this defensive projection that accounts for the confusion as to its site. Is the marvelous a subjective experience? Is chance an objective event?) Thus, on the one hand, the surrealists exploit the uncanny return of the repressed for disruptive purposes, while on the other they resist its consequences regarding the death drive. To argue this will require two steps: first the marvelous as convulsive beauty will be seen as an uncanny confusion between animate and inanimate states; then the marvelous as objective chance—as manifest in the sudden encounter and the found ob-ject—will be revealed as an uncanny reminder of the compulsion to repeat. Both these terms, convulsive beauty and objective chance, connote shock, which suggests that the marvelous also involves traumatic experience, that it may even be an attempt to work through "hysterical" experience. In this way too the marvelous can be understood in terms of the repetition that governs the uncanny and the death drive.

In the "Manifesto" Breton offers, without explanation or illustration, two examples of the marvelous: romantic ruins and modern mannequins (M 16). Both are prized emblems in surrealism, the first evocative of the space of the unconscious, the second of its status as both intimate and alien, but what renders them marvelous? Each combines or conflates two opposed terms: in the ruin the natural and the historical, and in the mannequin the human and the nonhuman. In the ruin cultural progress is captured by natural entropy, and in the mannequin the human figure is given over to the commodity form—indeed, the mannequin is the very image of capitalist reification.[11] In short, in both images the animate is confused with the inanimate, a confusion that is uncanny precisely because it evokes the con-servatism of the drives, the immanence of death in life.

In this light we may begin to see the uncanniness of the Bretonian marvelous in general. Breton resists this grim connection; he would not otherwise have associated the marvelous with the beautiful. Nevertheless, if the marvelous is beautiful, as is announced in the "Manifesto" (M 14),

Raoul Ubac, *Fossil of the Paris Opera*, 1939.

and if this beauty is convulsive, as is proclaimed at the end of *Nadja* (N 160), then its convulsive force must involve an uncanny return of repressed material. Provisionally, then, we might amend the famous dictum of surrealist aesthetics that concludes *Nadja* as follows: Beauty will be not only convulsive or will not be, but also compulsive or will not be. Convulsive in its physical effect, compulsive in its psychological dynamic, surrealist beauty partakes of the return of the repressed, of the compulsion to repeat. That is to say, it partakes of the uncanny.

The examples of the marvelous in the "Manifesto" only point to the uncanny; to grasp this connection we must turn to the definition of convulsive beauty in *L'Amour fou:* "Convulsive Beauty will be veiled-erotic, fixed-explosive, magical-circumstantial or will not be" (AF 19). Famously cryptic, this riddle comes with different clues. For the category of the veiled-erotic Breton offers these images: a limestone deposit shaped like an egg; a quartz wall formed like a sculpted mantle; a rubber object and a mandrake root that resemble statuettes;[12] a coral reef that appears like an underwater garden; and finally crystals deemed by Breton a paradigm of automatist creation. All are instances of natural mimicry, which relates them to other phenomena prized by the surrealists: e.g., the Blossfeldt photographs of flowers that resemble architectural forms; the Brassaï photographs of "involuntary sculptures," or everyday materials subconsciously molded into strange shapes; and the Man Ray photographs of hats that subliminally elaborate upon genital forms.[13] But what is the particular nature of the Bretonian veiled-erotic? In each example, Breton states, "the animate is so close to the inanimate" (AF 11). Here the veiled-erotic brushes up against the uncanny, and each example does evoke a petrified nature in which not only natural form and cultural sign but also life and death become blurred. It is this indistinction that renders the veiled-erotic marvelous, i.e., uncanny, for it suggests the inertia of life, the dominance of death.[14]

This uncanny indistinction also has a phylogenetic register, for such substances as limestone, coral, and crystal all exist in subterranean or submarine realms that are evocative of primal states, both ontogenetic (i.e., in

Photograph of Great Barrier Reef in *L'Amour fou*, 1937.

the womb) and evolutionary (i.e., in the sea). Moreover, the images of the veiled-erotic that do not evoke such fantasies of intrauterine existence, or the return to the mother, suggest the converse: fantasies of phallic intercession, or the law of the father, as is the case with the totemic rubber and root figures. (Is it significant that Man Ray titled the first *Moi, Elle* [1934] and Breton saw the second as Aeneas bearing Anchises [AF 16]?) As I will remark on other occasions, surrealism oscillates between these two uncanny fantasies of maternal plenitude and paternal punishment, between the dream of a space-time before bodily separation and psychic loss and the trauma of such events. Indeed, this Oedipal conundrum might be taken to structure the surrealist imaginary. [15]

In sum, the veiled-erotic is uncanny primarily in its in/animation, for this suggests the priority of death, the primordial condition to which life is recalled. The fixed-explosive, the second category of convulsive beauty, is uncanny primarily in its im/mobility, for this suggests the authority of death, the dominant conservatism of the drives. Again the definition is cryptic: the fixed-explosive involves an "expiration of motion" (AF 10), and Breton provides but two examples. The first is only described: a "photograph of a speeding locomotive abandoned for years to the delirium of a virgin forest" (AF 10). The second is only illustrated: a Man Ray photograph of a tango dancer caught, body and dress ablur, in midtwirl. In the first image, which deepens the ambiguous role of nature in convulsive beauty, an old train engine lies engulfed in a bed of vines. Nature here is vital yet inertial: it grows but only, in the guise of death, to devour the progress of the train, or the progress that it once emblematized. [16] The sexual import of this drama is obvious: the phallic engine exhausted in the virgin forest, a vulgar image of feminine sexuality common in surrealism. Under this sexual sign, nature, like pleasure, is seen to serve death: this image of expiration suggests not only the inertia of the entropic, the regression toward the inanimate, but also the immanence of death in sexuality. This evocation also renders the fixed-explosive marvelous, i.e., once again uncanny, for accord-

Photograph of abandoned train in *Minotaure*, 1937.

ing to Freud it is only thus "tinged with eroticism" that the death drive is sensed.[17]

The second image of the fixed-explosive also attests to this uncanny mutuality of erotic and destructive impulses. Here the fixed-explosive is the counterpart of the veiled-erotic: rather than the "spontaneous action" (AF 11) of the inanimate become animate, we have the arrested motion of a body become an image. The beauty of the dancer is indeed convulsive, at once disruptive and suspended, in a photograph that evokes the sadomasochistic nature of sexuality as posed by the death drive theory: "an enormously productive, decentering sexuality and a sexuality identical with its own explosive and definitive end."[18] In this regard the dancer complements the train precisely, albeit in ways not fathomed by Breton. For whereas the stalled train represents the expiration of sexuality for a patriarchal subject, the suspended dancer images the sadistic projection of this masochistic expiration onto the figure of the woman: here it is her vital activity that is violently arrested. Again the uncanny confusion of the psychic role of sexuality: does it serve life or death?

This violent arrest of the vital, this sudden suspension of the animate, speaks not only of the sadomasochistic basis of sexuality posed by the death drive theory, but also of the photographic principle that informs so much surrealist practice. This suggests that convulsive beauty must also be thought in terms of photographic shock, and Breton does relate beauty to shock at the end of *Nadja*. As his examples attest, photography captured this beauty most effectively, and together they become more important to surrealism over time. Automatically as it were, photography produces both the veiled-erotic, nature configured as a sign, and the fixed-explosive, nature arrested in motion; this is in part why Rosalind Krauss has argued that it supplies the very conditions of the surrealist aesthetic. However, my psychoanalytical principle, the uncanny logic of the death drive, subsumes this important photographic (or grammatological) account.[19] The veiled-erotic, or reality convulsed into a writing, is a photographic effect, but fundamentally it concerns an uncanny trace of a prior state, i.e., of the compulsion to return

27

to an ultimately inanimate condition: the mineral death of limestone, quartz, crystal. The fixed-explosive, or reality convulsed in shock, must also be seen in these terms; the subject suddenly suspended is again a photographic effect, but here too its fundamental import is psychic: the shot that arrests one is an uncanny fore-image of death.

That photography arrests movement was its distinctive characteristic for Brassaï; so it was too for Roland Barthes, who in *Camera Lucida* (1980) developed an implicitly surrealist theory of photography in terms related to the uncanny.[20] Photography points to the logic of the death drive in two ways: in its shock (for Barthes the *punctum,* prick or wound, of the photograph or shot) and in its tense (the future anterior of the photograph: this will have been). Before a camera, Barthes writes, "I am neither subject nor object, but a subject who feels he is becoming an object: I then experience a micro-version of death (of parenthesis): I am truly becoming a specter. . . . Death is the *eidos* of that Photograph."[21] This photographic process of in/animation is bound up with trauma, anxiety, and repetition: "I shudder, like Winnicott's psychotic patient [or Freud's shock victim?], over a catastrophe which has already occurred."[22] Convulsive beauty is bound up with these same effects. Indeed, as I will suggest, repetition keyed not only to primordial death but also to personal trauma is the basis of its third category, the marvelous as magic-circumstantial.

In/animate and im/mobile, the veiled-erotic and the fixed-explosive are figures of the uncanny. Breton recodes the "morbid anxiety" provoked by this uncanniness into an aesthetic of beauty. And yet finally this aesthetic has to do less with the beautiful than with the sublime. For convulsive beauty not only stresses the formless and evokes the unrepresentable, as with the sublime, but it also mixes delight and dread, attraction and repulsion: it too involves "a momentary check to the vital forces," "a negative pleasure."[23] In surrealism as in Kant, this negative pleasure is figured through feminine attributes: it is an intuition of the death drive received by the patriarchal subject as both the promise of its ecstasy and the threat of its extinction. However transformed the map, the terrain of this surrealist sublime is not much changed from that of traditional beauty: it remains the female body.[24]

Like the sublime, then, convulsive beauty involves the patriarchal subject in the inextricability of death and desire. Breton seeks to distinguish the two, to oppose to this death a beauty that is in fact bound up with it, and it is this contradiction which, never resolved, drives him to crisis after crisis. The pattern is repeated with the magic-circumstantial or objective chance. In retrospect Breton regarded objective chance as "the problem of problems";[25] it is one I want to consider in some depth.

Objective chance has two related aspects, the encounter and the *trouvaille,* defined by Breton as both "fortuitous" and "foreordained" (AF 19), "super-determinant in the Freudian sense of the word" (N 51).[26] Breton insists on the spontaneity of objective chance, and yet this claim suggests its opposite: that the encounter is a rendezvous, that the *trouvaille* or found object is a lost object regained. Here again a paradox basic to surrealism emerges: a category of experience that appears at once underdetermined and overdetermined, *imprévu* and *déjà vu.*

However spontaneous, objective chance is not free of causality. Derived in part from Engels, this category is intended to reconcile both Marxian and Freudian models of determination (AF 21). To this end Breton apparently stresses the psychic or internal aspect of necessity (such terms as "disturbing links" and "paroxysmal disturbances" [AF 24] even invoke the uncanny), yet he actually privileges its external aspect: "Chance is the form of manifestation of an exterior necessity as it opens a path in the human unconscious" (AF 23).[27] This definition, which does not fully overturn conventional causality, again betrays a defensive projection at work, according to which an unconscious compulsion associated with a real event is seen instead as a real event that produces an unconscious effect. (This projection of the psychic onto the world is as crucial to surrealism as it is common: it is why Ernst feels a passive "spectator" of his own work, or Breton an "agonized witness" [N 20] of his own life.)[28] Like convulsive beauty, objective chance *is* this "hysterical" confusion between internal impulse and external sign; unlike convulsive beauty, however, objective chance points to the mechanism that underlies this confusion: the compulsion to repeat.

In the compulsion operative in objective chance, the subject repeats a traumatic experience, whether actual or fantasmatic, exogenous or endogenous, that he does not recall. He repeats it because he cannot recall it: repetition occurs due to repression, in lieu of recollection. This is why each repetition in objective chance seems fortuitous yet foreordained, determined by present circumstances yet governed by "some 'daemonic' force at work."[29] Bretonian surrealists intuit this force: it fascinates them even as they defend against it. The result is that, just as the uncanny is recoded as the marvelous and arrested animation is sublimated as convulsive beauty, so repetition compulsion is inverted as objective chance: its instances are taken as external "signals" (N 19) of future events rather than internal signs of past states; the anxious is projected as the portentous. At this point, however, this is simply a hypothesis that I must test.

In the three principal Breton novels, *Nadja, Les Vases communicants,* and *L'Amour fou,* objects are "rare," places "strange," meetings "sudden" (N 19–20), yet all are haunted by repetition. So is Breton, to the point where he experiences being as haunting. "Perhaps my life is nothing but an image of this kind," he writes early in *Nadja;* "perhaps I am doomed to retrace my steps under the illusion that I am exploring, doomed to try and learn what I should simply recognize, learning a mere fraction of what I have forgotten" (N 12). Such repression and recurrence structure objective chance as a paradox: a serial repetition of unique encounters, a repetition governed not only by compulsion but also by identification and desire. Here it becomes difficult to distinguish the types of repetition at work. On the one hand, repetition in desire drives the Breton narratives; on the other hand, when a connection between desire and death is sensed (at the end of *Nadja,* intermittently throughout *L'Amour fou*), the narratives break down. It is this psychic tension that convulses the novels.

In the novels the encounters with men are strangely similar, and Breton often hails them as doubles (in *Nadja* Paul Eluard, Philippe Soupault, Robert Desnos, and Benjamin Péret all appear in this uncanny register). His encounters with women are also uncannily reiterative, but in a different way; each woman appears to Breton as a potential substitute for a lost love object. At the end of *Nadja* even he tires of this "substitution" (N 158), but this move from surrogate to surrogate is the very metonymic motion of his desire. And so it is enacted, indeed exacerbated, to the point where Breton comes to figure it as such, as repetition, in *L'Amour fou,* which opens with an extraordinary image of two rows of ambiguous figures, one of his former selves (the axis of identification), another of his former lovers (the axis of desire). In *Nadja* Breton poses the Oedipal riddle in three ways: first "Who am I?," then "Whom do I 'haunt'?" (N 11), and finally Who haunts me? In *L'Amour fou* it is clear that this otherness is within, that this uncanniness is intimate.[30]

Breton terms his encounters and *trouvailles* "signals" (N 19). Enigmatic, they are laced with anxiety, yet less as portents of things to come than as reminders of repressed events, past stages, the compulsion to repeat. As Freud theorized in 1926 (almost contemporaneously with *Nadja*), anxiety in Bretonian surrealism is a "signal" (*Angstsignal*), a repetition of a reaction to a past trauma triggered by a perception of a present danger.[31] Repressed, the trauma is subsumed by the signal, just as in the uncanny the referent is subsumed by the sign. The enigma of the signal, then, attests not to a lack of signification to be filled in the future but to an overdetermination produced in the past. This is why Breton is an "agonized witness" of these signals, and why they provoke both "surprise" (a term derived from de Chirico) and "loss," "anxiety," and "ennui" (N 12–17): although the trauma has always already occurred, each repetition comes as a shock.[32] In rare moments of recognition Breton grasps the stake of these repeated signals:

"our very instinct of self-preservation," he says in *Nadja* (N 20); "of Eros and the struggle against Eros!," he exclaims in *L'Amour fou* (AF 37).

Such is the stake as Breton pursues these signals in the three novels: like the infant of the *fort/da* game, he seeks to master actively what previously he had suffered passively—only to suffer again and again. The novels provide several analogues to the specific types of compulsive repetition that Freud related to the uncanny and the death drive: repetition to master the loss of the love object, as in the *fort/da* game; repetition to "prepare" for a shock already come, as in traumatic neurosis; and repetition that occurs in lieu of recollection, as when the analysand, in a condition of transference with the analysis, reenacts the repressed. These types of repetition can be associated respectively with the *trouvaille*, the encounter, and the relationships that emerge from these events (especially between Breton and Nadja in *Nadja*, and between Breton and Giacometti in *L'Amour fou*, each of whom plays both analyst and analysand to the other). In *Beyond the Pleasure Principle* Freud sketches one more type of repetition pertinent here: *Schicksalszwang* or fate compulsion, in which the subject feels "pursued by a malignant fate or possessed by some 'daemonic' power," usually experienced as a series of similar misfortunes.[33] For Freud this subject wishes these events; but the wish is unconscious, so its fulfillment appears as fate. This compulsion is also active in the Breton novels, where he misrecognizes this daemonic power from the past as an ambiguous love promised in the future.[34]

As noted in chapter 1, such repetitions may serve very different ends. In the *fort/da* game and in traumatic neurosis, repetition appears pledged to self-preservation, to the erotic binding of the subject against the loss of the object or the shock of the trauma. But repetition can also act to undo the subject as a defusive agent of the death drive. In the Breton novels as in the Freud texts it is often difficult to distinguish these two ends (as it is to determine the degrees of in/volition and un/pleasure involved in the repeated events). Breton seeks a mastery in repetition, or at least a binding in these events, but he often experiences, especially with Nadja and Giacometti, a repetition that is regressive, generally defusive, even deadly. In my reading, the drama of the Bretonian text is keyed to this conflict of the drives as evoked in the repeated objects and events of objective chance.

＊ ＊

Two examples each of the *trouvaille* and the encounter from *Nadja* and *L'Amour fou* must suffice to support this point; as uncanny reminders of past loss or future death for Breton, they do indeed test his instinct of self-preservation. My first example is one of the many ambiguous objects in *Nadja*: a bronze glove. However unusual (*insolite* is a privileged term for the surrealist object), the glove has art-historical associations from Klinger through de Chirico to Giacometti, but this lineage hardly explains its uncanny effect on Breton. Breton was intrigued by the blue gloves worn one day by a female visitor to the "Centrale Surréaliste" (the Bureau of Surrealist Research). He both wanted her to remove the gloves and dreaded that she might; eventually she left the bronze glove as a substitute, a compromise that suited him psychically (N 56). The eerie appeal of the object is not difficult to decode, for it not only casts a human form in a deathly mold, but also captures a fetishistic response to castration, which Breton can both recognize (in the displaced form of a "severed" hand) and disavow (although empty, the hardened glove remains on, as it were, to cover any absence). It is thus a doubly uncanny reminder of both the primordial condition of inanimation and the infantile fantasy of castration. (The Benjaminian definition of the fetish as "the sex appeal of the inorganic" neatly captures both aspects of the glove, which is similar in this regard to many surrealist objects.)[35] Significant here is that this instance of objective chance is an imaged repetition of a past (fantasmatic) event, a fetishistic substitute for a lost object, one that returns in the guise of the uncanny to be repeated in this text (e.g., in a drawing by Nadja that endows the glove with a female look and so effectively glosses it as desired object, castrative threat, and fetishistic figure all in one) and elsewhere (e.g., the equally fetishistic slipper spoon of *L'Amour fou*). In this way the bronze glove is a typical Bretonian

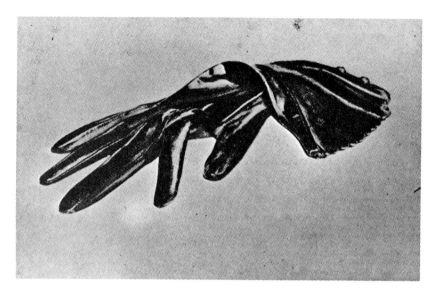

Photograph of bronze glove in *Nadja*, 1928.

object uncanny in its repetition, and Breton moves from one such object to another as from loss to loss (or, more precisely perhaps, as from *fort* to *da*).

My second example of objective chance is the prototypical Bretonian encounter, the liaison with Nadja, which Breton enters in the hope that she will stay his repetition of loss, staunch his desire as lack: if he seizes the glove as a fetishistic stopgap, he turns to Nadja (as to his other lovers) for erotic binding. But he finds less a lover than a double who enthralls him for another reason altogether: as a figure of his own compulsion to repeat, his own struggle with the death drive. With all her inhibitions and recriminations, fixed ideas and compulsive acts, Nadja is an obsessional neurotic.[36] Her symptomatic repetition of repressed material disturbs Breton, but it also fascinates him precisely because it is marked by repetition, destruction, death. In her transference Nadja implicates him in this defusion, and it is only then that he breaks away from it (and so condemns her to it).[37] Melancholic about past loss, anxious about future trauma, Breton had turned to Nadja for erotic binding, only to discover through her "a more or less conscious principle of total subversion" (N 152). This recognition comes after the fact, with Nadja ensconced in an asylum, in a note about a "nocturnal ride." Once in a car Nadja, "desiring to extinguish us" (N 152), had blinded Breton with a kiss. This death wish tempted him; its sexuality aroused him (a page later he confesses a "convulsive" impulse to suicide). But in a grandiose act of will ("What a test of life, indeed!") Breton opts for the other principle, that of love and life, also represented by a woman, Suzanne Musard, his next love object. Yet this move hardly frees him of repetition, of desire as lack and in death; it is simply its next manifestation. And indeed in *L'Amour fou* Suzanne Musard is soon associated with death, and his *next* love object, Jacqueline Lamba, with love and life.[38]

Jacqueline Lamba is the heroine of the famous encounter in *L'Amour fou,* "the night of the sunflower," my third example of objective chance. By this episode Breton is desperate to think objective chance in terms of unique love rather than deathly repetition. In *Les Vases communicants* he argued contra Freud that the dream can be prophetic; so here he claims that poetry

---

can be "predictive" (AF 53, 61), specifically that his 1923 poem "Sunflower" about a Parisian *flâneuse* prophesied his 1934 encounter with Jacqueline Lamba (AF 65). Breton obsessively decodes the poem as a cryptic map of their nocturnal *dérive,* yet clearly the poem does not predict the encounter so much as the encounter enacts the poem: this is a repetition that he has compulsively sought out à la *Schicksalszwang.*[39] As such it produces "a mixture of *panic-provoking* terror and joy" (AF 40); once again objective chance is linked to traumatic anxiety. Breton senses the uncanniness of the encounter but resists its implication in the compulsion to repeat: thus he insists on the *imprévu* as a defense against the *déjà vu.* Nevertheless, this implication cannot be repressed again; in the end Jacqueline Lamba appears as "the all-powerful commander of the night of the sunflower" (AF 67), an ambiguous cipher of a double tropism toward light and dark (*la nuit de tournesol*), of a difficult struggle between life and death.

The ambiguity of this figure seems that of the role of sexuality in the drives: again, which does it serve, life or death? Unlike Nadja, Jacqueline Lamba remains ambiguous, for with her Breton thinks desire in relation to its origin rather than its end: "To love, to find once more the lost grace of the first moment when one is in love" (AF 44). The prototype of this lost love is clear: the mother (Breton speaks of "the path lost with the loss of childhood" [AF 49]). Each new love object is then a repetition of this maternal term: "Are you, at last," Breton asks Jacqueline Lamba, "this woman?" (AF 49) As I will suggest, this search for the lost object, which is the surrealist quest par excellence, is as impossible as it is compulsive: not only is each new object a substitute for the lost one, but the lost object is a fantasy, a simulacrum.

My fourth and final example of objective chance will clarify this relation among desire, object, and repetition. It comes in *L'Amour fou* in the form of the twin paradigm of the surrealist object: the spoon and the mask found by Breton and Giacometti in the Saint-Ouen flea market in 1934. This instance of objective chance reveals its uncanny logic; as a crucial moment in the psychic economy of mature Bretonian surrealism, it warrants protracted scrutiny.

Accompanied by Giacometti, Breton places the episode under the sign of *The Invisible Object* (or *Feminine Personage,* 1934), a sculpture that had preoccupied both men at the time.[40] For Breton this abstracted nude evokes the *"desire to love and to be loved"* through *"the invisible but present object"* apparently held in her empty hands (AF 26). In a moment of "feminine intervention" Giacometti had lowered the hands to reveal the breasts—a disastrous move, according to Breton, in which the invisible object was lost (with the return of the breasts, we might say, the lost object was lost again). This underlined connection among desire, breast, and lost object, shrouded in "painful ignorance," is important to retain. In psychoanalytical terms it recapitulates the carving out of desire from need, or sexuality from self-preservation. (Significantly Breton suggests that the relation between object and breast in the sculpture was somehow disturbed, rendered less necessary, when Giacometti had a lover [AF 26].)

At this point, however, Breton turns to the head, which Giacometti could not realize. To Breton this difficulty was due to a "sentimental uncertainty" (AF 26), a "resistance" that Giacometti had to overcome, and this occurred through the intercession of a found object: a metal half-mask. This object, which attracted both men (though Breton would later deny it), partakes equally of a miliary helmet and an amorous mask. As ambivalent as it is ambiguous, Giacometti finally bought it, and its immediate effect was salutary: it helped him resolve the head and finish the sculpture. In retrospect the mask filled a formal gap in the series between *Head* (1934) and *The Invisible Object,* and this "catalytic role" (AF 32) inspires Breton to associate the finding of such objects with the wish fulfillment of dreams: just as the dream expresses a psychic conflict, so the found object resolves a "moral contradiction," and this in turn allowed Giacometti to resolve the "plastic contradiction" (AF 32) of the sculpture, to render form, style, and

Alberto Giacometti, *The Invisible Object*, 1934.

Man Ray, *A Highly Evolved Descendant of the Helmet*, 1934.

affect one. And yet, as I will suggest, this object has no more to do with wish fulfillment than the dreams of traumatic neuroses. It too points beyond the pleasure principle.

For Breton the mask restored the feminine personage to a "perfect organic unity" (AF 32); in effect, its shielded gaze rendered her a woman without lack. This brings great relief to both men as the threat of this lack is lifted, and this is the moral of the *trouvaille* for Breton. But there is another story, counter to this one of wish fulfillment, in which the figure sustains rather than occludes the psychic conflict at its source. To tell this story we must rearticulate the role of the mask and the effect of the sculpture. Like any negation, the underlined insistence that the mask was *"never seen"* (AF 28) points to its opposite: that it is a repetition of a prior object, a reminder of a primal state (we have encountered this trope before). So, too, its symbolic evocation of both war and love, death and desire, suggests that it is the psychic representative of a conflict or confusion between these principles, which renders it so tensely ambiguous. Breton suspects that "this blind face" represents a "necessity not known to us" (AF 28), but he resists its revelation—at least he does so until its point is brought uncannily home to him through his own *trouvaille,* a wooden spoon with a little boot for a base.

Initially for Breton the spoon, like the mask, is simply a manifestation of objective chance, i.e., a marvelous resolution of "internal finality" and "external causality" (AF 21), desire and object. If for the sculptor the resolution was formal, for the poet it is linguistic: the spoon appears as the answer to a riddle, the phrase is *le cendrier Cendrillon* (Cinderella ashtray) which had obsessed Breton at the time. And yet no more than the mask is this riddle about resolution; rather, it concerns the slippage of the subject, Breton, in language and desire—a slippage in which meaning is never fixed and desire cannot be satisfied. As with the sculpture, then, the only resolution here is a fetishistic one: through the slipper, a classic fetish, conjoined with the spoon, a common surrealist symbol of woman, Breton attempts to arrest this slippage.[41] He points to its fetishistic nature when he terms the

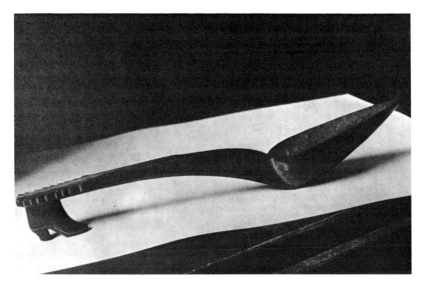

Man Ray, *From a Little Shoe That Was Part of It*, 1934.

spoon both a "lack" ("of which I think there was already a trace in my childhood" [AF 33]) and a "unity" (the same fetishistic term used for *The Invisible Object*). This unity, however, is so precarious that the spoon becomes for Breton a figure not only of a fetishism, i.e., of a disavowal of castration or sexual difference, but also of a primordial union, i.e., of a preemption of castration or sexual difference (like Freud, Breton was fascinated by the myth of androgyny). Not just a subjective phallic substitute, Breton sees it as an "objective equation: slipper = spoon = penis = the perfect mold of this penis." "With this idea," he concludes prematurely, "the cycle of ambivalences found an ideal closure" (AF 36).

But this too is wish fulfillment, and the ideal closure is undone when the "associative" nature of the spoon, i.e., of his desire, is revealed to Breton in this trope: the single slipper spoon becomes for him an open series of shoes, large and small, that corresponds psychically to the series of lost objects in his life. That is, the spoon becomes "the very *source* of the *stereotype*" (AF 33) not of a "perfect organic unity" but of an originary psychic split. It is a representative of the Lacanian *objet petit a,* the object from which the subject must separate in order to become a subject—the object that must be "lost" in order for the subject to be "found," the object that is the origin-cause of desire, not its end-satisfaction.[42] In short, in the very figure onto which Breton projects a primal unity (with the mother), he confronts an image of desire based on an originary separation (from her) and driven by an infinite substitution (of her). In this way the paradigmatic surrealist object is not simply a fetish that covers up lack (if it were, the surrealist object search would end here for both men); it is also a figure of lack, an analogue of the lost object that is keyed to the maternal breast, as "the invisible object" of the sculpture is so keyed. We arrive then at this paradoxical formula of the surrealist object: just as the unique encounter of objective chance is an uncanny repetition, so too the found object of objective chance is a lost object that, never recovered, is forever sought, forever repeated.[43]

In this way Breton points to a profound psychoanalytical insight. In *Three Essays on the Theory of Sexuality* (1905) Freud links the stirring of sexuality to the taking of nourishment; the maternal breast is thus the first external object of the drive. Soon the infant "loses" this object (as he must for sexuality to arise); significantly, regarding *The Invisible Object,* this occurs precisely when he is "able to form a total idea" of the mother.[44] Thus deprived, the infant becomes autoerotic before he seeks outwardly again, and "not until the period of latency has been passed through is the original relation restored." Freud concludes: "The finding of an object is in fact a refinding of it."[45]

Later, in "On Narcissism: An Introduction" (1914), Freud elaborates on this "anaclitic" type of object choice where the prototype is the parental nurturer. In this model the sexual drive is propped upon the self-preservative function: the infant sucks milk out of need, which can be satisfied, but experiences pleasure, a desire to repeat pleasure, which cannot be so satisfied. (In the Lacanian formulation, desire is this demand once need is subtracted.) The real object, milk, is the object of self-preservative need, not the object of sexual desire; this object is the breast, which in the autoerotic "sensual sucking" of the infant becomes hallucinated, fantasmatic.[46] The infant seeks this object of desire, which appears lost to it. On the one hand, then, the finding of an object is indeed a refinding of it, while on the other hand this refinding is only and ever a seeking: the object cannot be rediscovered because it is fantasmatic, and desire cannot be satisfied because it is defined as lack. The found object is always a substitute, always a displacement, that drives on its own search. Such is the dynamic that propels not only the surrealist object but the surrealist project in general: this surrealism may propose desire-as-excess but it discovers desire-as-lack, and this discovery deprives its project of any real closure. For any art as staked in such desire as is surrealism, there can be no origin that grounds the subject and delivers the object: here this foundational ambition of modernism is frustrated from within.

In the metal mask and the slipper spoon the stirring of sexual desire in the losing of the maternal object is intuited. Again, this lost object is ghosted in the surrealist object, and in *The Invisible Object* Giacometti configures it, or rather he conveys its impossibility: in the hands of the supplicant figure the lost object is shaped *in its very absence*. Indeed, the sculpture not only evokes the lost object but also figures its supplicant-subject. In this way it signifies not the fulfillment of desire (as Breton hopes) but the desire *to* desire (as Breton knows: "the desire to love and to be loved"[AF 26]).[47] Apparently the surrealist search for the lost object proved too psychically difficult for Giacometti. Certainly his ambivalence as expressed in such works as the two *Disagreeable Objects* is more extreme, more defusive, to the point where they appear riven by the very conflict of the drives, the very struggle within sexuality between erotic binding and thanatonic destruction.[48] In any case, in 1935, a year after *The Invisible Object,* Giacometti repudiated his surrealist objects and renounced his surrealist search. In so doing he effectively passed from a psychoanalytic (quasi-Lacanian) problematic to an existentialist (quasi-Sartrean) one, which questions the very existence of the unconscious.

Breton had too much at stake to make this turn. As he toils on in mad love, he develops a notion of desire intuitive of the Freudian formulation and proleptic of the Lacanian one. Like Lacan, Breton locates desire "in excess of the need" (AF 13); he even states that the *trouvailles* assume "the meaning of the *lost object*" (the allusion is to the slipper of "folklore" [AF 36]).[49] And if he does not quite consider the object the cause of desire, he does not exactly regard it as its fulfillment either: he calls it a "marvelous precipitate" (AF 13–15). Finally Breton appears aware of both the fetishistic aspect and the maternal reference of the *trouvailles*. Certainly he senses the psychic connection among the mask, the lost object, and the maternal wholeness of the figure; here he also refers the slipper spoon to the phallic mother: "it symbolized for me a woman *unique and unknown*" (AF 37), i.e., originary and unconscious. As Guy Rosolato has written,

> The multiple dialectic between the partial and the total object, the breast and the mother as a whole, between the genitals and the entire body but also between the lost object and the found object is centered on the fantasy of the maternal penis, around which the identifications of the two sexes are organized.[50]

This multiple dialectic is teased out through the two *trouvailles:* both the spoon and the mask speak of fantasies of maternal reunion, of a love before lack or beyond loss, even as they also attest to anxieties about paternal interdiction, castration, death.

Of course, to seek this total object—a unity before separation, an immediacy before language, a desire outside of lack—may be mad. It may also be necessary, for without such mad love, such erotic binding, Breton is psychically prey to deathly defusion, to thanatonic breakdown.[51] However, it is precisely with these *trouvailles* that the repetition pledged to this breakdown emerges most strongly. The slipper spoon is not only a fetish that combines a perception of castrative "lack" with an image of phallic "unity"; it is also a "Cinderella ashtray" that conflates a figure of desire (Cinderella) with an image of extinction (ashes). With its associations of love and war, maternal gaze and military death, the mask combines similar terms even more incisively.[52] Breton first published his account of these objects in 1934.[53] In a 1936 postscript in *L'Amour fou* he was forced to reconsider it for two reasons (AF 37–38). In the interim he learned from the Belgian surrealist Joë Bosquet that the mask was a military helmet with an "evil role" (Bosquet was paralyzed in the war). He also learned that Suzanne Musard had encountered the same object, indeed had witnessed the entire episode of the flea market. These two signs, the first of death in war, the second of loss in love, transform the mask for Breton into a "precipitate" not only of desire but also of "the 'death instinct'" (AF 38).

And yet this recognition is immediately resisted. Breton cannot tolerate the ambivalence that such ambiguity produces, and so he opposes the spoon

---

and the mask as respective "disguises" of the life and death drives. The spoon (associated with Jacqueline Lamba) now represents erotic binding alone, the mask (associated with Suzanne Musard) destructive defusion alone. Through this forced opposition Breton attempts to balance the two drives—to separate sexuality from death (i.e., from pain and aggression), to claim desire for life. But this opposition cannot hold: as we have seen, the spoon and the mask have a similar psychic value as mixed images of desire and death.[54] "Of Eros and the struggle against Eros!" Breton exclaims more than once. This line is in fact a quotation from *The Ego and the Id,* from a section that reprises the conflict of life and death drives proposed in *Beyond the Pleasure Principle* (which was included in the same 1933 French translation). Here Breton seeks to purify the opposition between the two drives, but his citation from Freud deconstructs it absolutely: "'The two instincts, the sexual instinct and the death instinct, behave like preservation instincts, in the strictest sense of the word, because they tend, both of them, to reestablish a state which was troubled by the apparition of life'" (AF 38).[55] In short, Breton opposes the two drives, only to quote Freud to the effect that they cannot be so opposed: on the one hand, both draw on the same sexual energy, the same libido (there is no "destrudo"), and, on the other hand, both are governed by a repetition in thrall to a dominant instinctual conservatism that conduces to death. "But," Breton intervenes with the classic signifier of disavowal, "But I had to start loving again, not just to keep on living!" Whereas Giacometti surrenders to this intuited recognition, Breton resists it in a blind testament to love. It may be a necessary leap of faith, but that is all it is. At this moment surrealism as an aesthetics, indeed a politics, of desire is deconstructed.

Two final points should be drawn from this lesson, the first concerning the valuation of sexuality in surrealism, the second regarding the role of trauma. Along with the new model of the drives presented in such texts as *Beyond*

the Pleasure Principle and *The Ego and the Id* comes a new conception of sexuality. No longer are the sexual drives opposed to the self-preservative (ego) drives; the two are united in Eros against the death drive. Sexuality is no longer seen as so disruptive of the subject; on the contrary, it is devoted to its binding. Consciously or not, the surrealists long operated according to the first model of a subversive sexuality, and as would-be Sadeans they exploited it as such. Later, however, at least the Bretonian surrealists regarded sexuality in terms of Eros, as a synthetic principle rather than a disruptive force, which is in keeping with the new Freudian formulation just as the prior practice was in keeping with the old. I believe this transformation is clinched for Breton in the face of the events narrated in *L'Amour fou:* the perception of desire as lack, the recognition of the found object as impossible lost object, the encounter with the death drive. Perhaps he could no longer avoid the stake of this model of a subversive sexuality, the risk for the subject, and his thought turned at the point of the moral of the mask and the spoon. (No doubt he glimpsed it before—in his relationship with Nadja certainly, in his disapproval of perversions perhaps, in his denunciation first of Bataille and later of Dalí maybe—but here the crisis could no longer be parried.) As a cult of desire in a culture of the death drive, surrealism had to resist the collapse of the one into the other. As suggested in chapter 1, the defusion proposed by the death drive theory undermines the binding necessary for the making of an artistic movement, let alone of a political revolution. Breton had to disavow this drive at the potential cost of psychic splitting: "But I had to go on. . . ."

My second point concerns trauma, which is how this recognition comes to Breton: these "disguises" of the drives, he says of the mask and the spoon, tested him "blow by blow" (AF 38). More than the marvelous, convulsive beauty and objective chance involve shock. So, too, Breton writes in a Baudelairean line from *L'Amour fou,* "interpretive delirium begins only when man, ill-prepared, is taken by a sudden fear in the *forest of symbols*" (AF 15). On the basis of this famous clue other fundamental concepts of surrealism—the paranoid-critical method, the posture of *disponibilité,* the city as array of anxious signs—might be read in terms of traumatic neurosis. Indeed, all these surrealist practices might be seen as so many attempts, compulsively repeated, to master trauma, to transform the anxious into the aesthetic, the uncanny into the marvelous.[56]

Traumas are as varied as individuals, but prototypical scenes are few, and in his evocations of convulsive beauty and objective chance Breton suggests what his are. As we have seen, convulsive beauty involves states (veiled-erotic and fixed-explosive) that recall death or, more precisely, the inextricability of desire and death. "Neither static nor dynamic" (N 160), this beauty is like a *petite mort* in which the subject is shocked free of identity—in an experience of *jouissance* that is also a fore-image of death.[57] This too is why Breton terms this beauty convulsive, and why we must see it as uncanny.

Objective chance also involves situations (found objects and enigmatic encounters) that recall primal loss. For Breton and Giacometti this is the trauma of the disappearance of the mother, the loss of the primal love object, which Breton seeks to recapture in his serial lovers and Giacometti seems to resent in his (dis)agreeable objects. It is also the trauma of the fantasmatic perception of castration, a related loss that overdetermines all the others. And the objects that Breton and Giacometti find (or rather that find them, that *interrogate* them, as Breton says) are ciphers in this Oedipal conundrum too. In this way the marvelous, convulsive beauty, and objective chance are founded on traumas that involve the origin of desire in loss and its end in death, and surrealist art can be seen as different attempts to repeat and/or work through such events. (Such at least is the formulation that I want to test in the next chapter in relation to three crucial figures, de Chirico, Ernst, and Giacometti.)

A final word about surrealist beauty. At the end of *Nadja* Breton introduces the term through this simile: convulsive beauty is "like a train . . . destined to produce one *Shock*" (N 160). This association is not as strange as it seems, for the discourse of shock was developed in the nineteenth century partly in relation to railway accidents, the traumatic effects of which were regarded first physiologically, then psychologically, and finally psychoanalytically.[58] In short, shock is an alternate route to the unconscious, the discovery of which is so often traced first to hysteria, then to dreams. Significant here is that convulsive beauty invokes both these discourses fundamental to the psychoanalytic apprehension of the unconscious: shock *and* hysteria.[59] In 1928, the year that Breton proclaimed the ideal of convulsive beauty, he and Aragon also celebrated hysteria as "a supreme means of expression."[60] This celebration included several photographs of "the passionate attitudes" of the hysteric Augustine from the Charcot *Iconographie photographique de la Salpêtrière*. This is not coincidental, for convulsive beauty is patterned on hysterical beauty as an experience of the world convulsed, like the body of the hysteric, into "a forest of symbols." What are we to make of this problematic analogy?

In the celebration, Breton and Aragon cite Hippolyte Bernheim, Joseph Babinski, and Freud, and they also allude to Charcot and Janet. All these theorists regarded hysteria as a "malady through representation,"[61] but they differed, of course, on its etiology. As is well known, Charcot referred hysteria to an organic basis, and Janet to a constitutional deficiency. Freud and Breuer broke with this account in *Studies on Hysteria* (1895): they too saw dissociation as "the basic phenomenon of this neurosis," but they referred it to psychological conflict, not physiological fault.[62] Freud went further: the hysterical symptom is a somatic "conversion" of a psychic conflict, a repressed idea, wish, or desire. In his early texts he understood this effect to be born of an actual event (hence the famous formula that "hysterical patients suffer principally from reminiscences"),[63] specifically the trauma of sexual seduction.

Breton and Aragon assume this "laborious refutation of organic disturbances." They even quote Bernheim to the effect that hysteria eludes definition, and Babinski (with whom Breton interned briefly) to the effect that its symptoms can be produced by suggestion and removed by countersuggestion.[64] They do so not to debunk hysteria but to exploit its "dismemberment": as before with automatism and later with paranoia, they revalue it from "pathological phenomenon" to "poetic discovery." More, they re-define hysteria as a "mental state" based on "a reciprocal seduction" that subverts all relations "between the subject and the moral world." For Breton and Aragon, then, the hysteric is a paragon of a liberated love that, like the marvelous, suspends rational relations and that, like convulsive beauty, shatters moral subjecthood. In a sense, it is a form of ecstasy, and the "seduction" is "reciprocal": it produces its effects in others—in doctor or analyst, in artist or viewer. In this way hysteria becomes a paradigm for surrealist art, for it too is to render its subject hysterical, sympathetically convulsive, seized by signs of desire; it too is a continuation of sexual ecstasy by other means.[65] The emblematic image of this convulsive beauty is the Dalí *Phenomenon of Ecstasy* (1933), a photomontage of ecstatic faces (most female, some sculpted), an anthropometric set of ears, and an art nouveau ornament.[66]

The association between hysteria and art is not original to the surrealists. For years Charcot sifted through art history for signs of the hysteric in images of the possessed and the ecstatic, and more than once Freud re-marked, ambiguously enough, that "a case of hysteria is a caricature of a work of art."[67] Moreover, as Jan Goldstein has shown, there is in nineteenth-century France a *pre*psychoanalytic association of hysteria and art.[68] Whereas medical discourse used hysteria as a way to stereotype gender (the hysteric, even the male hysteric, as "feminine," i.e., as passive and pathological), literary discourse tended to exploit it as a way to play with difference. Some male writers assumed the position of the hysteric in order to take on a "feminine" perspective, an "hysterical" sensibility. The most famous in-stance, of course, is the identification of Flaubert with Madame Bovary, an identification that Baudelaire saw as an androgynization. But Baudelaire is his own best example of this hysterical move: "I have cultivated my hys-teria," he once wrote, "with *jouissance* and terror."[69] As we have seen, the surrealists cultivated hysteria through a similar association of the artist with the hysteric, both of whom were regarded as ecstatic and sublime (as in

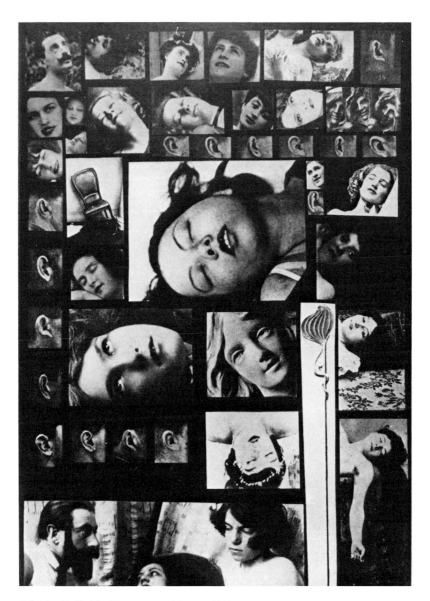

Salvador Dalí, *The Phenomenon of Ecstasy*, 1933.

Le peintre Max Ernst vu par la Photomaton

Photomat portraits of Max Ernst in *Variétés*, 1929.

convulsive beauty) or passive and pathological (as in poetic *disponibilité* or the paranoid-critical method).

And yet how subversive is this hysterical move? For Goldstein the nineteenth-century instances disturbed the strict gender coding of the time, but they hardly displaced, let alone exceeded, the stereotypical image of the feminine. Perhaps this recourse to hysteria only extended the purview of the male artist, who could thereby assume "female modalities" without any sacrifice of "male perogatives."[70] In effect, he could appropriate both the privilege of identity and the possibility of its subversion. The same may be true of the surrealist appeal to the hysteric. Granted, the surrealists attempted to rescue this figure from psychiatric discipline and to reinscribe her as a heroine of the movement, as a paragon of the artist (along with other "female ecstatics": the anarchist Germaine Barton, the patricide Violette Nozière, the murderous Papin sisters, all subjects of testimonials or texts in surrealist journals). But does this appeal constitute "a new vision of femininity . . . a new modernity"?[71]

In some feminist theory hysteria is seen as a ruse category that serves to exclude women as *subjects* from the very discourses that they help to constitute as *objects*. Classical psychoanalysis is one example of this discursive foundation-as-exclusion; traditional art (history) is another. The surrealist association of hysteria and art might function in a similar way: precisely because it is celebrated, the feminine, the female body, remains the silenced ground of this art.[72] However, this association departs from traditional aesthetics (if it does not improve on it): the female body is not the sublimated image of the beautiful but the *desublimated site of the sublime—i.e., the hysterical body inscribed with signs of sexuality and marks of death. Moreover, the surrealists not only desired this image, this figure; they also *identified* with it. And this identification should not be dismissed too quickly as an appropriation. In a simple sense they *wanted* to be hysterics, to be by turns passive and convulsive, *disponible* and ecstatic. In a more difficult sense they *were* hysterics, marked by traumatic fantasy, confused about sexual identity. Out of this condition some surrealists were able to develop a subversive association between sexual trauma and artistic representation—an association only suggested in Freud (and ambivalently too). It is to this development—from the problematic ideal of "convulsive beauty" into the provocative practice of "convulsive identity"—that I want to turn.

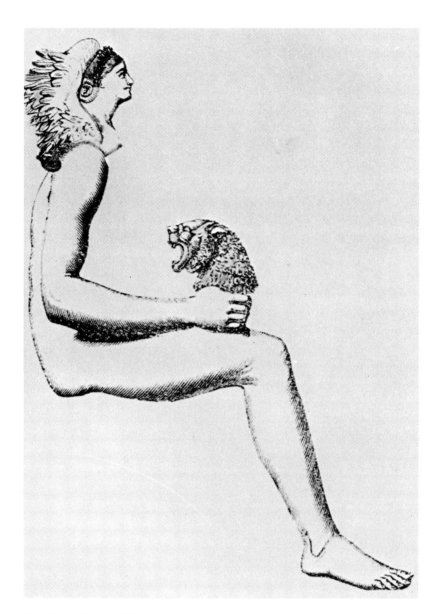

Max Ernst, *Oedipus*, 1931.

Convulsive Identity

If the marvelous as the leitmotif of surrealism involves the uncanny, and if the uncanny as the return of the repressed involves trauma, then trauma must somehow inform surrealist art. Such is the hypothesis I want to test here in relation to de Chirico, Ernst, and Giacometti. Again, according to Freud, the uncanny is evoked not only by reminders of death but also by evocations of traumatic scenes—scenes that put the subject in play, as it were. More than any others these three surrealists were obsessed by such scenes, to the point that they made them over into origin myths of art. Now to posit an origin in order to ground a self, to found a style, is a very familiar trope of modernism. The difficult difference here is that the primal fantasies of these surrealists render all such origins problematic: in this case at least, the modernist search for foundations leads to subversively non-foundational scenes.[1]

Freud distinguished three primal fantasies (*Urphantasien*) in our psychic life: that of seduction, the primal scene proper (where the child witnesses parental sex), and that of castration. First called scenes, they were later termed fantasies when it became clear that they need not be actual events to be psychically effective—that they are often constructed, in whole or part, after the fact, frequently with the collaboration of the analyst. Yet, though often contrived, these fantasies also tended to be uniform; in fact, the narratives appeared so fundamental that Freud deemed them phylogenetic: given schemas that we all elaborate upon. They are fundamental, he speculated, because it is through these fantasies that the child teases out the basic riddles of origins: in the fantasy of seduction the origin of sexuality, in the primal scene the origin of the individual, and in the fantasy of castration the origin of sexual difference. Freud added another primal fantasy, that of intrauterine existence, which might be seen as an ambiguous salve to the other, traumatic fantasies, especially that of castration, to which it is technically anterior. (At least this is how it functions in surrealism, where it is fundamental to the apprehension of space as uncanny.)[2] Here, however, I will focus on the first three types of fantasy, specifically on the ways that they appear to govern the art of de Chirico, Ernst, and Giacometti.

The return of such traumas in art is uncanny in its own right, but so is the very structure of the original scenes, formed as they are through a reconstructive repetition or "deferred action" (*Nachträglichkeit*). Again, in his early work on hysteria Freud referred each case to an actual event: for every hysteric there was a perverse seducer. Although he abandoned the seduction theory as early as 1897, he retained the essential idea of a trauma that is psychically originary though frequently fantasmatic. Enigmatically sexual, this initial event cannot be comprehended by the child (Freud described his state as one of fright [*Schreck*]). The memory of this event becomes pathogenic only if it is revived by a second event that the now sexual subject associates with the first, which is then recoded as sexual and so repressed.[3] This is why trauma seems to come from within and without, and why it is the memory, not the event, that is traumatic. Not strictly real for the child nor merely contrived by the adult, these primal scenes, Freud proposed, may be fantasies, intended at least in part "to cover up the autoerotic activity of the first years of childhood, to gloss it over and raise it to a higher level."[4] And yet they have all the effectivity of real events— even more so, Freud argued, for the subject often reworks actual experience according to the given scenarios of seduction, parental sex, and castration.[5]

Of course, fantasy cannot be reduced to these three types, nor do they appear in pure form. As I will suggest, the seduction fantasy of de Chirico has a castrative aspect; the primal scene of Ernst betrays a seductive side; and the castration fantasy of Giacometti begins as an intrauterine wish. These fantasies are also inflected by screen memory and conscious design; they are thus not temporally primary so much as structurally originary. Yet it is precisely in this way that primal fantasy may illuminate surrealist art. As expressly visual scenarios in which the psychic, the sexual, and the perceptual are bound together, primal fantasy does much to explain the peculiar pictorial structures and object relations of surrealism—specifically why subject positions and spatial constructions are rarely fixed. The scene of a daydream, for example, is relatively stable because the ego is relatively centered. This is not the case in primal fantasy where the subject not only is *in* the scene but also may identify with any of its elements. Such participation renders the scene as elastic as the subject is mobile, and this is so because the fantasy is "not the object of desire, but its setting," its mise-en-scène.[6] Such fantasmatic subjectivity and spatiality are put into play in surrealist art, where the first is often passive and the second often perspectivally skewed or anamorphically distorted.[7]

Breton struggled to articulate this basis of surrealist art in two well-known metaphors. In the "Manifesto of Surrealism" (1924) he points to the fantasmatic position of the surrealist subject with the automatist image of "a man cut in two by a window."[8] This image suggests neither a descriptive mirror nor a narrative window, the familiar paradigms of postmedieval art, but a fantasmatic window, a "purely interior model"[9] in which the subject is somehow split both positionally—at once inside and outside the scene—and psychically—"cut in two." Later in *L'Amour fou* (1937) Breton complements this image of the subject in fantasy with an image that suggests its projective aspect: surrealist art as a grid inscribed with "letters of desire" (AF 87). Implicitly in both accounts the artist does not invent new forms so much as he retraces fantasmatic scenes.[10]

Two points should be stressed here. All three fantasies touch upon the castration complex, which the surrealists evoke in scenarios fetishistic, voyeuristic, and/or sadistic in import. Theodor Adorno, no great friend of surrealism, once argued that its images are fetishes on which the "libido was once fixated. It is through these fetishes, not through immersion in the self, that the images bring back childhood."[11] This is indeed the rule in surrealism, but the presence of the primal fantasies points to exceptions: they suggest a self-immersion that might complicate sexuality, identity, and difference, a surrealism that might *defetishize* these terms. In short, the surrealist subject is more various than its heterosexist types otherwise imply (again, such mobility is characteristic of fantasy). After all, the primal fantasies are riddles about origins, not resolutions: they question rather than fix these terms.

Second, the source of surrealist fantasies is uncertain, as is registered by the paradoxical language used to describe them. Breton says that he "looks out" into a pure interior (SP 4), Ernst that he limns "what is visible inside him."[12] This uncertainty may be related to that of the source of the trauma narrated in the primal fantasy. As Jean Laplanche and J.-B. Pontalis gloss the theory of seduction:

> The whole of the trauma comes *both* from within and without: from without, since sexuality reaches the subject from *the other;* from within, since it springs from this internalized exteriority, this "*reminiscence* suffered by hysterics" (according to the Freudian formula), reminiscence in which we already discern what will be later named fantasy.[13]

As I noted in chapter 2, this uncertainy of inside and outside, psychic and perceptual, is fundamental to the talismanic concepts of surrealism: the marvelous, convulsive beauty, and objective chance. Indeed, the distinctive character of surrealist art may reside in the different ways that it works through psychic trauma in scenes that register as both internal and external, endogenous and exogenous, fantasmatic and real—in a word, surreal.

Primal fantasy structures other surrealist oeuvres too, and it also informs the contradictory and simulacral aspects of surrealist images more generally.[14] I focus on de Chirico, Ernst, and Giacometti because each not only evokes a different primal fantasy but also accounts for a different aesthetic method or medium: the development of "metaphysical painting" by de Chirico, of surrealist collage, frottage, and grattage by Ernst, of "symbolic objects" by Giacometti. These origin myths are the manifest content of the elaborated fantasies, but again they are grounded in more basic questions concerning the origins of sexuality, identity, and difference. Here degrees of awareness become difficult to determine.[15] The Ernst text seems consciously to exploit a screen memory of a primal scene in order to upset given ideas of identity (which, he writes after Breton, "will be convulsive or will not exist" [BP 19]). The Giacometti text also involves a screen memory—of a castration fantasy that encompasses both an Oedipal threat and a pubertal dream of sadistic revenge—but it is never fully worked through. Finally, the de Chirico text is somewhere between the other two. Set in an adult moment, his fantasy of seduction is traumatic, and yet he deploys its sublimated signs too; indeed, they are basic to his aesthetic of "enigma."

In a recent text Laplanche uses this de Chirican term to rethink all the primal fantasies as forms of seduction: not as sexual assaults but as "enigmatic signifers" received by the child from the other (parent, sibling, etc.).[16] It is this enigmatic, even seductive nature of primal fantasy that moves the artists not simply to simulate it but to elaborate the very origins of art in its terms. They cannot, however, escape the trauma of such fantasy, and it is finally this trauma that, never tamed, compels them to reenact such scenes—an uncanny reenactment of which they often appear more victim than master.

-❀ ❀-

In several short texts from 1911 to 1919 de Chirico speaks of "revelation" and "surprise," "enigma" and "fatality."[17] During the period that Freud drafts "The Uncanny" de Chirico works to depict the world as "an immense museum of strangeness," to reveal the "mystery" in insignificant things.[18] This topos seems to be the estrangement that comes of repression and returns as enigma, an enigma that he once refers to "the great questions one has always asked oneself—why was the world created, why we are born, live and die. . . ."[19] His "metaphysical" terms are thus so many riddles about origins—but to what origin do "surprise" and "enigma" speak? What origin estranges even as it founds? "Art is the fatal net which catches these strange moments," de Chirico tells us, and these moments are not dreams.[20] What are they then?

In his early texts de Chirico dwells on a memory that is elaborated in his early paintings, especially *Enigma of an Autumn Afternoon* (1910), to which it is directly referred, and *The Enigma of a Day* (1914).[21] In some sense it is elaborated in all his work. The first version comes from the 1912 text "Meditations of a Painter":

> One clear autumnal morning I was sitting on a bench in the middle of the Piazza Santa Croce in Florence. It was of course not the first time I had seen this square. I had just come out of a long and painful intestinal illness, and I was in a nearly morbid state of sensitivity. The whole world, down to the marble of the buildings and the fountains, seemed to me to be convalescent. In the middle of the square rises a statue of Dante draped in a long cloak, holding his works. . . . Then I had the strange impression that I was looking at all these things for the first time, and the composition of my picture came to my mind's

Giorgio de Chirico, *Enigma of an Autumn Afternoon*, 1910.

eye. Now each time I look at this painting I again see that moment. Nevertheless, that moment is an enigma to me, for it is inexplicable. And I like also to call the work which sprang from it an enigma.[22]

However enigmatic, this scene has its own sense. The space of the piazza is transformed by two temporalities that coexist within it: an event of "not the first time" that triggers a memory of "the first time," a structure characteristic of deferred action in primal fantasy. So, too, the scene is traumatic in the aforementioned sense that the enigma comes to de Chirico both from within and without, in the symptom of the intestinal illness and in the guise of the Dante statue. The illness alone is not enough to render the scene an originary "revelation"; it has this effect because it evokes a primal fantasy through a resisted, retrospective association—perhaps of *sick* with *sexual,* of *intestinal* with *genital.* Thus the scene reads as a displaced version of a fantasmatic seduction, a hypothesis that figures the statue as the father, the other who initiates the subject into sexuality (another section of this text is titled "The Statue's Desire").[23] Here de Chirico rewrites a traumatic initiation into sexuality into an origin myth of art.

Yet why is the scene partly seductive, or at least not entirely traumatic? Consider how it is treated in the two most relevant paintings. The "atmosphere" of the 1910 *Enigma* is "warm,"[24] and the space welcomes artist and viewer. Yet a few ambiguous signs disturb this relative calm: two obscured portals; an acephalic, almost androgynous statue; and two tiny figures in antique dress posed like Adam and Eve in an expulsion. This tension constitutes the "enigma" of the painting, sexual in nature, to be referred perhaps to a precocious initiation. For Freud a related seduction was crucial to the formation of Leonardo: an initiation by the mother that produced a sexual ambivalence, as worked over, never openly, in the enigmatic smile of the Mona Lisa and the androgynous features of other figures. A similar trauma seems to inform de Chirico, but here the fantasmatic seducer appears paternal, and the seduction produces an especially ambivalent Oedipal subject. In the first *Enigma* this ambivalence seems worked over in terms more "negative" than "positive," i.e., by a subject more amorous than jealous of the father.[25]

The treatment of this ambivalence is dramatically different in the 1914 *Enigma*. The space now threatens artist and viewer with its extreme perspective, and the mysterious portals are replaced by a steep arcade, "symbol of the intransigent will."[26] This arcade submits our look to the patriarchal statue that dominates the scene; meanwhile, the Adam and Eve figures are all but banished by this modern god. In the two *Enigmas,* then, a primal fantasy of seduction appears replayed first in its seductive (negative-Oedipal) aspect and then in its traumatic (positive-Oedipal) form.

In his 1913 text "Mystery and Creation" de Chirico restages this fantasy in the anxious terms that become standard in his paintings after the second *Enigma*:

> I remember one vivid winter's day at Versailles. . . . Everything gazed at me with mysterious, questioning eyes. And then I realized that every corner of the place, every column, every window possessed a spirit, an impenetrable soul. I looked around at the marble heroes, motionless in the lucid air, beneath the frozen rays of that winter sun which pours down on us *without love*. . . . At that moment I grew aware of the mystery which urges men to create certain forms. And the creation appeared more extraordinary than the creators. . . .
>
> Perhaps the most amazing sensation passed on to us by prehistorical man is that of presentiment. It will always continue. We might consider it as an eternal proof of the irrationality of the universe. Original man must have wandered through a world full of uncanny signs. He must have trembled at each step.[27]

Giorgio de Chirico, *The Enigma of a Day*, 1914.

Again a later scene appears to trigger a memory of a prior event, which returns here less as a seductive enigma than as a traumatic threat. However repressed or sublimated, the agent of this provocation remains the father. At this point this hypothesis may seem fully absurd, for where is the father in this fantasy? In the first version he appears in proxy (the statue), and so he does here. In this scene the look of de Chirico is returned as a gaze back at him (in the guise of the "marble heroes"), and it may be this gaze, castrative in import, that stands in for the father. Endowed with a gaze, objects appear more alive than de Chirico, and they query his lack. His active seeing has reversed into a passive being-seen.[28]

In this form of the gaze as threat de Chirico works over his enigma, especially in still lifes of spectral objects and cityscapes of paranoid perspectives. In these paintings perspective works less to ground any depicted figure than to unsettle the expected viewer; it is often thrown so forward that things appear to see us. Thus if de Chirico partially revives perspective he does so in a way that disturbs it from within.[29] Both points of coherence, viewing and vanishing, are decentered, sometimes to the point where the "seer" appears *within* the scene as a sightless, degendered mannequin, a "Medusa with eyes that do not see."[30] As rational perspective is deranged, the visual array as such becomes uncanny: a forest less of iconographic symbols than of enigmatic signifers concerning sexuality, identity, and difference. In the second version of the fantasy, as in the first, de Chirico almost grasps its significance. Once more he senses that origins are at stake, but again he displaces them—here not to his art but to creation as such. As in the primal fantasy according to Freud, he "fills in the gaps in individual truth with prehistoric truth."[31] That is, he refers his fantasy, his confusion about origins that upset as well as ground the subject, to "prehistorical man," as if his primal fantasy, its uncanny signs, were always already there to seduce and threaten.

But why see this enigma as a primal fantasy, and, more outrageously, why claim it to be a fantasy of seduction, especially when the de Chirico texts, though clearly concerned with origins, are scarcely sexual? One might invoke repression or sublimation, but the de Chirico of this period does evince seduction in two ways at least: in a thematic register of a welcomed seduction in which paternal figures appear, and in an enigmatic register of a traumatic seduction whose deflected signs are everywhere—in the gaze of objects, the corruption of space, the uncanniness of repeated symbols and shapes. The first register is most apparent in a theme that de Chirico repeats in different ways: the return of the prodigal. Here the fantasmatic seduction is perfectly disguised: in this traditional subject the father can be represented as fully ambiguous, a desired persecutor. In one drawing of 1917, for example, the mustachioed figure is partially derobed in petrified drag, while in another drawing of 1917 he is a statue come down from its plinth. In both images the son is a sightless, armless mannequin, submissive in the first, struggling in the second. These identities hold for many other appearances of the statue and the mannequin in de Chirico, and this encounter recurs throughout his work.

The more important enigmatic register of seduction is more difficult to locate. Breton once suggested that the de Chirican "revelation" concerning "our instinctual life" is effected through a revision of time and space,[32] and it is here that his fantasy of seduction seems folded into his art: according to de Chirico, in the "inhabited depth" that disturbs like a "symptom" the array of his metaphysical painting,[33] or, in our terms, in the psychic time (i.e., the deferred action of primal fantasy) that corrupts his pictorial space. De Chirico tends to think this strange revision of time and space in symbolic, even iconographic terms. Influenced by *Geschlecht und Charakter* (Sex and Character), the notorious 1903 text by the Austrian Otto Weininger that touches on the psychological effects of geometric forms, de Chirico advocates "a new metaphysical psychology of things" that might capture "the terror of lines and angles . . . [the] joys and sorrows . . . hidden within a portico, the angle of a street or even a room, on the surface of a table between the sides of a box."[34] This psychology seems to involve a traumatic vision, one of ambivalent uncanny signs. And these signs always appear

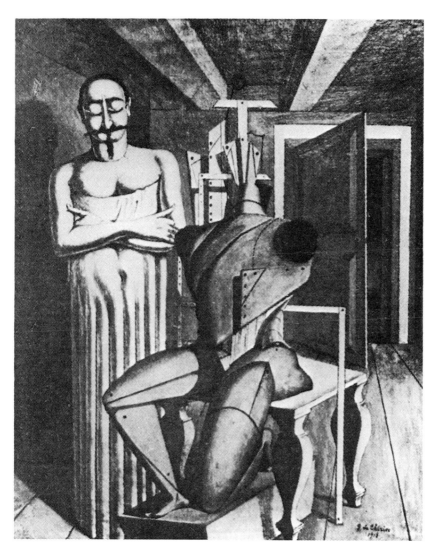

Giorgio de Chirico, *The Return*, 1917.

associated with his engineer father whose traces (tools, easels, drawings) are everywhere in the work.

The subject doubled by strange figures, surveyed by uncanny objects, threatened by anxious perspectives, decentered by claustrophobic interiors: these enigmatic signifiers point to a sexual trauma, a fantasy of seduction. This reading is supported by the more manifest complexes that govern the oeuvre, paranoia and melancholy, the first associated with de Chirico by the surrealists, the second evoked by the artist in various titles.[35] Both underscore the fantasmatic basis of his art.

The fantasy of seduction stirs a sexuality that the subject defends against. According to Freud, paranoia may also be a defense against sexuality—homosexuality—whereby the subject transforms the loved parent of the same sex into a persecutor.[36] This projection may account, at least in part, for the ambiguity of the surrealist father, split as bad object and good, philistine castrator and benevolent protector, as well as for the ambivalence of the surrealist son, contemptuous of the father yet obsessed by him (as Ernst, Dalí, and Bellmer, to name a few others, all were). Though more manifest elsewhere, this surrealist topos of paranoia begins with de Chirico, and it is he who develops its basic pictorial formulas.[37] Suggestive in this regard is the mannequin, doll, or dummy as a disguised self-portrait, the paranoid significance of which is intimated in "The Uncanny" where Freud discusses the E. T. A. Hoffmann story "The Sandman." In this story the father is split as if by the Oedipal ambivalence of the son Nathaniel into two sets of figures, the one kind and protective, the other castrative and pledged to blind him—a familiar association between castration and blindness central to surrealism. Important here is the desire of the son for the good father, a "feminine attitude" figured by the doll Olympia: "Olympia is, as it were, a dissociated complex of Nathaniel's which confronts him as a person, and Nathaniel's enslavement to this complex is expressed in his senseless obsessive love for Olympia."[38] This may be the psychological import of this surrealist self-representation. Sexually ambiguous in the de Chirican oeuvre, this figure suggests that the fantasmatic persecution of the

70

father may be a reversed form of the desired seduction by him. And in de Chirico as in Ernst (who follows him closely here) the two terms are in fact mixed: in some works the paranoid term is dominant (e.g., most famously, in the de Chirico *The Mystery and Melancholy of a Street* [1914] and the Ernst *Two Children Are Threatened by a Nightingale* [1924]), while in other works the seductive term is paramount (e.g., *The Child's Brain* [1914] and *Pietà, or the Revolution by Night* [1923]).[39] Though opposite representations of the father, both terms may elaborate upon a disguised love for him.

This reading is supported by the third psychic trope that governs the de Chirico oeuvre: melancholy. In certain ways the melancholic incorporation of the dead father overcodes the other two scenarios of welcomed seduction and paranoid projection. From "surprise" and "enigma" de Chirico passes to "nostalgia" and "melancholy": from scenarios of seduction and persecution he moves to compulsively repeated homages to the dead seducer. Evariste de Chirico died in 1905 when Giorgio was seventeen. The son was devoted to the father, but de Chirico never refers the melancholy in his oeuvre to this loss. He assigns it to other terms (which the critical literature mostly reiterates): a nostalgia for Italy, neoclassical styles, old master techniques, and so on. These lost objects pervade his work in the form of ruined references and failed recoveries. Psychically, however, they may be charged as representatives of the dead father.[40]

For the melancholic the lost love object is partly unconscious. Unable to give it up, he clings to it "through the medium of a hallucinatory wish-psychosis" in which deeply cathected memories are obsessively repeated.[41] Along with the sublimation of seduction, this process effects the uncanny nature of de Chirican scenes, hallucinatory and reiterative as they are; it also compounds the ambivalence that they register. For just as the subject of the fantasmatic seduction is ambivalent vis-à-vis the seducer, so too is the melancholic vis-à-vis the lost object. As the melancholic de Chirico internalizes his lost object, he also internalizes his ambivalence for it, which is then turned round on the subject.[42] This ambivalence for both subject and object is most apparent in de Chirico, and for a time he sustains it. However,

Max Ernst, *Pietà, or the Revolution by Night*, 1923.

its destructive aspect soon becomes dominant, as he comes to identify with images of the dead (dead father, traditional motifs, old master methods), as is evident in the self-reification of *Self-Portrait* (1922). Here melancholy seems to pass over into masochism.

The working over of seduction, the paranoid projection of persecution, the melancholic repetition of loss: all these processes in de Chirico fascinate. Certainly they fascinated the surrealists—that is, until they could no longer ignore his necrophilic turn. In 1926 Breton wrote: "It took me, it took us, five years to despair of de Chirico, to admit that he had lost all sense of what he was doing."[43] But did he really lose this sense, or was he finally overcome by it? That is, was his deathly repetition (first of historical motifs, then of his own images) a willed break in bad faith, or an involuntary development of an uncanny psychologic? As Breton knew with Nadja, a disruptive subject may intrigue, but a truly defusive one repels, and so it was finally with de Chirico and the surrealists. Compulsive repetition was always the motor of his obsessional work. For a time he was able to recoup it as a mode of art, to make a muse of uncanny returns, as he did in *The Disquieting Muses* (1917). Eventually he could inflect it no further, and his work petrified in melancholic repetition, as is evident in the many versions of this painting.[44] As petrification became its condition rather than its subject, his art came to intimate, as Freud once said of melancholy, "a pure culture of the death instinct."[45]

-❦ ❦-

In 1924 in *La Révolution surréaliste* 1 de Chirico was asked to recount his most impressive dream:

> I struggle in vain with the man whose eyes are suspicious and very gentle. Each time I grasp him, he frees himself by quietly spreading his arms which have an unbelievable strength, an

Giorgio de Chirico, nine versions of *The Disquieting Muses*.

incalculable power. . . . It is my father who thus appears to me in my dreams. . . .

The struggle ends with my *surrender: I give up*: then the images become confused. . . .[46]

In effect, this dream conflates aspects of a fantasy of seduction with a primal scene. No longer returned as a persecutory gaze from the scene, the look becomes embodied within it, as the subject assumes a "feminine attitude" to the father. Yet this relation is overcoded by the traumatic schema of seduction, so that the father remains a menace as well. In this way images of seduction and struggle, desire and anguish are indeed "confused." In Ernst such confusion regarding sexuality, identity, and difference is programmatic; he consciously puts into play the trauma of the primal scene (in which a similar fantasmatic relation to the father is suggested) in order "to hasten the general crisis of consciousness due in our time" (BP 25).

In 1927 in *La Révolution surréaliste* 9-10 Ernst published "Visions de demi-sommeil." This short text was the origin of his 1948 book *Beyond Painting,* in which Ernst deploys infantile scenarios, family romances, and screen memories (with echoes of the Freud studies of Leonardo, the Wolf Man, and Judge Schreber), many of which are also invoked in his art.[47] The title text of the book, "Au-delà de la peinture" (1936), has three parts. The first, titled "History of a Natural History," opens with a "vision of half-sleep" dated "from 5 to 7 years":

I see before me a panel, very rudely painted with wide black lines on a red ground, representing false mahogany and calling forth associations of organic forms (menacing eye, long nose, great head of a bird with thick black hair, etc.).

In front of the panel, a glossy black man is making gestures, slow, comical and, according to my memories of a very obscure epoch, joyously obscene. This rogue of a fellow wears the turned-up moustaches of my father. (BP 3)

Menacing eye, long nose, great head of a bird, obscene gestures, rogue father: this is an obvious chain of signifiers—a first encounter with painting cast in terms of a primal scene. In a near parody of deferred action this screen memory layers three moments: (1) "the occasion of my own conception" (BP 4), the fantasy of the primal scene that is the retrospective origin of the vision; (2) the described encounter with the father-painter (in the period of latency), which both evokes the primal scene as sexual and represses it as such; and (3) the act of memory ("at the age of puberty" [BP 4]), in which the first two scenes are recoded as an artistic initiation. Yet this artistic origin or identity is refused, as the father is made to appear both ridiculous and oppressive (Ernst *père* was a Sunday painter of academic art). However, it is only as such that he is rejected; as his paranoid preoccupations suggest, Ernst is ambivalent about the paternal.

However contrived, this primal scene remains traumatic for Ernst, for he elaborates it many times over in his text—to master its charge, to transform its affect, to rework its meaning.[48] In "History of a Natural History" it is followed by a reference to Leonardo, an artist also said to work over a traumatic fantasy. Specifically Ernst refers to his exemplum (cherished by the surrealists) that even a stain on a wall might inspire pictorial invention. If Ernst rejected his paternal artistic origin, he embraces this self-invented one:

On the tenth of August, 1925, an insupportable visual obsession caused me to discover the technical means which have brought a clear realization of this lesson of Leonardo. Beginning with a memory of childhood (related above) in the course of which a panel of false mahogany, situated in front of my bed, had played

Max Ernst, *La Femme 100 têtes*, 1929: "The might-have-been Immaculate Conception."

the role of optical provocateur of a vision of half-sleep, I was struck by the obsession that showed to my excited gaze the floor-boards upon which a thousand scrubbings had deepened the grooves. I decided then to investigate the symbolism of this obsession. (BP 7)

This investigation takes the form of his first frottages or rubbings (published in a 1926 portfolio *Natural History*), to which Ernst responds: "I was surprised by the sudden intensification of my visionary capacities and by the hallucinatory succession of contradictory images superimposed, one upon the other, with the persistence and rapidity characteristic of amorous memories" (BP 7). Here again the visionary develops out of the voyeuristic; once more artistic identity is framed in terms of a primal scene (hallucinatory, contradictory, amorous). In this case, however, the primal scene is rewritten as an aesthetic invention, one that redeems the original event even as it is rooted in it: in its scopophilic look, in its autoerotic rubbing.[49] According to Freud, the significant "rubbing" in the primal scene is not that of the parents but that of the child whose fantasy is designed to "cover up" his autoerotic activity, to "elevate" it in fact. The frottage technique reprises this hypothetical moment: it is an artistic origin in which fantasy, sexuality, and representation are all bound together, at once covered up and elevated.

But how covered up and elevated, i.e., how sublimated? Here Ernst diverges from the Freud account of Leonardo, which he otherwise parallels, perhaps follows. There Freud argues that the investigative powers of the artist derived from a sexual curiosity never checked by his absent father. Ernst shares this curiosity, which is finally about origins, and in "Some Data on the Youth of M.E." he plays with this portrait (as with Freud on Leonardo, he keys the beginning of his curiosity to the birth of a sibling rival). However, the crux of the Leonardo analysis concerns his precocious initiation, a trauma that emerged as a sexual ambiguity in his art. It is this that Ernst seeks to reproduce—but with a difference. He does not sublimate

it; in his techniques of collaging, rubbing, and scraping he *resexualizes* it—
in part to flaunt his father (who was far from absent), to shock his petit-
bourgeois society.

In his analysis Freud thinks this sexual ambiguity through the famous
fantasy of Leonardo—that as an infant his lips were brushed by the tail of a
vulture. In this story, according to Freud, Leonardo "remembers" the nurs-
ing of his solitary mother—a memory of love that he later reciprocates in
his devotion to the subject of the Virgin and Child.[50] However, Freud
argues, this memory of a maternal nipple also conceals a fantasy of a
maternal penis, and it is finally this paradox—of a seduction both pleasant
and assaultive, of a parent both tender and terrible—that Leonardo works
over in his enigmatic figures. A related enigma, I have claimed, is treated
in different ways by de Chirico. So is it too by Ernst, most consciously in
his ambiguous persona Loplop, variously bird and/or human, male and/or
female.[51] But Ernst also works over this sexual ambiguity in formal or
procedural ways (as with de Chirico, this is no simple iconographic connection). Indeed, his aesthetic privileges the "passive" (homosexual) position
that Leonardo assumes in his fantasy; more generally it prizes "the continuously shifting positions of traumatic sexuality."[52] It is this sentient, sexual
motility that Ernst seeks in his art.

In this way Ernst not only puts this traumatic sexuality into play but
also recoups it as a general theory of aesthetic practice. "It is," he writes,
"as a spectator that the author assists . . . at the birth of his work. . . . The
role of the painter is to . . . *project that which sees itself in him*" (BP 9).
Though complicated, this formula suggests why the primal scene is so
important to Ernst, for it allows him to think the artist as both active creator
(of his aesthetic identity) and passive receiver (of his automatist work), as
both participant inside and voyeur outside the scene of his art. Like the
subject in the fantasy "A Child Is Being Beaten," he is not fixed in any one
position: hypothetically at least, the usual oppositions of subject and object,
active and passive, masculine and feminine, heterosexual and homosexual,

are suspended. But how exactly is this done? What is the psychic mechanism at work?

Ernst focused his first memory of the primal scene on an active, even sadistic object: the father-painter (the child often interprets parental sex as paternal aggression). In his second scene, however, there is a turning round from the object to the subject and a reversal from active to passive: a move from an active seeing almost to a passive being-seen (as occurs in de Chirico). For Freud sexuality first emerges in this turn to the autoerotic, to the fantasmatic hallucination of the lost object, and it is this originary turn that Ernst wants to recapitulate in his art. It is a moment that, recovered, suspends the aforementioned oppositions that constrain identity. In *Instincts and Their Vicissitudes* (1917) Freud defines this in-between state thus: "The active voice is changed, not into the passive, but into the reflexive middle voice."[53] Though understood here as a linguistic position, this state is eminently visual and tactile, and it is in these terms that Ernst poses it as the basis of his art: in the reflexive moment of looking, in the autoerotic sense of touching. If de Chirico swings between seeing and being-seen, Ernst privileges the state in between—when one is caught up in the sequence of fantasmatic images, "surprised and enamored of what I *saw* wishing to identify with it all" (BP 9). For Ernst this is the ideal condition of art—to be "engrossed in this activity (passivity)" (BP 8), to be suspended in a sentience disruptive of identity, a convulsive identity in which axes of desire and identification cross. It is a "hysterical" condition that the surrealists prized above all others: in its benign form they called it *disponibilité,* in its anxious form "critical paranoia" (BP 8).

In the second section of "Au-delà de la peinture" Ernst continues this art-treatise-*cum*-auto-analysis in relation to collage (its title, "The Placing under Whiskey-Marine," was that of his 1921 Paris show of dadaist collages). "One rainy day in 1919 . . . I was struck by the obsession which held under my gaze . . . an illusive succession of contradictory images . . . peculiar to love memories and vision of half-sleep" (BP 14). Obsession, gaze, contradictory images, visions of half-sleep: once again Ernst frames an aesthetic discovery in terms of an infantile one, the visual fascinations and (pre)sexual confusions of the primal scene. This association determines not only his definition of collage, "the *coupling* of two realities, irreconcilable in appearance, upon a plane which apparently does not suit them" (BP 13), but also his understanding of its purpose: collage disturbs "the principle of identity" (BP 19), even "abolishes" the concept of "author" (BP 20).[54]

Not just another rehearsal of Lautréamont, this definition is fundamental to surrealism, for it implicitly characterizes the surrealist image as a transvaluation of dadaist collage. In surrealism collage is less a transgressive montage of constructed social materials (i.e., of high art and mass-cultural forms) located in the world, as it is in dada, and more a disruptive montage of conductive psychic signifiers (i.e., of fantasmatic scenarios and enigmatic events) referred to the unconscious. To the social reference of dadaist collage the surrealist image deepens the unconscious dimension: the image becomes a psychic montage that is temporal as well as spatial (in its deferred action), endogenous as well as exogenous (in its sources), subjective as well as collective (in its significations). In short, the surrealist image is patterned upon the symptom as an enigmatic signifier of a psychosexual trauma.

Again, for Ernst the primary trauma is the primal scene; it is this coupling that his collage aesthetic works over. As with de Chirico this working over is not only thematic; it occurs at the level of process and form—if only to undo both. In his early work Ernst did not simply reject painting as paternal and traditional; rather, he moved "beyond" it to collage modes as more effective ways to transform the principle of identity. One early example of such coupling must suffice here. *The Master's Bedroom* (1920) alludes to the primal scene thematically, but it is in the construction of the scene that the trauma is treated, the charge released in the subject, the *punctum* inscribed in the viewer: in its contradictory scale, anxious perspective, and mad juxtaposition (table, bed, cabinet, whale, sheep, bear). Together these procedural elements produce the de Chirican effect of a returned gaze that positions the spectator both in and out of the picture,

Max Ernst, *The Master's Bedroom*, 1920.

that makes him (like the eponymous child) both master and victim of the scene.[55]

Such couplings are repeated in his collages, frottages, grattages, and decalcomanias, all of which, driven by trauma and structured in repetition, are pledged, consciously or not, to transform the principle of identity. In "Instantaneous Identity," the last section of "Au-delà de la peinture," Ernst speaks of this subjectivity in the very language of the primal scene: "he displays [note the characteristic split in personal reference] two attitudes (contradictory in appearance but in reality simply in a state of conflict) that . . . are convulsively fused into one" (BP 19). Here an "hysterical" trauma is recouped as a convulsive identity, and it is precisely in the shock of the collaged image—in the "exchange of energy" (BP 19) between its psychic signifiers—that this is achieved. In the coupling of two scenes, in the deferred action of fantasy, subjectivity is indeed convulsed.

Of course, such a convulsive identity is difficult to sustain; and rather than a reflexive middle voice Ernst tends to swing between active and passive modes, sadistic and masochistic scenes. Paranoid fantasies (scenerios of domination or submission, delusions of grandeur or persecution, hallucinations of the end or of the beginning of the world) come to govern the work. Especially evident in the collage novels, such extreme visions also pervade "Some Data on the Youth of M.E.," where Ernst writes that "he came out of the egg which his mother had laid in an eagle's nest" and that "he was sure he was little Jesus Christ" (BP 27). Both these fantasies are related family romances, i.e., stories that reconfigure the family in ideal terms. The first fantasy of the egg displaces the father, but the second fantasy reveals this to be less a psychotic disavowal than an incestuous apotheosis: little Max as Christ positions the father as God.[56] Gradually, however, this attachment is broken, partly through the figure of Loplop. At first the desired father paranoiacally projected as the "menacing bird," Loplop eventually represents the lawful father introjected as the superego (the appellation "Bird Superior," the vocation "my private phantom" [BP 29], even the castrative onomatopoeia all suggest this). Especially as he loses his hybrid character,

———

Loplop comes to figure the "positive" Oedipal passage of Ernst whereby he assumes a normative heterosexual position; i.e., he becomes "perturbed" about castration and identifies "voluntarily" with the father (BP 29). And yet for Ernst to arrive at this end is to become fixed in a way that his own aesthetic credo argues against. After the early collages his work tends to illustrate more than to enact a convulsive identity.[57]

If in de Chirico the origin of metaphysical painting is refracted through an enigmatic seduction and in Ernst that of surrealist collage through a primal scene, then in Giacometti the origin of symbolic objects is refracted through a fantasy of castration. For Freud artistic inventions may stem from sexual inquiries made as children, two of which he stresses: where do I come from? And what distinguishes the sexes, i.e., which one am I? While Ernst elaborates on both questions, Giacometti focuses on the second. Like Ernst, he poses this riddle in a way that troubles sexual difference, that places conventional subject positions in doubt; however, unlike Ernst, he is profoundly troubled by this riddle. Some of his surrealist objects attempt to suspend the putative castration that subtends sexual difference, or at least to render sexual reference ambiguous. Others seem to disavow this castration fetishistically, while still others appear to punish its female representative sadistically. Although the surrealist fetish quickly became a cruel cliché, Giacometti was able to sustain his psychic ambivalence and to recoup it as a symbolic ambiguity—at least for a few years.[58]

Three texts will guide my reading. The first is the last in date, the famous statement regarding *The Palace at 4 A.M.* published in *Minotaure* in December 1933. Here Giacometti writes that his objects come to him "entirely completed" like so many psychic readymades that, if modified at all, are totally lost.[59] Automatist in bias, this remark also suggests the fantasmatic basis of his work, which Giacometti elsewhere describes in terms of "projection."[60] And in fact his favored formats of the cage, the game board,

Max Ernst, *La Femme 100 têtes*, 1929: "Germinal, my sister, the hundred headless woman. (In the background, in the cage, the Eternal Father.)"

Alberto Giacometti, *The Palace at 4 A.M.*, 1932–1933.

and the fetish do project a fantasmatic space between the actual and the virtual. That the fantasies are traumatic is implied in the *Minotaure* text: "Once the object is constructed, I tend to find in it, transformed and displaced, images, impressions, and facts that have moved me profoundly (often unknown to me), and forms that I feel to be very close to me, although I am often incapable of identifying them, which makes them all the more disturbing to me."[61]

His test case is the *The Palace at 4 A.M.,* which seems to reprise a dream or screen memory that, prompted by a love affair, concerns a traumatic memory. Besides a skeletal bird and a spinal column, both of which Giacometti relates to his lover, the stage contains three primary figures: a scaffold of a tower; an abstracted woman in front of three "curtains" associated with his mother; and a pod form on a "red" plank with which Giacometti identifies (again the subject is *in* the fantasmatic scene). Within the Oedipal triangle these figures are indeed "displaced," for here the paternal term, the tower, is "unfinished" or "broken," while the mother appears dominant in her long "black" dress. Yet this displacement reveals more than conceals the fetishistic scenario of the piece: a vision "in my earliest memories" of his mother, a glance diverted to her dress which "seemed to me like part of her body." A site of a fetishistic displacement, the dress still provokes "fear and confusion." This implies that the castrative charge of the vision cannot be blunted; indeed, its stake is figured in the spinal column that hangs, like some phallus dentatus, at once cut and whole, from a string. That this fantasy is not simply scripted is suggested by its genuinely disarticulative aspect, which appears both obscure in meaning and layered in time.[62] That is to say, the scenario of *Palace* seems constructed out of the deferred action of traumatic fantasy.

Giacometti almost intuits this process in an earlier text published in *Le Surréalisme au service de la révolution* in December 1931, which presents sketches of works such as *Cage, Suspended Ball,* two *Disagreeable Objects,* and *Project for a Square* (all c. 1931) under the rubric "objets mobiles et muets."[63] Below the drawings is an automatist caption that runs together

OBJETS MOBILES ET MUETS

Toutes choses... près, loin, toutes celles qui sont passées et les autres, par devant,

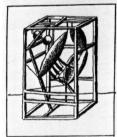 

trois personnes, de quelle gare? Les locomotives qui sifflent, il n'y a pas de gare par ici,

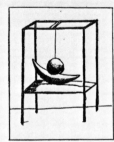 

qui bougent et mes amies — elles changent (on passe tout près, elles sont loin), d'autres approchent, montent, descendent, des canards sur l'eau, là et là, dans l'espace, montent,

on jetait des pelures d'orange du haut de la terrasse, dans la rue très étroite et profonde — la nuit, les mulets braillaient désespérément, vers le matin, on les abattait — demain je sors —

descendent — je dors ici, les fleurs de la tapisserie, l'eau du robinet mal fermé, les dessins du rideau, mon pantalon sur une chaise, on parle dans une chambre plus loin ; deux ou

elle approche sa tête de mon oreille — sa jambe, la grande — ils parlent, ils bougent, là et là, mais tout est passé.

ALBERTO GIACOMETTI.

Alberto Giacometti, "Objets mobiles et muets," *Le Surréalisme au service de la révolution*, 1931, including *Cage* and *Suspended Ball* above, and two *Disagreeable Objects* and *Project for a Square* below.

different memories in a delirious cadence: "All things . . . near, far, all those that passed and the others, in front, moving; and my lady friends—they change (we pass, very near, they are far away); others approach, ascend, descend. . . ."[64] In this verbal dislocation spatial juxtaposition comes to represent temporal spacing, and it is out of this layering of scenes that Giacometti constructs his objects. At this point, however, there is no indication of what the ur-scene or primal fantasy might be; this comes only a year and a half later, after most of the relevant objects are made.

Between these two brief texts Giacometti published a recollection, "Hier, sables mouvants" (Yesterday, Quicksand), in *Le Surréalisme au service de la révolution* in May 1933, that does not deal directly with any work. Instead it presents several memories dated, as was the case with the Ernst "visions of half-sleep," from latency to puberty. The first one begins:

> As a child (between four and seven), I only saw the things of
> the world that delighted me. . . . During two summers at least
> I had eyes only for one big stone. It was a golden monolith, its
> base opening on a cave; the entire bottom was hollowed out by
> the action of water. . . . I considered this stone a friend at once
> . . . like someone whom we knew and loved a long time ago
> and whom we met again with infinite joy and surprise. . . . I was
> overjoyed when I could crouch in the little cave at the bottom;
> it could hardly hold me; all my wishes were fulfilled. . . .[65]

The story points to a primal fantasy of intrauterine existence, the cave as womb. However, the mother in Giacometti is as ambiguous as the father in de Chirico or Ernst: both desired lost object and feared agent of this loss. Conventionally these Oedipal roles are divided between maternal and paternal terms. And the fantasy of intrauterine existence, of reunion with the mother, does seem to be a response to a *prior* fantasy of castration, of interdiction by the father—for it is only this interdiction that causes the desire for the mother to be repressed, and only this repression that renders any return of the maternal, such as the memory of the cave, uncanny.[66] In short, the castration fantasy may determine the intrauterine fantasy; however, in this screen memory, the first follows the second:

> Once (I don't remember by what chance) I walked further than usual and found myself on a hill. Just below in a bunch of bushes rose a huge black rock in the shape of a sharp narrow pyramid. I can't tell you how bewildered and resentful I felt at that moment. The rock struck me as a living thing, hostile, menacing. It threatened everything: us, our games, our cave. Its existence was intolerable and I knew right away that, being unable to make it go away, I would have to ignore it, forget it, tell no one about it. I approached it nonetheless, but with a feeling of surrendering myself to something secret, suspicious, reprehensible. Fearful and disgusted I scarcely touched it. I walked around it, trembling to find an opening. No trace of a cave, which made the rock all the more intolerable. But then I felt a certain satisfaction: an opening in this rock would have complicated everything, and already I felt the loneliness of our cave. . . . I fled this rock, I never spoke about it to the other children, I ignored it and never returned to look at it.[67]

Here the castration fantasy comes through the screen memory as transparently as did the intrauterine fantasy, but two things are not so clear: how do the two fantasies function together, and how does Giacometti deploy them? For Freud the paternal threat alone does not convince the little boy of castration; this requires the sighting of the maternal genitals as well.[68] In this light the cave may figure the fantasm not only of the intrauterine mother

but also of the castrated one. This is more in keeping with the split significance of the maternal in the Giacometti oeuvre (e.g., the regenerative spoon
woman versus the castrative praying mantis) as well as with its volatile
ambiguity regarding sexual difference. In the heterosexist account of Freud,
the threat of castration typically dissolves the Oedipus complex for the little
boy, who surrenders the mother as love object, introjects the father as
superego, and accepts a heterosexual structure of desire and identification.
Here, however, Giacometti seems to retain an ambivalence. Like Ernst, he
refers his work to a fantasmatic memory, to the critical moment when the
child foregoes infantile sexuality and responds to cultural renunciation. He
returns to this critical moment to disturb the subject positions that are first
fragilely posed there: to render them ambivalent again. This ambivalence is
as difficult to sustain as is the reflexivity prized by Ernst; and just as that
reflexivity was often the point between active and passive modes, so is this
ambivalence often the movement between sadistic and masochistic impulses.
Nevertheless, it can produce a disruptive "oscillation of meaning."[69]

For Freud the fetish is a substitute for an absent (maternal) penis, a
substitute that parries the threat of castration that such absence signifies for
the little boy (the more ambiguous case of the little girl is mostly scanted).[70]
Fetishism is thus a practice of ambivalence in which the subject simultaneously recognizes and disavows castration: "Yes . . . but. . . ." This
ambivalence may split the ego, which, if disavowal becomes total, leads to
psychosis; it may also split the object, as it were, which thereby becomes
ambivalent too. After all, the fetish is as much a "memorial" to castration
as a "protection" against it, which is to say that both recognition and
disavowal are often evident in the fetish, as are both contempt and reverence
in its treatment. (The respective examples offered by Freud are fig leafs and
bound feet; the latter is particularly suggestive here.) This ambivalence is
fundamental to the Giacometti objects, as he seems to intuit: "all this alter-
nated, contradicted itself, and continued by contrast."[71]

Giacometti designates seven objects "mobile and mute"; at least five
were executed, while the other two evoke scenarios of sex and/or sacrifice

somewhere between *Cage* and *Point to the Eye,* i.e., scenarios in which sexuality and death are bound up with one another in a conundrum now clearly crucial to surrealism. *Cage* images two abstracted praying mantises, a familiar surrealist favorite for the way in which, as here, the female devours the male during or after copulation. As discussed by Roger Caillois, these figures de-define the order both of life and death and of reality and representation.[72] Just as importantly here, they also disturb the usual opposition of passive female and active male in a manner that symbolically deconstructs any strict binarism of the drives—erotic and destructive, sadistic and masochistic.

Suspended Ball figures a related ambivalence regarding sexual object rather than drive. If the mantises in *Cage* image desire preemptively consumed, the sphere in *Suspended Ball* that scarcely touches its wedge counterpart images desire forever frustrated.[73] At the same time the piece renders sexual reference indeterminate: neither form is simply active or passive, masculine or feminine; such terms become unfixed.[74] It is in sexual evocation, then, that both objects are "mobile and mute." The same holds true for the subject who, as in fantasy, can identify with either term or both; paradoxically identification may come to rest, if at all, only with the implied motion of the piece. The forms not only cross each other in sexual reference but also suggest two series of signifiers (e.g., for the ball: testicles, buttocks, eye . . .) that have no fixed beginning or end; they are opened to the *play* of difference in language.[75] Yet the "round phallicism" of *Suspended Ball* is equally pledged to the Bataillean project of a *collapse* of difference in form. It is in this paradox—in difference both opened in language and blurred in form—that the symbolic ambiguity of the piece lies. As for its psychic ambivalence, this affect stems as well from its implicit oscillation between the erotic and the autoerotic, the sadistic and the masochistic, an oscillation that, if posed in language, is as conundral as this question: who or what strokes or strikes whom or what? Here the paradox concerns not only a "round phallicism" but also a suspended motion or a mobile suspension—

a convulsive beauty that again points to the sadomasochistic basis of sexuality, a basis that surrealism both embraces and defends against.

This ambivalence is difficult to sustain. In the two *Disagreeable Objects* it is treated in a strictly fetishistic way; indeed, both objects are structural simulacra of the sexual fetish. Here the two elements that signify the two genders are not disconnected but rather combined, and the effect is less an indeterminacy of sexual reference and an oscillation of subject position than an immobile contradiction of both terms. No longer suspended, desire is fixed in fetishistic substitutes that are "disagreeable" because each evokes castration—or the hostility produced by its threat—even as it wards it away. In the first *Disagreeable Object* the wedge from *Suspended Ball* is now clearly phallic, but in its penetration of the convex board it is also cut. The second *Disagreeable Object* is more complicated: here the phallic wedge has become an embryonic body replete with eyes, a body that, like the suspended ball, suggests its own chain of signifers (penis, feces, baby . . .), a chain analyzed by Freud in terms of both separation or loss and its fetishistic defense.[76] Recognition of castration is literally inscribed on this phallic substitute in the form of several spikes: in this way "hostility" for the fetish is indeed mixed with "affection," the narcissistically disagreeable (the castrative) with the perversely desirable (the fetishistic).[77]

If fetishistic ambivalence is recouped as symbolic ambiguity in the "objets mobiles et muets," it is soon disarticulated, pulled apart. (Already in *Project for a Square* Giacometti appears to oppose genders in more normative, iconographic ways—negative, hollowed volumes versus positive, phallic forms.) It is almost as if the fetishistic structure of his work breaks down into its constituent parts, the sexual drive into sadistic and masochistic impulses. Some objects such as *Hand Caught* and *Point to the Eye* (both 1932) figure castration threat alone; others such as *Woman with Her Throat Cut* (also 1932) appear as symbolic acts of sadistic vengeance exacted on the figure of woman as representative of castration. Indeed, this splayed scorpion woman is the psychic complement of the devouring mantis of *Cage*:

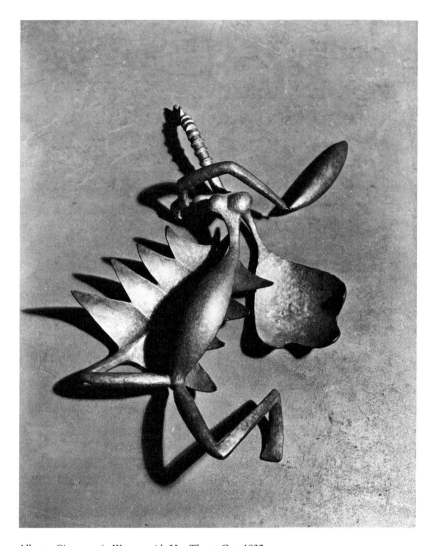

Alberto Giacometti, *Woman with Her Throat Cut*, 1932.

here the threat of castration is returned as a "horror of the mutilated creature or triumphant contempt for her."[78]

It is with such a fantasy that "Hier, sables mouvants," the text that places fetishistic ambivalence at the center of the work, ends:

> I remember that for months while a schoolboy I couldn't get to sleep unless I imagined first that I had gone through a thick forest at nightfall and reached a great castle rising in a most secluded and unknown place. There I killed two defenseless men . . . [and] raped two women, first the one who was thirty-two . . . and then her daughter. I killed them too, but very slowly. . . . Then I burned the castle and, satisfied, went to sleep.

This contempt for the feminine knows no bounds (mother, daughter . . .), but it begins at home. That is, it concerns a lack in the masculine subject that the feminine subject only represents (it is Giacometti who was 32 in 1933): the self-contempt of a castratable subject violently resentful of a female other who, far from castrated, is uncastratable.[79] This sadism appears as a turning round of a more fundamental masochism; and this is how the ambivalence in Giacometti seems to break down. As we saw in chapter 2, with the difficulty of desire compounded by the volatility of sexuality, he finally rejected the psychic as the source of his art. From the fantasmatic he turned back to the mimetic—obsessively: "I worked with the model all day from 1935 to 1940."[80] Giacometti too succumbs to petrification.

In these varied ways, then, primal fantasy seems to inform the symptomatic depth of de Chirico paintings, the psychic coupling of Ernst images, and the affective ambivalence of Giacometti objects. If the surrealist object may be related to the metonymic order of desire, the surrealist image may be related to the metaphoric order of the symptom (the Lacanian definitions of both—desire and symptom—appear to be inflected by surrealism).[81] Of course, the surrealist image is not a direct trace of a psychosexual trauma, any more than the surrealist found object is a simple refinding of a lost one. Unconscious as they are, these terms cannot be intentional referents or literal origins of this art; rather, they help us to understand its structure.[82] In this light we might grasp the contradictory nature of the surrealist image as an effect of a repetitive working over of fantasmatic scenes by a mobile subject, a working over that is never purely involuntary and symptomatic *or* controlled and curative.

However, I have not fully accounted for the other crucial aspect of the surrealist image: its simulacral quality, its paradoxical status as a representation without a referent, or a copy without an original. Despite its call to disorder, much surrealism is implicated in the partial restoration of mimesis in the *rappel à l'ordre* of the 1920s.[83] In its subversive modes, however, representation becomes other, fantasmatic—as if, repressed in high modernism, it returns there uncannily, its distortion the mark of its repression.

Michel Foucault pointed to this sea change in his 1963 essay on Magritte.[84] For Foucault the privileged terms of traditional representation are affirmation and resemblance (or similitude): in such art an affirmation of the reality of the referent is made through the iconic resemblance of the image to it. In modernism this paradigm is eroded in two fundamental ways, which Foucault associates with Kandinsky and Magritte respectively. In his abstractions Kandinsky frees affirmation of the real from resemblance to it: resemblance or similitude is (mostly) abandoned. This account is accurate as far as it goes, but if the referent is eclipsed in Kandinsky, reality, now located *beyond* resemblance (as spiritual or Platonic), is still affirmed (as it is in Malevich, Mondrian . . .). And this affirmation renders such abstraction far less subversive to both traditional mimesis and transcendental aesthetics than is usually thought, even by Foucault. In his simulations Magritte does the more radical converse: he frees resemblance from affirmation. Resemblance or similitude is here maintained, but no reality is affirmed: the referent, its reality, transcendental or otherwise, evaporates— significantly for us through devices of calligrammatic doubling and rhetorical repetition. "Magritte allows the old space of representation to prevail, but only on the surface . . . ; underneath, there is nothing."[85] In such surrealist art representation only seems to reappear; in fact, it returns uncannily as simulation. And it is this simulation that subverts the representational paradigm: in its cancelation of representation abstraction preserves it, whereas simulation unfounds it, pulls the real out from underneath it. Indeed, simulation confounds the entire opposition of representation and abstraction conventionally considered to control modern art.[86]

But what does simulation have to do with fantasy? Both can confound origins, and both are repressed within modernism for doing so. It is in the despised realm of fantasy that our aesthetic tradition long imprisoned simulation—that is, until its partial release in surrealism. For Plato, images were divided between proper claimants and false claimants to the idea, between good iconic copies that resemble the idea and bad fantasmatic simulacra that insinuate it. As Gilles Deleuze has argued, the Platonic tradition repressed the simulacrum not simply as a false claimant, a bad copy without an original, but because it challenged the order of original and copy, the hierarchy of idea and representation—the principle of identity, we might say after Ernst. In repression the fantasmatic simulacrum assumed a daemonic quality as well, and Deleuze describes it in terms similar to our "uncanny" definition of surrealist fantasy:

> The simulacrum implies great dimensions, depths, and distances which the observer cannot dominate. It is because he cannot master them that he has an impression of resemblance. The simulacrum includes within itself the differential point of view, and the spectator is made part of the simulacrum, which is transformed and deformed according to his point of view. In

short, folded within the simulacrum there is a process of going
mad, a process of limitlessness.[87]

The subject is *in* the simulacrum, as it were, just as he is *in* the fantasy; but
the similarity does not end there. Like the fantasy, the simulacrum is com-
prised of at least two different terms or series or events ("it interiorizes a
dissimilitude"),[88] neither of which can be fixed as original or copy, first or
second. In a sense the simulacrum is also produced out of a deferred action,
an internalized difference, and it is this difference that troubles the Platonic
order of representation. It is also this difference that not only renders the
fantasmatic art of surrealism simulacral, but structures the surrealist image
as a signifier of an involuntary memory, a traumatic fantasy.[89] It is to the
most difficult instance of this structuring that I want to turn: the *poupées*
(dolls) of Hans Bellmer.

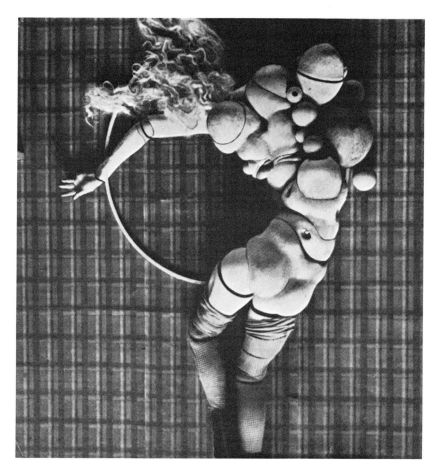

Hans Bellmer, *Doll,* 1935.

4

In chapters 2 and 3 I pointed to a traumatic uncanniness at work in such principles as convulsive beauty and such practices as symbolic objects. This intuition led me to complicate surrealist conceptions of love and art, to see, over the resistance of Breton, a deathly side to *amour fou*. Here I want to deepen this complication in relation to a body of work that pushes (beyond?) the limits of surrealist love and art: the two dolls constructed and photographed by Hans Bellmer, a German associate of the surrealists, in the 1930s.[1] In many ways these *poupées* comprise a summa of the surrealism delineated thus far: uncanny confusions of animate and inanimate figures, ambivalent conjunctions of castrative and fetishistic forms, compulsive repetitions of erotic and traumatic scenes, difficult intricacies of sadism and masochism, of desire, defusion, and death. With the dolls, the surreal and the uncanny intersect in the most difficult desublimatory ways—which is one reason why Bellmer is marginal to the literature on surrealism, devoted as it mostly is to the sublimatory idealisms of Breton.

The intersection between the surreal and the uncanny may also be most literal here, for one inspiration of the *poupées* was the operatic version of the E. T. A. Hoffmann tale "The Sandman" that Freud discusses at length in "The Uncanny."[2] But the *poupées* put into play less obvious aspects of the uncanny as well. Like de Chirico, Ernst, and Giacometti, Bellmer is concerned to work over cathected memories: he too restages primal fantasies and/or traumatic events concerning identity, difference, and sexuality.[3] In "Memories of the Doll Theme," the text that introduces the first doll in *Die Puppe* (1934), Bellmer speaks explicitly of seduction;[4] and his photographs often present both *poupées* in scenes evocative of sex as well as death. Like the other surrealists, he too returns to the scenes of such crimes in order to reclaim not only a power of perversion but also a mobility of position. In short, Bellmer is also devoted to compulsive beauty and convulsive identity; and the difficulties of these ideals may be most apparent in his work: i.e., that the psychic shattering (the convulsive identity) of the male subject may depend upon the physical shattering (the compulsive beauty) of the female image, that the ecstasy of the one may come at the cost of the dispersal of the other. But if this is so, how can Bellmer claim, as he insistently does, that the eroticism figured in the dolls is not his alone, that the "final triumph" is theirs?

Surrealism, we should recall, is pledged to the point where contraries meet, which I have termed the *punctum* of the uncanny. This point is very charged in the *poupées,* for these tableaux force together apparently polar opposites—figures that evoke both an erotogenic body and a dismembered one, scenes that suggest both innocent games and sadomasochistic aggressions, and so on. Here I want to consider the dolls in relation to this uncanny point of surrealism, to see what different apprehensions of love, (de)sublimation, and the body might converge there.

Made of wood, metal, plaster pieces, and ball joints, the *poupées* were manipulated in drastic ways and photographed in different positions. *Die Puppe* contains ten images of the first doll (1933–1934), and a suite of eighteen photographs was published in *Minotaure* 6 (Winter 1934–1935) under the title "Variations sur le montage d'une mineure articulée."[5] For

Bellmer these variations produce a volatile mixture of "joy, exaltation and fear," an intense ambivalence that appears fetishistic in nature, as the second doll (1935–), even less anatomical, makes even more manifest. For Bellmer manipulates this *poupée* very aggressively: as Rosalind Krauss has suggested, each new version is a "construction *as* dismemberment" that signifies both castration (in the disconnection of body parts) and its fetishistic defense (in the multiplication of these parts as phallic substitutes).[6]

This reading is not discouraged by Bellmer. In *Die Puppe* he speaks of the first doll as a way to recover "the enchanted garden" of childhood, a familiar trope for a pre–Oedipal moment before any impression of castration. Moreover, in *Petite anatomie de l'inconscient physique, ou l'Anatomie de l'image* (1957), he locates desire specifically in the bodily detail, which is only real for him if desire renders it artificial—that is, if it is fetishized, sexually displaced and libidinally overvalued. Such is the "monstrous dictionary of the image," Bellmer writes, "a dictionary of analogues-antagonisms."[7]

Yet the *poupées* involve more than fetishism. The production of the dolls is not concealed (as in the Marxian account of fetishism); the photographs of the first *poupée* display its parts openly. Moreover, the notion of a "dictionary of analogues-antagonisms" does not imply a fixing of desire (as in the Freudian account of fetishism); rather its shifting drives the many recombinations of the dolls.[8] We encountered such a shifting before in the paradigmatic story of the surrealist object, the slipper spoon of *L'Amour fou* (roughly contemporaneous with the *poupées*). There Breton thinks this shifting of desire in terms of the slippery associations of the spoon ("slipper = spoon = penis = the perfect mold of this penis"). Bellmer also makes a linguistic connection. "The anagram is the key to all my work," he attests more than once. "The body is like a sentence that invites us to rearrange it."[9] But there is an important difference here too. In Breton the shifting of desire follows the flight of the signifier that can only invoke another signifier; it produces the infinite surrealist quest for the lost object that, never found, is only ever substituted. In Bellmer the shifting of desire does not run on in this way; its line doubles back, turns in, as if to capture the object, to

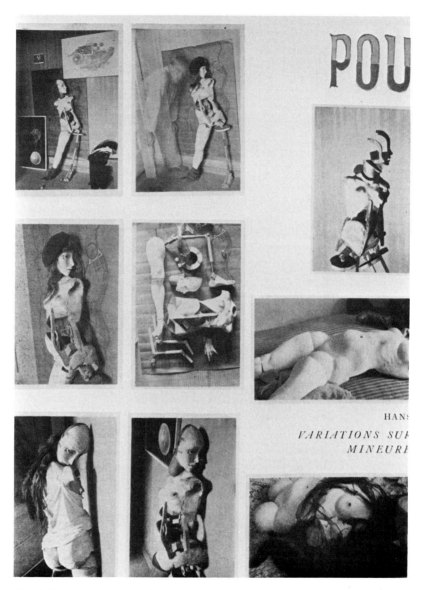

Hans Bellmer, "Variations sur le montage d'une mineure articulée," *Minotaure*, 1934–1935.

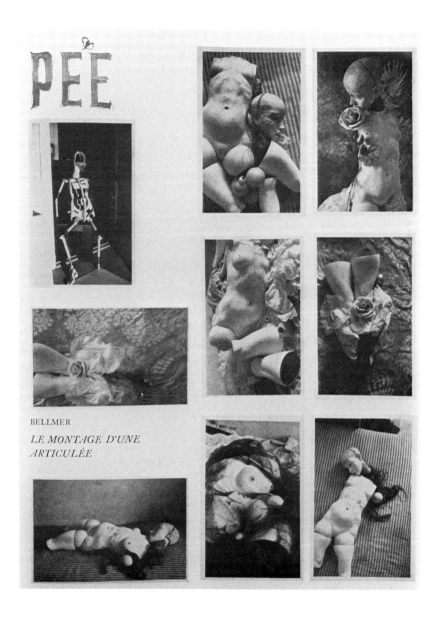

BELLMER

*LE MONTAGE D'UNE
ARTICULÉE*

make, unmake, and remake its image again and again. While Breton chases one sign of desire after another in *Nadja* (1928), Bellmer takes the path of Bataille in *Histoire de l'oeil* (also of 1928): he multiples signs and crosses them.

As read by Roland Barthes, *Histoire de l'oeil* is just that: the story of an object (or part-object) that summons its own set of metaphoric substitutes (eye, egg, balls . . .) and then a related set (now liquid: tears, milk, piss . . .). For Barthes, Bataillean transgression occurs only when these two metaphoric lines are metonymically crossed, when new encounters replace old associations (e.g., "an eye sucked like a breast"). "The result is a kind of general contagion of qualities and actions," he writes. "The world becomes *blurred*."[10] Such is Bataillean eroticism: a physical transgression, a crossing of the limits of the subject, underwritten by a linguistic transgression, a crossing of the lines of sense.[11] Breton approaches this transgressive eroticism only to swerve away from it, alien as it is to his sublimatory conceptions of love and art, of the integrity of object and subject alike. For his part Bellmer seeks this eroticism: in his anagrammatic work he not only substitutes part-objects (the same ball may signify "breast," "head," or "leg") but also combines them in ways that render the body blurred. (His drawings further this process through complicated superimpositions.) In short, the dolls are not slipper spoons: they emerge out of a difficult dictionary of analogues-antagonisms pledged to a transgressive anatomy of desire.

But what exactly is this desire? Again, it is not (only) fetishistic: sexual difference is not disguised; on the contrary, the sex of the *poupées* seems investigated, obsessively so. Like the little Hans analyzed by Freud in "Analysis of a Phobia in a Five-Year-Old Boy" (1909), Bellmer manipulates the dolls as if to ascertain the signs of difference and the mechanics of birth.[12] In this way castration seems almost staged, even prosecuted, as if the *poupées* not only represented this condition but were punished for it as well. As with Giacometti, so with Bellmer: erotic delight is mixed with "horror at the mutilated creature or triumphant contempt for her."[13]

In short, a sadism is inscribed in the dolls as much as a fetishism, although the two should not be opposed, as they are not here.[14] This sadism is hardly hidden: Bellmer writes openly of his drive to master his "victims," and to this end he poses the *poupées* very voyeuristically. In the second doll this look masters through its many mises-en-scène, while in the first it is also made internal to the mechanism of the *poupée*: its interior is filled with miniature panoramas intended "to pluck away the secret thoughts of the little girls."[15] A patriarchal fantasy of control is thus at work—not only over creation but over desire as such. Although Bellmer may claim that other desires are figured, it is obvious who the masterful subject is, what the mastered object.

Or is it? Again, what is this desire? If it is so masterful, why does it call out for master*ing*? The dolls not only trace a shifting of desire; they also represent a shattering—of the female object, to be sure, but also of the male subject.[16] Could this be what Bellmer means by "erotic liberation"? And by the "final triumph" of the *poupées*?[17] Paradoxically in "Memories of the Doll Theme" he places this triumph at the very moment that the dolls are "captured" by his look, by his grasp. How are we to understand this?

One way to begin is to consider how the sadism inscribed in the *poupées* points to a masochism as well. "I wanted to help people," Bellmer remarked in retrospect, "come to terms with their instincts."[18] Here we should take him at his word, for the dolls do seem to stage a struggle between erotic fusion and sexual defusion, between "the innumerable integrating and dis-integrating possibilities according to which desire fashions the image of the desired."[19] More starkly than any other surrealist, Bellmer illuminates the tension between binding and shattering as well as the oscillation between sadism and masochism so characteristic of surrealism. Elsewhere Breton attempts to sublimate such sadomasochistic impulses in new notions of beauty, and de Chirico, Ernst, and Giacometti seek to deflect them in new techniques of art. In Bellmer such sublimation is minimal, and the sado-masochistic nature of sexuality, indeed of surrealism, stands revealed. Is this

Hans Bellmer, mechanism of first *Doll*, 1934.

why he is marginal to the critical literature—not because his work is eccentric to surrealism but because it is all too central? Because the surrealist struggle between Eros and Thanatos, the one never pure of the other, is most blatantly performed in his work, and most blatantly its theater is the female body?[20]

For Freud, we should recall, there is a nonsexual drive to master the object that, when turned inward, is made sexual for the subject. When turned outward again, this drive is sadistic. Yet there remains an aggressivity within the subject that the Freud of the death drive theory termed an "original erotogenic masochism."[21] It is this interrelation between sadism and masochism, the erotogenic and the destructive, that the *poupées* evoke. For in his sadistic scenes Bellmer leaves behind masochistic traces; in his destruction of the dolls he expresses a self-destructive impulse. He sets up an anatomy of his desire only to display the deathliness of his eroticism, which the dispersed image of the female body is made to represent. In this regard the *poupées* may go beyond (or is it inside?) sadistic mastery to the point where the masculine subject confronts his greatest fear: his own fragmentation, disintegration, and dissolution. And yet this is also his greatest wish: "All dreams return again to the only remaining instinct, to escape from the outline of the self."[22] Is this why Bellmer appears not only to desire the (dis)articulated female body but also to identify with it, not only to master it sadistically but also to become it masochistically? (In one photograph of the first doll he is less its separate creator than its spectral double, and in many drawings he commingles his image with hers.)[23] "Should not that be the solution?" Bellmer asks at the end of "Memories." And does he not implicate us in this fatal crossing of desire and identification? But then who is this "us" here? Again, which subjects are permitted this oscillation of gender identity and sexual position, and which are displaced, even elided thereby?

To understand this conflicted motive "to escape from the outline of the self," we might see the *poupées* not only as an excessive elaboration of surrealist notions of love but also as an immanent critique of fascist conceptions of the body.[24] This is treacherous terrain, especially where these two isms cross, but two notions may help to guide us through: sublimation and desublimation.

Freud never defines sublimation in clear distinction from repression, reaction-formation, idealization, and so on. But very simply one can say that sublimation concerns the diversion of sexual drives to civilizational ends (art, science) in a way that purifies them, that both integrates the object (beauty, truth) and refines the subject (the artist, the scientist). Whether seen as a rescue of the subject from the anarchy of the drives (as Freud seems to suggest), or as a reparation of the object feared by the subject to be destroyed (as Melanie Klein seems to suggest), sublimation retains "the main purpose of Eros—that of uniting and binding."[25] For Freud such is the pained path of civilization: the renunciation of some aims, the sublimation of others.[26]

Yet this is a path that can be trodden in the opposite direction too, the way of *de*sublimation, where this binding is loosened. In art this may mean the (re)erupting of the sexual, which all surrealists support; but it may also lead to a (re)shattering of object and subject alike, which only some surrealists risk. It is at this point where sublimation confronts desublimation that surrealism breaks down, and I mean this literally: such is the stake of the split between official Bretonian and dissident Bataillean factions circa 1929, a stake that the *poupées* do much to illuminate (and vice versa). Although both groups recognize the uncanny power of desublimation, the Bretonian surrealists resist it, while the Bataillean surrealists elaborate it—especially, I want to suggest, along the line of its imbrication with the death drive.

Ambivalence about desublimation characterizes Bretonian surrealism. On the one hand, Breton infuses the sexual into the aesthetic, traditionally defined in Kantian terms of disinterest, and he supports the symptomatic model of the surrealist image as advanced by Ernst, Giacometti, and others. On the other hand, Breton insists that the sexual not explode the symbolic, and he refuses to equate regression with transgression (actual perversion outrages him).[27] And yet what is the surrealist project without such transgression? So here too Breton is ambivalent. On the one hand, he is drawn to its anticivilizational force: in his program for *L'Age d'or* (1930) he disputes the faith of the elderly Freud in a renunciation of the destructive drives, and in his notion of convulsive beauty he almost invokes the "negative pleasure," the sexual shattering, at work in the sublime.[28] On the other hand, Breton is wracked by the ramifications of such transgression, by the defusion, even the death, at its core. This is why he ultimately values sublimated form and idealist Eros, and upholds the traditional function of the aesthetic: the normative reconciliation of contrary modes of experience (in Kant nature and reason, judgments of fact and value, and so on). Recall once more his formulation of the surrealist point: "Everything tends to make us believe that there exists a certain point of the mind at which life and death, the real and the imagined, past and future, the communicable and the incommunicable, high and low, cease to be perceived as contradictions."[29]

Double and other to Breton, Bataille stands on the far side of this ambivalence. Often he rises to support the Bretonian formulation, only to supplement it in a way that subverts it, pushes it beyond the pleasure principle: "Good and evil, pain and joy," Bataille adds to the Bretonian list. "Divine ecstasy and its opposite, extreme horror." "The persistence of life and the pull of death." And finally: "Life and death, being and nothingness."[30] Breton cannot abide this subversion, and so he overcomes his ambivalence, most famously in the "Second Manifesto of Surrealism" (1929), where he explicitly advocates "sublimation" and repudiates "regression" (M 160), whose name here is Bataille.[31]

Ironically Breton mocks the way Janet and company pathologize him, only to pathologize Bataille in turn, whose "anti-dialectical materialism" is reviled as so much infantilist perversion (M 183). In this regard Breton not only advocates sublimation; he practices it as well. Orderly, parsimonious, obstinate—that is to say, in a classic reaction-formation against his own anal eroticism—Breton condemns Bataille as an "excrement-philosopher" (M 185) who refuses to rise above big toes, mere matter, sheer shit, to raise the low to the high, to proper form and sublimated beauty. Breton reacts against Bataillean materialism precisely because it celebrates the coincidence of life and death. Strange to say, then, this revolutionary manifesto of surrealism is also a reactive display of "shame, disgust and morality."[32] (At one point Breton sets "moral asepsis" as the necessary condition of "the Surrealist endeavor" [M 187].) And yet the "Second Manifesto" does score its points. The portrait of Bataille is uncannily accurate (is it not true that he "wallows in impurities" [M 185]?). And Breton does sense his double bind: how can Bataille deploy reason against reason, desublimate art within its sublimatory forms?

For his part Bataille turns this critique around. If Bretonian surrealists are so committed to "low values," why are they "full of disgust for this too base world"?[33] And why do "they invest these values with an elevated character," disguise "claims from below" as "claims from above" (V 39)? Is this not to turn the *sub*versive into the *sur*real, to sublimate in the pretense of desublimation? For Bataille the Bretonian project is an "Icarian subterfuge," an Oedipal game concerned not to transgress the law but to provoke its punishment, to play "the role of juvenile victims" (V 40). Elsewhere Bataille terms this game *le jeu des transpositions,* and he implies that Bretonian surrealism, despite its claim to liberate sexual desire, is as committed to its sublimatory elevation, to its symbolic substitution, as any other formal modernism. For Bataille no such art of sublimation can match the sheer power of perversion: "I defy any lover of painting to love a picture as much as a fetishist loves a shoe."[34] If this were only an attack on sublimation or a celebration of perversion for its own sake, the Bretonian critique might stick. But Bataille develops these ideas into a philosophical praxis, one of transgression that, in the crucial point of difference from Bretonian surrealism, elaborates rather than resists an intuition of the death drive. This elaboration is undertaken in two related areas of most relevance here: his

112

origin myth of art and his theory of eroticism. Together they will help us to grasp the psychic effectivity of the Bellmer *poupées*.

In an early reflection on cave and child figuration, Bataille develops a reading of representation at odds with realist, rationalist, and instrumentalist accounts. In its beginnings, Bataille argues, representation is driven not by an imperative of resemblance (this is first fortuitous and only later encoded) but by a play of *altération*—by which he means that the formation of an image is its *de*formation, or the deformation of its model. For Bataille, then, representation is less about formal sublimation than about instinctual release, and this position leads him to an extraordinary formulation: "Art . . . proceeds in this way by successive destructions. To the extent that it liberates libidinal instincts, these instincts are sadistic."[35]

Such a desublimatory account of representation contradicts our most cherished narratives of the history of art, indeed of civilization: that it develops through instinctual sublimation, cognitive refinement, technical progression, and so on. More modestly here it also helps us to understand the Bellmer dolls, driven as they are not by sublimatory *transpositions* but by desublimatory *altérations*. In this regard two elaborations of this term are especially pertinent. First, Bataille suggests that the sadism at work in *altération* is also masochistic, that the mutilation of the altered image is an automutilation as well—a thesis that he poses vis-à-vis van Gogh and that I have entertained vis-à-vis Bellmer.[36] Second, in a note appended to his original definition Bataille suggests that *altération* also signifies both a "partial decomposition analogous to that of cadavers" and a "passage to a perfectly heterogeneous state" related to the sacred and the spectral.[37] It is precisely this *altération* that marks the dolls, many of which read simultaneously as a corpse and a *corps morcelé,* as the body "after" subjecthood, absolutely delimited, and as the body "before" subjecthood, given over to its heterogeneous energies. In this regard the *poupées* may appear doubly uncanny— as fantasmatic reminders of a past erotogeneity on the one hand, and of a future death on the other.

In this way the dolls participate in Bataillean eroticism, as Bellmer was aware.[38] From the early novels and essays to such late texts as *Lascaux, ou la Naissance de l'art* (1955), *L'Erotisme* (1957), and *Les Larmes d'Eros* (1961), Bataille develops this problematic notion along with his ideas about representation; the two are bound together in his general economy of energy and expenditure, life and death. For Bataille eroticism is sexual activity informed by death; as such it distinguishes the human from the animal. But eroticism also de-distinguishes us, linked as it is to death in a more profound way. For eroticism returns us, if only for a moment, to the continuity of death, a continuity that is disturbed by life defined as a discontinuous limit, and broken by subjecthood defined as a bounded body-ego.[39] And yet Bataillean eroticism does not simply oppose life to death; rather, like the death drive theory, it pushes them toward identity.[40] Thus Bataille defines eroticism as an "assenting to life up to the point of death" (E ii), which might be understood here as an intensifying of discontinuity to the point where it touches upon continuity once again. "The final aim of eroticism is fusion," Bataille argues, "all barriers gone" (E 129). And Bellmer agrees; in fact, the dolls epitomize the paradoxical "erotic object" proposed by Bataille: "an object which implies the abolition of the limits of all objects" (E 140). Here this "final aim," this instinct "to escape from the outline of the self," must be seen in terms of the death drive. But again, why is it played out on the compulsively (dis)articulated image of a female body?

In search of an answer we might do well to consider the other historical frame of the dolls, against which they were expressly posed: Nazism. Too young for World War I, Bellmer was sent by his father, an engineer with fascist sympathies, to study engineering at the Berlin Technical School of Art (where he met George Grosz and John Heartfield among others). But he rejected this dictated profession in favor of publicity, which he also rejected when the Nazis came to power lest he abet them in any way. It was then that Bellmer turned to his *poupées*—explicitly as an attack on fascist father and state alike. How are we to understand this attack? Can his avowed politics be reconciled with the apparent sadism of the dolls? What is the relationship of the fantasies figured in the *poupées* to the fascist imaginary? Might the dolls evoke a similarly damaged ego, one that seeks a sense of corporeal stability not only in an armoring of the male body but also in an aggression against other bodies somehow deemed feminine (Jews, communists, homosexuals, "the masses")?[41] Or do the *poupées* challenge this fascist armoring of body and psyche alike with the very force against which it is pledged: the unconscious and sexuality, also coded in this fascist imaginary as feminine?

If we see the dolls as sadistic, then the object of this sadism is clear: woman. But if we see the dolls as representations of sadism, then the object becomes less obvious.[42] Two remarks seem helpful to me here. The first was offered by Walter Benjamin in the midst of the same fascism that confronted Bellmer: "Exposure of the mechanistic aspects of the organism is a persistent tendency of the sadist. One can say that the sadist sets out to substitute for the human organism the image of machinery."[43] This formulation was then focused by Theodor Adorno and Max Horkheimer toward the end of World War II: the Nazis "see the body as a moving mechanism, with joints as its components and flesh to cushion the skeleton. They use the body and its parts as though they were already separated from it."[44] In this light the sadism of these mechanistic dolls might be seen, at least in part, as second-degree: a reflexive sadism aimed as an exposé at the sadism of fascist father and state. This may not render them any less problematic (the ground of this "Oedipal" challenge remains the female body, and "woman" remains a trope for other things), but it does suggest what they seek to problematize.

Bellmer constructed the first *poupée* under the erotic inspiration of his young cousin, with the technical assistance of his brother and out of childhood things provided by his mother. In its very making, then, the doll is an incestuous assault upon the father. As his friend Jean Brun graphically

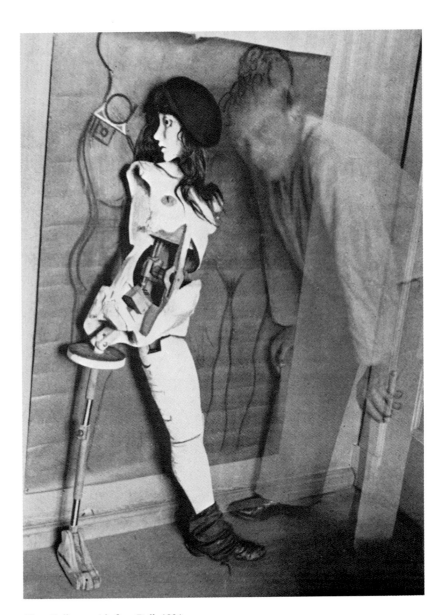

Hans Bellmer with first *Doll*, 1934.

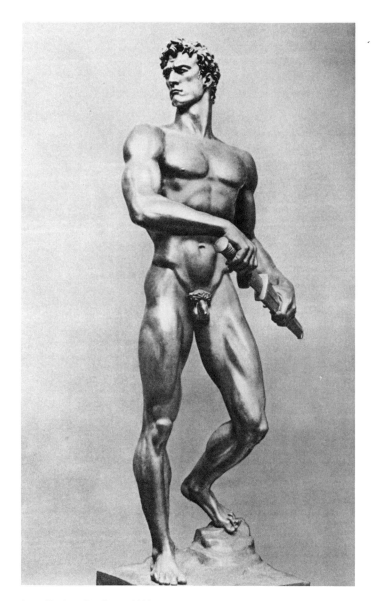

Arno Breker, *Readiness*, 1939.

stages it, this attack turns the tools of the fascist engineer perversely against him:

> The father is vanquished. He sees his son holding a hand-drill, securing a dolly's head between his brother's knees, and telling him: 'Hold on to her for me, I've got to pierce her nostrils.' Pallid, the father goes out, while the son eyes this daughter, now breathing as it is forbidden to do.[45]

Upon this incestuous transgression of the *poupées* Bellmer experiences "a matchless pleasure,"[46] a *jouissance* that defies the phallic privilege of the paternal. Here the *perversion* of the dolls is precisely a *turning away* from the father, a disavowal of his genital monopoly and a challenge to his preemptive law through an "erosion of the double difference between the sexes and the generations."[47] Bellmer enacts this erosion in several ways: not only as he usurps the creative prerogative of the father, but also as he identifies, even interpenetrates, with the female figures on the one hand, and as he seduces "the little girls" of his memory on the other. This erosion of sexual and generational difference is so scandalous because it exposes an archaic order of the drives, "the undifferentiated anal-sadistic dimension."[48] Surrealism, I have argued, is drawn to this dimension, against which Breton reacts (with "shame, disgust and morality") and out of which Bataille philosophizes (with excremental abandon). More fully than any other artist Bellmer situates surrealism in relation to this dimension.

But what does all this have to do with Nazism? I think it suggests how Bellmer contests it from within its own construction of masculine subjectivity—contests it with that which this subjectivity represses and/or abjects. Consider the account of the German fascist male in the 1920s and 1930s offered by Klaus Theweleit in *Male Fantasies* (1977/78). Theweleit does not hesitate to think this subject in terms developed for the psychotic child:

unable to bind his body image, let alone cathect it, the fascist male is formed not from the inside out, as it were, but *"from the outside, by the disciplinary agencies of imperialist society"*—hierarchical academy, military school, actual battle, and the like.[49] These agencies do not bind this subject so much as they armor his body and psyche, an armoring he deems necessary not only for self-definition but for self-defense, forever threatened as he is by the fantasmatic dissolution of his body image. For Theweleit it is this double demand that compels the fascist male to attack his social others (again, Jews, communists, homosexuals), in part because all appear as guises of this feared dissolution. In so doing, however, what he targets is his own unconscious and sexuality, his own drives and desires, coded, like his social others, as fragmentary, fluid, feminine.

Fascist armoring, then, is pledged against all comminglings urged by sexuality or produced in death. This armoring is psychic, to be sure, but it is also physical; indeed, it is represented in fascist aesthetics as a physical ideal—for example, in the steeled male figures of celebrated Nazi sculptors such as Arno Breker and Josef Thorak, pumped up phallically as these vessels of purity are. Although Nazi art is often used as the antitype of modernist art, its principal aesthetic is not as aberrant as it may seem; it has much in common with other European classicisms of the 1920s and 1930s, other *rappels à l'ordre* reactive against the modernist fragmentations of cubism, expressionism, dadaism, and surrealism. But the Nazi version is extreme precisely in its reaction, for it seeks to block not only these modernisms, and not only the mutilated bodies of World War I (which haunt these modernisms as well), but also the "feminine" forces of sexuality and death that threaten the Nazi male.[50]

That Nazism cannot abide these forces is clear from its antimodernist polemics as well as its artistic ideals. For example, in "Entartete Kunst" (Degenerate Art), the infamous 1937 exhibition that condemned modernist art, the most reviled work was not necessarily the most abstract or the most anarchic. Greatest anathema was reserved for art that represented the body— but disfigured it, opened up its image to its own heterogeneous energies, impressed its form with its own "feminine" forces of sexuality and death, and (most importantly) connected these forces to the social figures that threatened the Nazi male with "degeneration" (here not only the Jew, the communist, and the homosexual, but also the child, "the primitive," and the insane). In this sense the most reviled work was also the most intimate to the Nazis—like expressionism (which included Nazi supporters such as Emil Nolde). For there disfiguration, dissolution, and "degeneration" are most pronounced; there the heterogeneity of sexuality and death is impressed all but directly on the body. Had they known them, the Bellmer dolls would have provoked the Nazis even more profoundly, for not only do they shatter all sublimatory idealisms, but they also attack fascist armoring with the effects of sexuality. Not only do the *poupées* trope the sadism at work in this armored aggressivity, but they also confound the fascist insistence on bodily separation and challenge the fascist persecution of desire. As opposed to such separation, the dolls suggest a release from "the outline of the self"; as opposed to such persecution, they represent "a physical unconscious."[51]

According to Theweleit, even as the fascist male requires armoring, he also strives to be free of it; thus even as he fears all comminglings, he is also drawn to them. This ambivalence is best treated in war, for there, all at once, this subject can be defined, defended, and discharged—as if he were a weapon. For Theweleit this configuration of the subject as weapon is fundamental to fascist aggression, for it allows "desiring production" to be expressed as "murdering production." Bellmer tropes this configuration critically in *Machine-Gunneress in a State of Grace* (1937). This doll almost images what Theweleit postulates: that it is only in violence against its feminine others that the fascist male can be confirmed. But it also suggests that imbricated in this sadism is a masochism, that the other attacked here may also be "the female self within."[52] One way to develop this argument may be to see this self in terms of the masochistic aspect of the psyche (which Freud does describe, problematically, as feminine). In this respect the fear of the feminine within may also be the fear of this diffusive or destructive drive within. And this in turn may be where the Bellmer dolls

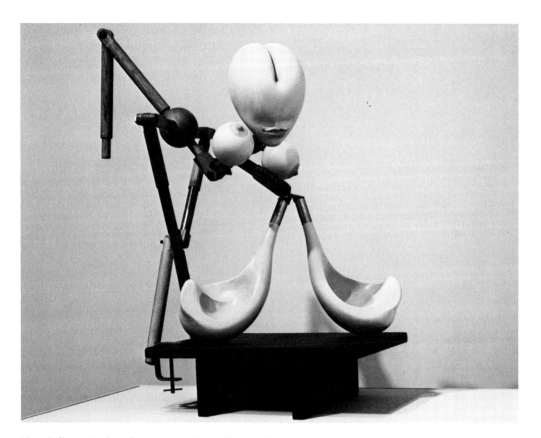

Hans Bellmer, *Machine-Gunneress in a State of Grace*, 1937.

participate most deeply in the fascist imaginary, only to expose it most effectively. For in the *poupées* this fear of the diffusive and the destructive is made manifest and reflexive, as is the attempt to overcome it vis-à-vis the feminine. Such is the scandal but also the lesson of the dolls.[53]

There are problems with this work that cannot be resolved away.[54] The *poupées* produce misogynistic effects that may overwhelm any liberatory intentions. They also exacerbate sexist fantasies about the feminine (e.g., associations with the fragmentary and the fluid, the masochistic and the deathly) even as they exploit them critically. So, too, they persist in the association of avant-gardist transgression with psychosexual regression, an association often made through violent representations of the female body.[55] And, finally, however much they may disturb oppositions of the masculine and the feminine, the very move to merge the two may be another form of displacement: i.e., as with the surrealist identification with the figure of the hysteric, there may be an appropriation around the position of the masochistic.[56] There may be problems with my analysis as well; in particular my reading of the sadism of the dolls as second-degree may be difficult to accept. This is a risk that I have wanted to run, however, for more directly than any other corpus the *poupées* expose the desires and fears of the surrealist subject bound up with the uncanny and the death drive. It is to two generic ciphers of such desires and fears that I want to turn: the surrealist figures of the automaton and the mannequin.

La protection des hommes

"Protection of Men," photograph in *Variétés*, 1930.

5

E X Q U I S I T E   C O R P S E S

In chapters 2 and 3, I argued that crucial surrealist definitions and practices revolve around the uncanny as so many signs of a confusion between life and death, a compulsion to repeat, a return of repressed desires or fantasmatic scenes. These marvelous confusions blur distinctions between inside and outside, the psychic and the social: the one is not seen as prior or causal to the other (one of many insights offered official Marxism but rejected by it). In chapter 4 this blurring led me to suggest that the surrealist uncanny is imbricated in social processes, in particular that the uncanniness of the Bellmer *poupées* can be seen in critical apposition to the deathliness of the fascist subject. In the next two chapters I want to deepen this historical dimension of the surrealist uncanny: to argue first that it concerns the shocks of industrial capitalism as well as the traumas of individual experience, and second that it involves the recovery of obsolete cultural materials as well as the return of repressed psychic events.

In chapter 2 I noted that Breton presents in the "Manifesto" two cryptic examples of this marvelous confusion of the animate and the inanimate: the modern mannequin and the romantic ruin, the first a crossing of the human and the nonhuman, the second a mixing of the historical and the natural. Here I want to propose that these emblems also interested the surrealists because they figured two uncanny changes wrought upon bodies and objects in the high capitalist epoch. On the one hand, the mannequin evokes the remaking of the body (especially the female body) as commodity, just as the automaton, its complement in the surrealist image repertoire, evokes the reconfiguring of the body (especially the male body) as machine. On the other hand, the romantic ruin evokes the displacing of cultural forms by this regime of machine production and commodity consumption—not only archaic feudal forms but also "outmoded" capitalist ones. I borrow this term from Walter Benjamin, for whom Breton and company were "the first to perceive the revolutionary energies that appear in the 'outmoded', in the first iron construction, the first factory buildings, the earliest photos, the objects that have begun to be extinct"—objects that Benjamin elsewhere describes as "the wish-symbols of the previous century," "the ruins of the bourgeoisie."[1]

Two points should be stressed here. First, as the Bretonian pairing of mannequin and ruin implies, the mechanical-commodified and the outmoded are dialectically related: the mechanical-commodified produces the outmoded through displacement, and the outmoded in turn defines the mechanical-commodified as central—and may be deployed to contest it as such symbolically.[2] Second, the mechanical-commodified and the outmoded, the mannequin and the ruin, are both uncanny but in different ways: the first in a demonic register, the second in an auratic register. Disruptive of traditional social practices, the machine and the commodity were long seen as infernal forces (Marx often draws on this folk language to describe capital in general as vampirish).[3] But the very nature of the machine and the commodity is also demonic, for both evoke an uncanny confusion between life and death. It is precisely this confusion that fascinated the surrealists, obsessed as they were by the strange (non)human character of the mannequin, the automaton, the wax figure, the doll—all avatars of the uncanny and all players in the surrealist image repertoire.[4] As I will argue in the next chapter, the outmoded is uncanny in another way: as familiar images and objects made strange by historical repression, as *heimisch* things of the nineteenth century returned as *unheimlich* in the twentieth century.

Since they define each other, the mechanical-commodified and the outmoded cannot always be distinguished (e.g., the old automatons cherished by the surrealists may belong to both categories). Nevertheless, bound to different productive modes and social formations, the figures that evoke them do produce different affects. Provisionally we can see this difference as that between the aura of the crafted object in which human labor and desire are still inscribed, and the fascination of the fetishistic machine or commodity in which such production is either incorporated or effaced.[5] This dialectical relation between the outmoded and the mechanical-commodified in surrealism echoes that between aura and shock in Baudelaire, at least as read by Benjamin. As Baudelaire reflects on "the disintegration of aura [i.e., of the ritual elements in art] in the experience of shock [i.e., of industrial-capitalist modes of perception],"[6] so the surrealists, involved as they are in this Baudelairean tradition, attempt to redeem the outmoded and to mock the mechanical-commodified.

Like other surrealist activities not often regarded as political (e.g., bizarre collections of tribal and folk artifacts), the deployment of such images and figures serves as a rhetorical *détournement* of the high capitalist order of things—of the projected totality of industrial production and consumption, of the becoming machine and/or commodity of both the human body and the object world. Often in surrealism mechanical-commodified figures parody the capitalist object with its own ambitions, as when the body is rearticulated as a machine or a commodity (a device held over from dada, e.g., *The Hat Makes the Man* of Ernst). So, too, outmoded images may challenge the capitalist object with images either repressed in its past or outside its purview, as when an old or exotic object, redolent of a different productive mode, social formation, and structure of feeling, is recalled, as it were, in protest. This double contestation of the high capitalist order by the mocked mechanical-commodified and the recovered outmoded is intimated in Breton texts on the surrealist object, from the 1924 "Introduction to the Discourse on the Paucity of Reality" to the 1936 "Crisis of the Object." In the "Paucity of Reality" the surrealist object (only emergent in 1924) is conceived along the double lines of the mechanical-commodified and the outmoded: on the one hand Breton calls for "idle machines of a very specific construction," "absurd automatons perfected to the last degree," and on the other hand for such objects as a fantastic book crafted in the world of dreams.[7] "I would like to put into circulation certain objects of this kind," Breton writes, "to throw further discredit on those creatures and things of 'reason'."[8] And in "Crisis of the Object" the useless, singular surrealist object (pervasive by 1936) is posed against the efficient, serial commodity.[9]

In our discussion two examples of the outmoded and the mechanical-commodified are already in circulation: the flea market objects of *L'Amour fou,* the auratic slipper spoon "of peasant fabrication" and the demonic military mask of industrialized war. In the next chapter I will attend to the auratic outmoded set of figures and affects; here I want to focus on the demonic mechanical-commodified set.

For Freud the uncanniest objects are "wax-work figures, artificial dolls and automatons."[10] In his account such figures not only provoke a primordial confusion about the (in)animate and the (non)human, but also recall an infantile anxiety about blindness, castration, and death.[11] In chapter 3 I touched on the connection made in surrealism between blindness and castration; here it is the status of these figures as deathly doubles that interests me. In the phylogenetic thought of Freud (who follows Otto Rank here), the double or *Doppelgänger* is a primordial protector of the ego that, repressed, returns as a present harbinger of death. A related doubleness is possessed by both the tool-become-machine and the object-become-commodity, and it is this uncanniness that the surrealists intuited in the automaton and the mannequin. From this intuition we might immediately speculate further: might the very apperception of the uncanny, in Freud no less than in surrealism, depend on the historical development of reification, of the ghostly doubling of the human by the mechanical-commodified, by *the thing*?[12]

In his definition of commodity fetishism, Marx argues that producers and products under capitalism trade semblances: social relations take on "the fantastic form of a relation between things," and commodities assume the active agency of producers.[13] In effect, the commodity becomes our uncanny double, evermore vital as we are evermore inert. As for the machine, I noted its reception as demonic; also pertinent here is the ironic inversion remarked by Marx in its technical history. In the premodern instance the machine is thought to mimic the organic movements of the human (or animal) body that is its model (residual, say, in the description of the early train as "the iron horse"); the machine remains a tool, suited to the craftsman and subservient to him. In the modern instance, however, the machine becomes the model, and the body is disciplined to its specifications, first in mechanistic terms (as in the eighteenth-century model of man-as-machine), then in energistic ones (as in the nineteenth-century paradigm of the human motor); here, as the worker resembles the machine, it begins to dominate him, and he becomes its tool, its prosthetic.[14]

The modern machine thus emerges not only as an uncanny double but as a demonic master. Like the commodity, it is uncanny both because it assumes our human vitality and because we take on its deathly facticity. Both machine and commodity thus draw out human labor and will, animation and autonomy, and return them in alien forms, as independent beings; both are thus other yet not-other, strange yet familiar—"dead labor" come back to dominate the living. This uncanniness is announced in automatons and mannequins, where machine and commodity appear as if embodied. With such figures the surrealists could insist on the uncanny effects of mechanization and commodification; more, they could exploit these perverse effects to critical ends. This points to a primary surrealist politics (which official Marxism also rejected): to oppose to the capitalist rationalization of the objective world the capitalist *irrationalization* of the subjective world.

The surrealists intimated this process of (ir)rationalization in many ways. As one instance consider the skit published by Benjamin Péret in a 1933 issue of *Minotaure* under the title "Au paradis des fantômes." In this satire, which, in a manner typical of the genre, associates the human with the mechanical, several inventors from Alexandria to the Enlightenment are confronted by automatons.[15] Péret sees these automatons as *fantômes,* more marvelous and irrational than mechanistic and rational: "These mobile sphinxes," he concludes, "have not yet ceased to propose enigmas to men, the solution of which in turn calls up a new enigma."[16] However, the images in the text relate these irrational phantoms to modern *rationalization*—which implies that they are enigmatic, indeed uncanny, precisely because they resemble men and women under industrial capitalism.

The first spread of images presents four examples of the automaton from its greatest era, the late eighteenth century. Three of the four satirize class positions and gender relations in this turbulent period (e.g., a monkey dressed as a marquis playing "La Marseillaise," a submissive woman wheeling a pompous man in a barrow). The primary figure, however, is the famous *Young Writer* (c. 1770) constructed by Pierre Jacquet-Droz, the most prominent automaton maker after Jacques Vaucanson. According to Péret, this uncanny figure so cherished by the surrealists writes the word *merveilleux* again and again—as if to confirm the primary definition of the marvelous as that which escapes rational causality. Yet its presentation here foregrounds not its marvel but its *mechanism:* with head and arm devices exposed, this automaton is the very figure of mechanistic man. This connection is also suggested by the image sequence on the second spread of the text: two more eighteenth-century automatons juxtaposed with three modern automaton-mannequins (a man in evening clothes, a woman in a café, another man in safari garb), plus a robot. Implicitly the Enlightenment automaton is posed here as the historical prototype of modern producers and consumers alike. Though clearly distinct from the robot, the automaton remains its ancestor: an outmoded curiosity, it is also the ur-form of the "slavery of the machine."[17]

The historical connection between Enlightenment automaton and capitalist producer-consumer is quite close. In 1748 Julien Offray de La Mettrie (a surrealist favorite) published *L'Homme machine,* a systematic attempt to redefine man in terms of mechanical laws: man as automaton. Developed by Enclopedists like Diderot and d'Alembert from Descartes (who wrote that "the human body may be considered as a machine"),[18] this materialist rationalism challenged the metaphysical claims on which the feudal institutions of the ancien régime were based. But it also legitimated new rational and reticulated disciplines of the body that supplemented the old arbitrary and immediate subjugations of absolutist power. "La Mettrie's *L'Homme-machine* is both a materialist reduction of the soul and a general theory of *dressage,*" Michel Foucault writes, "at the centre of which reigns the notion of 'docility', which joins the analysable body to the manipulable body."[19] Of course, this docile body was broken down to be reconstructed in many different institutions—school, army, hospital, prison. But its automatic behavior was perfected in the factory and emblematized by the automaton.

In Jacques Vaucanson these two terms, automaton and factory, are directly related. In 1738 he presented his famous automatons (flutist, drummer, and duck) to the Académie Royale des Sciences, but his story only begins here. For in 1741 Vaucanson was named Inspector of the Silk Manufactures, in which capacity he worked to mechanize fabric production (his mechanical loom was the basis of the automatic Jacquard loom of 1801), and in 1756 he designed a silk factory near Lyons that, rationalized in plan and power, is often considered the first modern industrial plant. Through this single figure, then, the automaton or machine-as-man announces the modern factory, the central site where man-as-machine, worker-as-automaton, is produced. This paradigmatic relation between Enlightenment automaton and docile worker was not lost on nineteenth-century theorists, whether celebrated as an ideal of productive efficiency as it was by the

GROUPE D'AUTOMATES — AU CENTRE, UN CORDONNIER ASSIS SUR UN ESCABEAU
TIRE LE FIL DE SA COUTURE, IL BAISSE LA TÊTE ET OUVRE LA BOUCHE. A SA DROITE
INCLINANT LE CHEF UN PHYSICIEN SOULÈVE LE COUVERCLE D'UN TONNEAU D'OÙ
ÉMERGE UNE TÊTE DE NÈGRE. A GAUCHE, UNE FIGURINE — PROBABLEMENT UN
BERGER — PORTE SUR SON DOS UNE HOTTE DE LAQUELLE SORT PAR INSTANTS UNE
PETITE CHÈVRE. AU SECOND PLAN, UNE FEMME AUX CHEVEUX DÉFAITS, COIFFÉE D'UN
CASQUE, PORTE UNE SORTE DE CORBEILLE DONT, DE SA MAIN DROITE, ELLE SOULÈVE
LE COUVERCLE, FAISANT APPARAÎTRE UN OISEAU. PUIS, LE CASQUE SE RABATTANT
SUR SON VISAGE, ELLE PRÉSENTE UNE FIGURE MASCULINE. DANS LE FOND, LES
BRANCHES D'UN PALMIER LAISSENT VOIR LORSQU'ELLES S'ENTROUVRENT UN
COUPLE ENLACÉ CACHÉ DANS L'ARBRE.

SINGE MUSICIEN HABILLÉ EN MARQUIS ET COIFFÉ D'UN BONNET
ROUGE A COCARDE TRICOLORE. JOUE LA MARSEILLAISE ET LA
CARMAGNOLE. FIN DU XVIIIᵉ SIÈCLE (COLLECTION CORTI).

FEMME POUSSANT UNE BROUETTE SUR LAQUELLE
EST ASSIS UN HOMME (MUSÉE DE CLUNY)

MÉCANISME DES YEUX
DE L' « ÉCRIVAIN » DE
JAQUET-DROZ.

MÉCANISME DE L' « ÉCRIVAIN »
DE JAQUET-DROZ

Nous devons à l'obligeance de M. Édouard Gélis, auteur, avec
M. Alfred Chapuis, du remarquable ouvrage « Le Monde des
Automates » (Paris, 1928) la plupart des illustrations de cet article.

Photographs of automatons and mannequins in *Minotaure*, 1933.

M. KERLY'S, L'HOMME AUTOMATE.

LA FUMEUSE (MUSÉE DES MASQUES DE CIRE, MOULIN-ROUGE).

HOMME AUTOMATE.

LE FUMEUR (COLL. COMTE DE RIBES).

LE ROBOT.

reactionary Andrew Ure, or denounced as a figure of capitalist subjection as it was by the radical Marx.[20]

However, a strange thing happens to this ideal of the automaton in its industrial application: it becomes less a paragon of rational society than a "threat to human life,"[21] less a figure of enlightenment than a cipher of uncanniness. In romantic literature at the turn of the nineteenth century, these mechanical figures become demonic doubles of danger and death (the tales of E. T. A. Hoffmann are only the most obvious examples). Moreover, as soon as they are coded as demonic, they are also gendered as female. In this way a social ambivalence regarding machines, a dream of mastery versus an anxiety about loss of control, becomes bound up with a psychic ambivalence, of desire mixed with dread, regarding women.[22] A similar patriarchal apprehension greets the commodity, indeed mass culture generally, throughout the nineteenth century, both of which are also associated with women.[23] This gendering is not fixed in surrealism (or, for that matter, in dada), but certainly ambivalence regarding both machine and commodity is figured in this way: in terms of feminine allure *and* threat, of the woman as erotic *and* castrative, even deathly. In this regard as in so many others, the surrealists presuppose a heterosexist subject, whose fetishisms they exacerbate. And yet they also exploit the anxieties of this subject vis-à-vis the machine and the commodity—a historical inheritance that they tap in defiance of modern(ist) celebrations of these forms.[24]

Again, this fetishistic ambivalence has a long history, and there are many artistic precedents of surrealist automatons and mannequins as well. Most familiar from the image repertoire of Baudelaire and Manet are the ragpicker and the prostitute, two related ciphers of the mechanical-commodified, which, decoded by Benjamin in the milieu of surrealism, are still active in its imaginary (particularly in texts and images concerning urban *dérives* and derelict spaces). Sphinxes of the social, the first at its edge, the second at its crossroads, the ragpicker and the prostitute were threats, enticements, doubles to the modern artist.[25] On the one hand, like the ragpicker, the artist was marginal to the industrial process, and he too recovered cultural refuse for exchange value.[26] On the other hand, like the prostitute, the artist had come onto the marketplace, "as [he] thought, to observe it—but in reality it was already to find a buyer"; thus his ambivalent identification with the whore as "seller and commodity in one."[27]

However, as mechanization and commodification intensify, these figures are transformed. In *Le Paysan de Paris* Aragon confuses a prostitute with a "living corpse," while in *Nadja* the wax figure of a whore strikes Breton more strongly than the real thing ("the only statue I know of with eyes, the eyes of provocation, etc.").[28] Here it is not only a question of ambivalent empathy with the commodity as figured in the prostitute or of ambiguous identification with industrial detritus as represented by the ragpicker. Reification has become more literal: the prostitute has become a mannequin, and the ragpicker is now replaced by a machine, a "bachelor machine."[29] In the first figure, the mannequin, sexual fetishism overdetermines commodity fetishism, and the result is "the sex appeal of the inorganic,"[30] an uncanny effect that some surrealists indulge. In the second figure, the bachelor machine, the human (body, sexuality, unconscious) is recast in terms of the mechanical (conjunctions, repetitions, breakdowns), and the result is another fetishistic overdetermination, one that some surrealists actually perform. For example, long before Andy Warhol, Ernst took the machine as a persona (as in "Dadamax, the self-constructed small machine"), just as his Cologne compatriot Alfred Gruenwald identified with the commodity (with the pseudonym "Baargeld" meaning "cash"). In such personas these artists assumed the trauma of mechanization and commodification in order to double it, to expose it—in short, to deploy its psychophysical effects against the very order that produced them. More important than the art-historical lineage of the surrealist deployment of the mechanical-commodified, then, is its psychosocial logic, the transformation of body and psyche that it works over, and here again the model of surrealist art as a repetition of trauma may be useful.[31]

This traumatic becoming machine and/or commodity of the body is not often figured in surrealism simply or as such. A becoming animal is more common in its image repertoire (e.g., the praying mantis or the minotaur), and these hybrids mean different things to different surrealists. For some (especially around Breton) they announce a redefining of the human in terms of the sexual and the unconscious. For others (especially around Bataille) they advance a related redefining of the human in terms of the base and the heterological. But these grotesques also bespeak a mechanizing and/or commodifying of body and psyche alike.[32] Indeed, these psychophysiological redefinings cannot be separated from such sociological transformations, and in surrealism the two are often expressed in terms of each other: the unconscious as an autonomous machine, the sexual as a mechanistic act, the commodification of sexuality as the sexualization of the commodity, the difference between male and female as the difference between the human and the mechanical, an ambivalence concerning women as an ambivalence regarding the mechanical-commodified, and so on.

In the early years after World War I, the becoming machine and/or commodity of the body was focused in the figure of the mutilated and/or shocked soldier. Then in the 1920s, with the spread of Taylorist and Fordist disciplines of the industrial body, the worker became the epitome of these processes. Finally, with the fascism of the 1930s a new figure, the Jüngerian worker-soldier, the armored body become weapon-machine, emerged to overdetermine the other two. Together these figures form the dialectical object of attack of the mechanistic grotesques that surrealism developed, after dada, to contest the modern cult of the machine—a cult variously promulgated not only in technophilic movements such as futurism, constructivism, purism, and the middle Bauhaus, but also in the everyday ideologies of the Fordist state, whether capitalist, communist, or fascist.

Although these types are not always distinct, I want to concentrate on the second one, the worker as machine, as elaborated in the surrealist milieu. To do so I will lean heavily on images rather eccentric to the canon: several suites of essayistic photographs of automatons, mannequins, and the like in *Variétés*, "an illustrated monthly review of the contemporary spirit" published in Brussels under surrealist influence from May 1928 to April 1930. This is surrealism at a remove, surrealism headed toward chic; yet, though some of its complexities are lost, some of its concerns are clarified. The photographs, by artists and nonartists alike, are grouped into complexes that are rarely credited.[33] Typical of journals across the cultural-political spectrum at the time, such complexes were especially important to surrealism, where they comprise a practice of juxtaposition in which surrealism appears precisely as the transformative *colle* of the collage.

In the early 1929 spreads of *Variétés* a proposition about fetishism emerges, one implicit in both Marxian and Freudian accounts: that we moderns are also fetishists; more, that our machine and commodity fetishes irrationalize us, even reritualize us.[34] In "Le Surréalisme en 1929," a special issue of *Variétés* edited by Breton and Aragon, one finds under the rubric "Fétiches" a female automaton from the Musée des Arts et Métiers juxtaposed with a totem figure from the Pacific Northwest coast. In another 1929 series (March 15) this fetishism of the body as machine is developed in terms of the body as commodity. Here two photographs, one of "a mannequin-man of fashion in the Paris streets," another of two "sandwichmen at the Leipzig fair," are juxtaposed with two photographs of masks, one from the Belgian Congo (used by priests who perform circumcisions), another apparently from a Greek tragedy. The primary initiations in high capitalist society, the spread suggests, involve the sacrificial rites of the commodity: to become a social being is to accede to its condition, literally to assume its character.[35] A later 1929 photo complex (October 15) makes a similar point in relation to the machine, specifically to medical apparatuses and technological prostheses. In one spread a modern woman behind an optometrical device is paired with a Tibetan dancer in a horrific mask; in another a deep sea diver is placed beside an expressionist ghoul.

The captions of these photographs frequently stress the term "masquerade," which suggests that these identities are performed. However, that

Masques

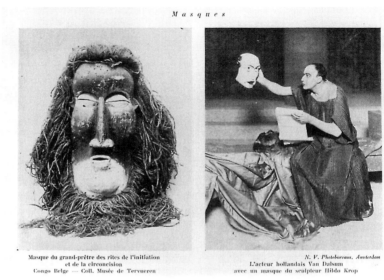

Masque du grand-prêtre des rites de l'initiation
et de la circoncision
Congo Belge — Coll. Musée de Tervueren

N. V. Photobureaux, Amsterdam
L'acteur hollandais Van Dalsum
avec un masque du sculpteur Hildo Krop

Mascarade publicitaire

Photo A. Dubreuil
Le mannequin-élégant dans les rues de Paris

Hommes-sandwich à la foire de Leipzig

Photographs in *Variétés*, 1929.

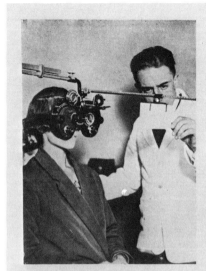

Masque de clinique

Danseur thibétain

Photo Meshrapom-Russ

Photo Germaine Krull

Mascarade d'atelier

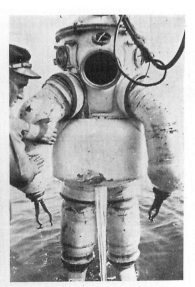

Scaphandre

Photographs in *Variétés*, 1929.

the disciplines of commodity and machine are not voluntary is underscored by several images. In one the face of a modern woman is usurped by a collaged advertisement, then paired with a prettified doll (October 15); in another the heads of two people have become photographic apparatuses (December 15). In the first image (captioned "to offend the aesthete") the commodity is no longer only associated with the female body or supported by it; it is inscribed on her very face, once the sign of unique subjectivity. In the second image (captioned "to see or to hear") the machine is no longer only a technical prosthesis; it becomes an organ substitute: modern vision as photographic gun. Just as the first image is hardly a proto-pop embrace of the modern commodity world, so the second is scarcely a Bauhausian celebration of a technological new vision. In these images the uncanny underside of the commodity and the machine is suggested, and the world views that might celebrate them are mocked.

Only in two *Variétés* photo complexes (January 15, 1930) is modernist art specifically related to the machine and the commodity, and in both the ur-form of such art is taken to be the mechanical-commodified body. The principal spread of the first complex includes three modernist works: an abstracted puppet by Man Ray (recurrent in his oeuvre), a primitivist *Child* by Brancusi, and a marionette *Soldiers* by Sophie Taeuber-Arp. All three images are referred to a fourth: "a steel automaton that performs human movements on command" (its chestplate bears the letters R.U.R., an allusion to the 1920 play by the Czech Karel Capek, *R.U.R. (Rossum's Universal Robots),* that popularized the term "robot" in the 1920s).[36] Here the paradigm of the modernist object is the worker-become-machine; the usual art-historical references to tribal, folk, or childhood objects are displaced—as if these other fetishes were now considered academic, even mystificatory (one grouping of such figures is captioned "L'Académie des fétiches").

The second photo complex addresses not only this ur-form of modernist figures but also the relationship of different modernisms to the machine. Titled "Aboutissements [effects] de la mécanique," it begins with three photographs of human–machine hybrids: two figures in gas masks, a third

140

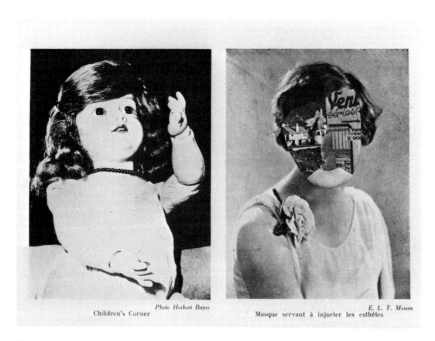

Children's Corner *Photo Herbert Bayer*

E. L. T. Mesens Masque servant à injurier les esthètes

Photographs by Herbert Bayer and E. L. T. Mesens in *Variétés*, 1929.

Voir ou entendre

Photograph in *Variétés*, 1929.

Man Ray : Le penseur

Brancusi : Enfant

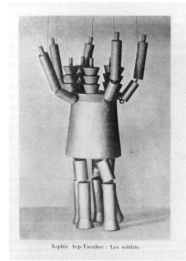
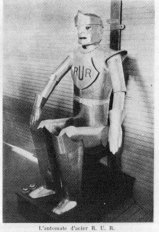

Sophie Arp-Taeuber : Les soldats

L'automate d'acier R. U. R.
qui accomplit au commandement les mouvements humains

Photographs of figures by Man Ray, Brancusi, and Sophie Taeuber-Arp in *Variétés*, 1930.

masked by an optometrical device. The caption, "the protection of men," is mordantly ironic: here technology does not extend, let alone protect, bodily limbs and senses; it constricts, even deforms them: these men have become mechanical insects.[37] This *aboutissement* nuances the constellation of four images that follow: a photograph of Fernand Léger on the laboratory set of the L'Herbier film *L'Inhumain* (1923), the stage apparatus designed by Lyubov' Popova for the Meierkhol'd production of *The Magnanimous Cuckold* (1922), and the painting *Usine de mes pensées* (1920) by Suzanne Duchamp, all of which are referred to a photograph of several military dirigibles captioned "traffic." The three art images suggest a partial map of machinist modernisms. Technological modernity is in turn represented by the fourth image, the dirigibles, the very emblem of new forms of mobility, visuality, spatiality, of new freedoms of the body. Yet, announced by the insectoid men, this image is not celebratory; here the freedoms are only apparent, grounded in a capitalist-militarist base—the *trafic* of weapons and soldiers, products and people.

I will return to this map in a moment; but first consider the bizarre way that these two photo complexes conclude. The dirigibles suite ends with two photographs of "refuse"; the robot spread with two images of "underwater life," a sea anemone and an octopus. Apparently incongruous, these conclusions actually possess an uncanny logic. Just as capitalist technology is seen to menace more than to protect the body, so here its *aboutissement* is revealed to be simple waste, destruction, death: "refuse" is not the other of the mechanical-commodified but its outcome. In a similar way the images of underwater life are not only opposed to the robotic images as organic to mechanistic; rather, they point to an uncanny deathliness at work in the mechanical-commodified forms too. In these two complexes, then, the "drive" of capitalist technology is implicitly referred, on the one hand, to a present waste, a destructiveness that belies any techno-utopia, and, on the other hand, to a primordial state, a regressiveness that belies any transcendental new man. However slight, the suggestion is that modernism is bound up not only with the dynamic of rationalist technology but also, through this dynamic, with the death drive. And from this implication we might again speculate: just as mechanization and commodification might prepare the apperception of the uncanny, might they also permit the formulation of the death drive? Further, might this drive be the internalization of these processes—and not just in the sense that Freud conceived the drive as a mechanism, indeed a motor, that was both compulsively repetitive and energistically entropic?[38] Finally, is this connection between machinist modernisms and the death drive somehow glimpsed in the compulsive figure of the bachelor machine?[39]

But what map of machinist modernisms is suggested here? In "Aboutissements de la mécanique" the works of Suzanne Duchamp, Popova, and Léger all represent different positions on the becoming industrial of culture (mechanical drawing in painting, constructivist design in theater, avantgarde film). In both idiom and title the Duchamp image, *Factory of My Thoughts,* suggests a mechanization of artistic craft as well as of (un)conscious thought. However, it does so to mock traditional representation and modernist expressivity rather than to embrace industrial production as such. The machine is parodic in dadaist work; here the parody remains within the given code of painting, and so affirms the very order that it otherwise dandyishly derides.[40] In this regard the Duchamp painting is dialectically opposed to the Popova construction. Hardly parodic, this constructivist stage set is an affirmative sketch of industrial communism to come, which the Meierkhol'dian actor is to evoke with biomechanical gestures (Meierkhol'd based these gestures on Taylorist studies of labor). Here the artist works not to annex industry thematically to art but to do the reverse—"to translate the task from the aesthetic plane to the Productivist plane."[41] The Léger position differs from both the Duchamp and the Popova: neither a parody nor a subsumption of art vis-à-vis industry, Léger proposes a populist aesthetic based on the "manufactured object."[42] In effect, he assumes capitalism as the motive force that modernism must somehow recoup: art became abstract under the demands of its "specialization," and in order to "renew the man-spectacle mechanically" the artist must adapt

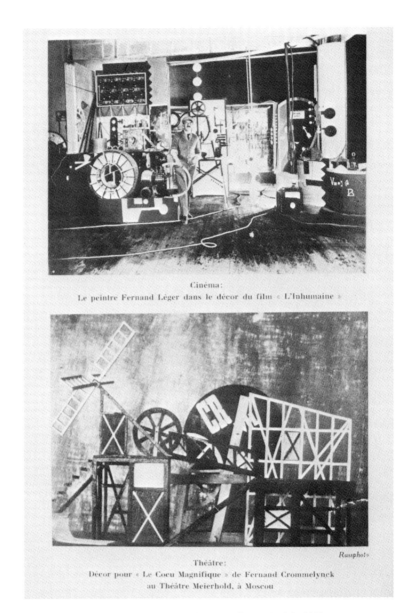

Cinéma:
Le peintre Fernand Léger dans le décor du film « L'Inhumaine »

Russphoto

Théâtre:
Décor pour « Le Cocu Magnifique » de Fernand Crommelynck
au Théâtre Meïerhold, à Moscou

"Aboutissements de la mécanique," photographs in *Variétés*, 1930.

Trafic

Peinture:
« Usine de mes pensées » par Suzanne Duchamp (1920)

the machine and the commodity, must address capitalist "spectacle" and industrial "shock."[43]

This position is the other to the surrealist position, the absent fourth term in this partial map. For if dada and constructivism form one dialectical pair, so too do the dysfunctional devices of surrealism and the machinist models of Léger (not to mention of Le Corbusier, the middle Bauhaus, and many others—all different, to be sure, but all alike in this opposition).[44] Whereas the mechanistic images of dada parody the institution of autonomous art only to affirm its individualistic practices, the productivist wing of constructivism seeks to transcend this institution in the collective production of industrial culture. And whereas Léger and company insist on the rational beauty of the capitalist object, surrealism stresses the uncanny repressed of this modern rationality: desire and fantasy. Under its gaze the dirigibles here may become so many fantastic fish and innocuous bombs, pneumatic penises and inflated breasts—part objects of desire rather than mass paradigms of objectivity. "In every [rational] object," Roger Caillois wrote in 1933, "[there is] an irrational residue,"[45] and it is this residue that the surrealist gaze seizes upon. It does so in order to save the object from strict functionality and total objectivity, or at least to ensure that the traces of the body are not entirely effaced. In short, in the (ir)rationalization of the object the surrealists seek "subjectivity itself, 'liberated' in the phantasm."[46] Though sited in different socioeconomic orders, both the Popova and the Léger represent modernisms that value industrialist objectivity: triumphantly they announce a new technological world, a new rational man. Surrealism takes a different view: mechanization does not produce a new objective being; it creates an uncanny hybrid beast—like the insectoid men in "Aboutissements de la mécanique."

Almost all machinist modernisms fix fetishistically on the machine as object or image; rarely do they position it in the social process. Even the surrealist critique is often (mis)directed at the machine as such rather than at its capitalist deployment. Nevertheless, this critique should not be dismissed as another liberal humanism or romantic anticapitalism. For surre-

alism does not reject the becoming machine and/or commodity of the body
in reactive nostalgia for a natural man (as expressionism mostly did). Often
surrealism resists it, in dialectical wit, with its own psychic effects, its own
psychic damage. Perhaps only a critic of surrealism like Theodor Adorno
could grasp the raggedness of this critical-redemptive move: "Surrealism,"
he wrote in retrospect, "forms the complement of the *Neue Sachlichkeit,* or
New Objectivity, which came into being at the same time. . . . [It] gathers
up the things the *Neue Sachlichkeit* denies to human beings; the distortions
attest to the violence that prohibition has done to the objects of desire."[47]

◦ ❧ ◦

Surrealism was well positioned to deride the mechanical-commodified in
this way, for the effects of mass production and consumption were first
pervasive only in its time.[48] Thus in 1922, at the very moment of the rise
of surrealism, Georg Lukács wrote that "the 'natural laws' of capitalist
production [i.e., fragmentation of both subject and object] have been extended to cover every manifestation or life in society."[49] And in 1939, at the
effective end of surrealism, Benjamin argued that the fragmented rhythm
of such production, of repetitive shock and reaction to shock, had become
the perceptual norm in the capitalist city—that even the simplest acts (light-
ing a match, making a telephone call, taking a photograph) were automatic.[50] This holds for psychic mechanisms as well, for it is at this time
too, according to Sigfried Giedion, that mechanization had "impinged upon
the very center of the human psyche."[51] It is this "impinging" that surrealism
limns: according to Giedion, it alone "has given us keys to the psychic
unrest" produced in these processes.[52]

Again, there are particular reasons why this is so. Surrealism was coeval
with the socioeconomic crises of the 1920s—at least two cycles of booms
and busts—after a war that cost France 1.7 million lives and consumed 30
percent of its national wealth.[53] In this era French capital was split not only
among the different demands of city, province, and empire (which began

to fall apart at this time)[54] but also between industrial production and craft manufacture—a contradiction that the surrealist interest in the mechanical-commodified and the outmoded addresses. Nevertheless, the rate of growth of production was high throughout the decade (5.8 percent per year), a growth based on labor productivity (which doubled between 1920 and 1938). This productivity depended on new techniques of rationalization: mechanization of labor, standardization of products, work planning, assembly line manufacturing, organization of offices, and so on. Even before the war French labor saw that these Taylorist and Fordist practices represented the reduction of the worker to "a machine without a soul," a "front-line soldier" in the economic war. Or as one labor activist wrote in a 1913 *Vie ouvrière:* "Intelligence is chased away from the workshops and factories. What remains are only arms without brains and robots of flesh adapted to the robots of iron and steel."[55]

The geniuses of this robotizing are well known. After decades of time studies of work Frederick W. Taylor published his *Principles of Scientific Management* in 1911, and his disciple Frank B. Gilbreth added his motion studies soon thereafter. Similar psychotechnical procedures were developed in France during this same period (e.g., Etienne-Jules Marey, Henri Fayol), and in time others were elaborated elsewhere (e.g., the industrial psychology of Hugo Münsterberg in Germany, the industrial sociology or "human relations" of Elton Mayo in the United States). Of greatest impact, of course, were the production principles of Henry Ford, who opened the first conveyor assembly line at his Highland Park factory in 1913. Almost as important, however, were the consumption principles of Alfred Sloan, who introduced market feedback as a way to control production flows at General Motors in the mid-1920s: here capital moved to integrate, indeed to "automatize," consumption as well. It is this robotizing of the producing body that Lukács theorized in 1922, this robotizing of the consuming body that Benjamin historicized in 1939, this robotizing of both that the surrealists doubled, exaggerated, and mocked throughout this period.

All these psychotechnical procedures were designed to increase capitalist profit through cuts in labor cost: "to reduce to a minimum the resistance offered by man," as Marx foresaw, "that obstinate yet elegiac natural barrier."[56] Taylor was explicit about this goal: the scientific management of labor was to eliminate extraneous movements and individualistic gestures; "elements of chance or accident" were also to be eradicated.[57] All such characteristics were henceforth considered *"mere sources of error."*[58] And yet what are these mere sources of error, these despised elements of chance and accident, if not the very *values* of surrealism—embraced precisely in order to spite such rationalization? In practice if not in principle this resistance is not undertaken in the name of a prior human nature; rather, it goes through such rationalization, uses its strange effects, its hybrid subjects, in order to critique it from within. On this view rationalization not only does *not* eliminate chance, accident, and error; in some sense it *produces* them. It is around this dialectical point that the surrealist satire of the mechanical-commodified turns.

Too often strategies of chance are seen as opposite rather than immanent to rationalization. And yet just as the modernist value of originality is incited by a world of increased reproductions, so the surrealist values of the singular and the *insolite* are articulated against a world of increased repetition and regularity. Chance, accident, and error are thus bound up with the advent of administered society (its very government depends on such "sciences" of chance as statistics and probability); not alien to such social life, they may even prepare us for it. "Games of chance," Benjamin once remarked, "paved the way for empathy with exchange value"; activities of leisure, Adorno and Horkheimer added later, are "afterimages" of mechanized labor.[59] While the first may ready us for speculations on the (stock) market, the second may reconcile us to routines of the workplace. My point is not about some grim total system that recuperates everything; rather, it concerns the very possibility of any immanent critique. Surrealist explorations of chance, dreams, *dérives,* and the like can confront the mechanical-commodified world only *because they are already inscribed within it:* only from there can this

world be *détourné*. Previously I have suggested that these surrealist explorations bespeak psychic mechanisms; here we may see that they are also
bound up with social mechanization. But rather than cancel them out, this
positioning gives them a dialectical edge. Take the famous surrealist game
of the *cadavre exquis* (exquisite corpse), whereby different parts of a drawing
or a poem were produced by different hands oblivious to what the others
had done. As is often said, such collaborations evaded the conscious control
of the individual artist, but do they not also mock the rationalized order of
mass production? Are these witty grotesques not also critical perversions of
the assembly line—a form of automatism that parodies the world of
automatization?[60]

The uncanniness of the machine and the commodity does not reside in these
forms; it is a projection of a particular subject—in surrealism as in Freud an
anxiously heterosexual male. It is important then to stress again the fetishistic
link made between a historical ambivalence regarding the mechanical-commodified and a psychic ambivalence regarding woman—a desire for mastery
over these figures mixed with a dread of servitude to them.[61] But this alone
does not explain the persistent association between woman and the mechanical-commodified. Is it that the (non)otherness of the first is paradigmatic for the patriarchal subject of the (non)otherness of the second? Or do
all these figures—woman, machine, commodity—converge through an overdetermined evocation of sexuality and death, a sex appeal of the inorganic?

For some male modernists the machine held out a more intimate promise than that of a new rational order of society: the promise of creation
outside woman, of identity free of difference, of self-conception without
death. This most fetishistic of all desires is not absent from surrealism: it is
active in its fascination with dolls (as we saw with Bellmer) as well as in its
marveling about automatons. Indeed, this fantasy is thematized by some
surrealists ("the child when speaking for the first time says 'Mama!' or

'Papa!,'" Péret writes in "Au paradis des fantômes," "but the automaton writes 'marvelous' because it knows itself to be essentially marvelous"). It is even ironized by some proto-surrealists: e.g., Picabia in *Girl Born without a Mother* (1916–1917) and Ernst in *Self-Constructed Small Machine* (1919), both of whom reflect on the becoming machine of the body at its very threshold, at birth. Such images evoke a peculiar family romance in which a machine dream substitutes for a biological origin, in which a patriarchal fantasy of technological self-creation outside the mother is expressed—but expressed to be mocked, not embraced. For these machines are figures not of a brave new world but rather of a sterile new condition. Amid the ironical wit they suggest a historical insight: that the capitalist *development* of the mechanical-commodified body can promote an uncanny *regression* to a quasi-autistic state.

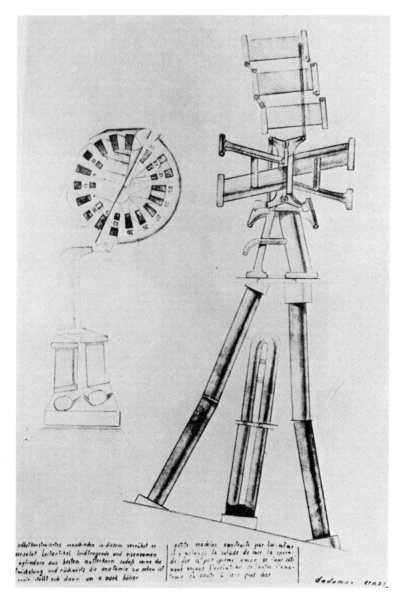

Max Ernst, *Self-Constructed Small Machine*, 1919.

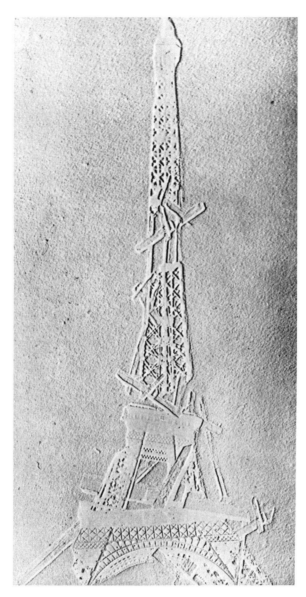

Raoul Ubac, *Fossil of the Eiffel Tower*, 1939.

6

OUTMODED SPACES

In chapter 5 I read the two emblems of the surrealist marvelous, the man-nequin and the ruin, as twin figures of a dialectical process: a modernization that is also ruinous, a progress that is also regressive. It is the outmoded figured in the ruin that concerns me here, and, as with the mechanical-commodified figured in the mannequin, I want to locate within it a historical dimension of the uncanny. Thus I will suggest that the uncanny return of past states discussed in individual terms in chapter 3 may also occur in a social register, that surrealism recovers repressed historical as well as psychic materials. Often these recoveries are intended as a disruptive return, but sometimes they intimate a transformative working-through too. This raises a set of difficult questions. Can the uncanny be recouped in this way? Can the repetition compulsion, indeed the death drive, be *détourné*? Or is such a redemption not only suspect but impossible?[1]

Again, I derive the notion of the outmoded from Walter Benjamin, whose own historical practice as a montage of past and present citations was thoroughly informed by surrealism (much to the chagrin of his rival angels, Adorno and Brecht, and sometimes of Benjamin too).[2] To extend the quo-tation begun in chapter 5: Bretonian surrealists were the first to perceive the revolutionary energies that appear in the "outmoded" [*veraltet*], in the first iron constructions, the first factory buildings, the earliest photos, the objects that have begun to be extinct, grand pianos, the dresses of five years ago, fashionable restaurants when the vogue had begun to ebb from them. The relation of these things to revolution—no one can have a more exact concept of it than these authors. No one before these visionaries and augurs perceived how destitution—not only social but architectonic, the poverty of interiors, enslaved and enslaving objects—can be suddenly transformed into revolutionary nihilism. . . . They bring the immense force of "atmosphere" concealed in these things to the point of explosion.[3]

Two aspects of this insight should be noted immediately. The first concerns the paradoxical inscription of a temporal category in spatial forms like old buildings and interiors: if the mechanical-commodified impacts primarily on the body, the outmoded is registered primarily in its architectures, which thus become "spatial allegories of a temporal crossing or historical change."[4] The second point is that in his extraordinary list of outmoded things Benjamin does not distinguish among the truly archaic, the magically old, and the simply *démodé*—among objects of precapitalist modes of production, objects of the era of surrealist childhood, and objects "of five years ago" that have fallen out of fashion. The surrealists do make such distinctions in practice if not in principle. On the one hand, they see an aura in outmoded things from the peasant spoon seized by Breton in *L'Amour fou* (1937), through the early nineteenth-century arcade detailed by Aragon in *Le Paysan de Paris* (1926), to the late nineteenth-century illustrations appropriated by Ernst in his collage novels (1929–1934). On the other hand, they also turn to *démodé* forms, such as the art nouveau architecture that infatuated Dalí (in texts of the early 1930s), but for reasons difficult to sort out: in a campy mode of retro-risqué but also as "anti-aphrodisiacal" reminders of the just-past, in antimodernist gestures but also as provocations against a modernism become chic.[5]

However, none of these deployments makes clear how the outmoded can be radical, the auratic explosive or cultural destitution transformed into "revolutionary nihilism." The outmoded as the archaic would seem associated with the traditional, even the reactionary, and the outmoded as *démodé* with the merely parodic, the ultimately affirmative; aura and shock would likewise appear to be opposed. How could it be otherwise? By way of an answer I want to press the term *outmoded* in a way that the German may not support: to key it to *mode* in the sense not only of fashion but also of mode of production (*veraltet* is closer to our "obsolete"). Even less than Benjamin did the surrealists see art, fashion, or culture in general as a superstructural expression of an economic base (a truly fundamental point of conflict with official Marxism).[6] Rather, they played upon the tension between cultural objects and socioeconomic forces, between mode as fashion and mode as means of production. In effect, the surrealist outmoded posed the cultural detritus of past moments residual in capitalism against the socioeconomic complacency of its present moment; and it did so through three different sorts of citations: of artisanal relics, of old images within bourgeois culture, and of outdated fashions.

Hence the classic site of the surrealist *dérive,* the flea market, where the temporally outmoded comes to rest in the spatially marginal. "I go there often," Breton writes of the Saint-Ouen market in *Nadja* (1928), "searching for objects that can be found nowhere else: old-fashioned, broken, useless, almost incomprehensible, even perverse . . . yellowed nineteenth-century photographs, worthless books, and iron spoons."[7] Again, it was there in 1934 that Breton found the slipper spoon described in *L'Amour fou.* To retrieve this object "of peasant fabrication," made for personal use rather than for abstract exchange, was not only a response to a private desire (as discussed in chapter 2). Implicitly it was also a gesture of social critique whereby the dominant system of commodity exchange was symbolically

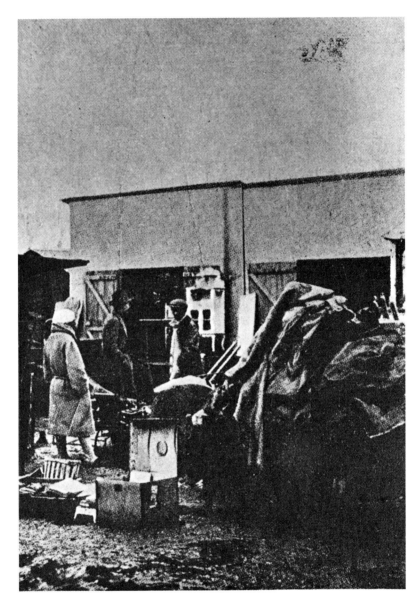

Photograph of Saint-Ouen flea market in *Nadja*, 1928.

queried by a fragile relic of the supplanted order of craft relations.[8] The spoon is thus an instance of the first order of the surrealist outmoded: a token of a precapitalist relation that commodity exchange has displaced or submerged. Here its recovery might spark a brief profane illumination of a past productive mode, social formation, and structure of feeling—an uncanny return of a historically repressed moment of direct manufacture, simple barter, and personal use. This is not to romanticize this old economic mode so much as it is to spark a connection between psychic and historical dimensions via a social object—a connection, however private, that might be both critical and curative in the present. As suggested in chapter 5, such little disruptions of the capitalist order of things constitute an important part of surrealist politics, one complementary to its local derangements of representation and language. In the case of objects such as the peasant spoon, the surrealists exploit the very effects of an expansive capitalism—not only artisanal objects rendered outmoded by industrialization but also tribal objects rendered *dépaysés* in imperialization—against its own system of commodity exchange. In this way they confront the bourgeois order with tokens of its repressed past (the outmoded) as well as its exploited outside ("the primitive").[9]

However, such precapitalist things make up only a small part of the surrealist reflection on the outmoded. As Benjamin suggests, this gaze focuses on the remains of the nineteenth century. "Balzac was the first to speak of the ruins of the bourgeoisie," he writes in his 1935 *Passagen-Werk* exposé "Paris—the Capital of the Nineteenth Century."

But only Surrealism exposed them to view. The development of the forces of production has turned the wish symbols of the previous century into rubble even before the monuments which represented them had crumbled. . . . All these products are on the point of entering the market as commodities. But they still linger on the threshold. From this epoch stem the arcades and interiors, the exhibitions and panoramas. They are residues of a dream world.[10]

This then is the second focus of the surrealist outmoded: "the situation of the middle class at the moment it shows its first signs of decline," when its cherished forms begin to crumble as "wish symbols," to become ruins before the fact—in short, when it begins to forfeit its own progressive values and utopian projections (here Benjamin follows Marx in his *Eighteenth Brumaire of Louis Bonaparte* [1852]).[11] To invoke such outmoded forms is to advance a twofold immanent critique of high capitalist culture (the precapitalist protests via artisanal or tribal objects is more transcendental). On the one hand, the capitalist outmoded relativizes bourgeois culture, denies its pretense to the natural and the eternal, opens it up to its own history, indeed its own historicity. In effect, it exploits the paradox that this culture, under the spell of the commodity, has any history at all.[12] On the other hand, the capitalist outmoded challenges this culture with its own forfeited dreams, tests it against its own compromised values of political emancipation, technological progress, cultural access, and the like. It may even intimate a way to tap the utopian energies trapped in these historical forms—to tap them for other political purposes in the present. Here we might glimpse how this "substitution of a political for a historical view of the past"[13] might turn cultural destitution into revolutionary nihilism. For the surrealist outmoded does invoke a "destitution," a loss or a lack productive of desire (as in the dominant psychoanalytic account), but because this destitution is "social" and "architectonic," because this lack is historical and material, the desire is not *necessarily* impossible, incapable of fulfillment (as again in the dominant psychoanalytical account). Such fulfillment, however, does necessitate a near-impossible move: a revolutionary leap "in the open air of history."[14]

What does all this have to do with the uncanny? I want to suggest that the surrealist concern with the marvelous and the uncanny, with the return of familiar images made strange by repression, is related to the Marxian concern with the outmoded and the nonsynchronous, with the persistence of old cultural forms in the uneven development of productive modes and social formations; more, that the first supplies what the second cannot do without: its subjective dimension.[15] To posit such a connection between the psychic and the historical is often problematic, and a familiar criticism of Benjamin is that he succumbed to a suspect notion of a Jungian collective unconscious in doing so. Yet he more often held to an "image sphere" *within* historical memory, and the same is true of the surrealists. In the "Manifesto" Breton alludes to this uncanny image sphere in terms of the nonsynchronous: "The marvelous is not the same in every period: it partakes in some obscure way of a sort of general revelation only the fragments of which come down to us: they are the romantic ruins, the modern mannequin."[16] These image fragments may be "residues of a dream world," as Benjamin calls them, but the surrealists did not wish to remain asleep in it, as he sometimes stated: they too sought to use these outmoded images to awaken this world.[17]

For both parties this dream world is auratic. In the surrealist outmoded the present is often recalled to the past, especially so in the citation of childhood images. "One day, perhaps," Breton writes, "we shall see the toys of our whole life, like those of our childhood, once more."[18] Such is the privileged realm of the outmoded for Benjamin too: it "speaks from our childhood," he tells us;[19] and for both Benjamin and surrealism, it speaks with a maternal voice. Indeed, in its auratic register the surrealist outmoded seems to evoke a maternal memory (or fantasy) of psychic intimacy and bodily unity.

This intimate affect of the outmoded is already inscribed in the Benjaminian definition of aura, which possesses a subjective as well as a historical dimension. On the one hand, an object is auratic if it appears to return our gaze, and the prototype of this returned gaze is the gaze of the mother. On the other hand, an object is also auratic if it bears the "traces of the practiced hand"—that is, if it retains the marks of human labor (though, again, Benjamin was hesitant to delimit it in this way).[20] In direct contrast to the mechanical-commodified, both these qualities are often active in the outmoded—the memory of the gaze as well as the mark of the hand—and they intersect in the mystery of the body, the forgotten human dimension that is related in the psychic register to the maternal and in the historical register to the artisanal. In many of the things cherished by the surrealists (again, the slipper spoon is a convenient example) these two terms, the psychic token of a lost object and the social relic of an artisanal mode of labor, converge to overdetermine the object, to cathect it intensely.[21] But this maternal cathexis active in the surrealist outmoded may also be more direct, less "prehistorical." This is the case with its second register—not the artisanal relics but the bourgeois ruins, among which the surrealists as children played. In *Camera Lucida* Barthes writes: "That is what the time when my mother was alive *before me* is—History (moreover, it is the period which interests me most, historically)."[22] So it is with the surrealists too.

However, for the surrealists if not for Benjamin the outmoded is never purely auratic. For the outmoded not only recalls the present to the past; it may also return the past to the present, in which case it often assumes a demonic guise. Thus for Aragon the old arcade is full of "sirens," "sphinxes," and other ciphers of desire and death, and the nineteenth-century interiors of the Ernst collage novels are overrun with monsters and grotesques. The Freudian uncanny may help us to see why: once repressed, the past, however blessed, cannot return so benignly, so auratically—precisely because it is damaged by repression. The demonic aspect of this recovered past is then the sign of this repression, of this estrangement from the blessed state of unity—whether with a childhood toy or (ultimately) with the maternal body. In surrealism this demonic aspect is often inscribed on the thing (the toy, the body) in the form of distortions—the distortions that, again in the formulation of Adorno, "attest to the violence that prohibition had done to the objects of desire."[23]

⁕ ⁕

None of these psychic affects yet explain why this interest in the outmoded arises in the 1920s and 1930s. The process of outmoding is continual in capitalism: why does it come into focus then? For the same reasons that the mechanical-commodified comes into relief then too: after World War I modernization intensified greatly. The period centered in the 1920s and 1930s is now seen as the long wave of the second technological revolution, defined technically by new uses of electricity and combustion and stamped culturally by new forms of transportation and reproduction.[24] As these techniques penetrated everyday practices, the outmoded was brought to consciousness as a category.

But Benjamin is specific: this critical perception—whereby an old cultural image is grasped as dialectical only at the moment of its eclipse—is not a general insight; it is a surrealist recognition, credited to Aragon in particular.[25] Early in *Le Paysan de Paris* (whose very title juxtaposes different social-spatial orders) Aragon describes the decrepit passages in this way:

> Although the life that originally quickened them has drained away, they deserve, nevertheless, to be regarded as the secret repositories of several modern myths: it is only today, when the pickaxe menaces them, that they have at last become the true sanctuaries of a cult of the ephemeral, the ghostly landscape of damnable pleasures and professions. Places that were incomprehensible yesterday, and that tomorrow will never know.[26]

Here Aragon echoes the famous Baudelairean definition of modernity: "By 'modernity' I mean the ephemeral, the fugitive, the contingent, the half of art whose other half is the eternal and the immutable."[27] Only now the transcendental half has evaporated, and the modern half has congealed into myth: the "vast picture-gallery" of pleasures and professions that delighted the Baudelairean flâneur has become a ruinous wax museum, a "ghostly landscape," for the surrealist specter. The ruin here is real, the work of the pickaxe of development. But it is also an effect of the surrealist vision of history: "Everything is crumbling under my gaze" (P 61). This gaze is not melancholic; the surrealists do not cling obsessively to the relics of the nineteenth century. Rather it uncovers them for purposes of resistance *through* reenchantment. If we can grasp this dialectic of ruination, recovery, and resistance, we will grasp the intimated ambition of the surrealist practice of history.[28]

In this regard a short text of 1939 by Benjamin Péret titled "Ruines: ruine des ruines" is suggestive. As Aragon exposed Baudelairean modernity as mythical, so Péret exposes the capitalist dynamic of innovation as a process of ruination: "one ruin," he writes, "drives out the one before and kills it."[29] This ruination is not the surrealist use of history; it is more akin to its abuse in fascist and totalitarian regimes. Consider the way Mussolini celebrates ancient Rome, only to betray its republican values, Péret suggests, or the way Stalin remembers Lenin, only to betray his vision. A remembering that represses, such history is opposed to the surrealist concept of history that ruins in order to recover through an active return of the repressed.

Péret underscores the uncanniness of this surrealist notion with photographs by Raoul Ubac of the Paris Bourse (1808/27–1902/3), Opera House (1861–1874) and Eiffel Tower (1889) all as so many fossils, "monuments of the bourgeoisie as ruins even before they crumbled."[30] Here Péret and Ubac regard these contradictory monuments, historicist and technologistic, as zoological remains; they appear arrested in time as if by natural catastrophe. In a gesture of defamiliarization also practiced by Benjamin the modern is seen as the primal, and cultural history is recast as natural history.[31] In this surrealist vision the historicity of the bourgeois regime is imaged through an accelerated archaism of its forms: its transcendental ambitions are contested through the very presentation of its wish symbols as ruins. And in this vision the present is also revealed as a ruin, a ruin (perhaps by 1939 the ruin of surrealism too) that must be recovered as well. In this regard, if the surrealist vision is related to the Benjaminian model of history, then both must be opposed to a third contemporaneous regime of history, one formulated most famously by Albert Speer in "A Theory of the Value of Ruins" (1938). There Speer argues for a culture that encompasses its own destruction in order to secure ruins which, hundreds of years later, "will inspire as many heroic thoughts as the models of Antiquity do today."[32] Here the ruin is posed as a way to dominate history continuously rather than as a means to crack open its historicist continuum.

At this point we might begin to solve the riddle of the surrealist outmoded—why sometime members of the Communist Party committed to future emancipation would be concerned with historical reclamation (of bourgeois ruins no less!). One part of my answer was that this reclamation relativizes the bourgeois order of things, opens it up to cultural revolution.[33] The other part is that this reclamation treats repressed moments in this order, in its official history. In this way the surrealist repetition of such historical material is undertaken not only to disrupt the present but also to work through the past.

This reading might illuminate the otherwise obscure remark of Benjamin that "surrealism is the death of the last century through comedy."[34] In the famous first lines of *The Eighteenth Brumaire of Louis Bonaparte* Marx paraphrases Hegel to the effect that all great events and characters are apt to occur twice—the first time as tragedy, the second time as farce.[35] But in an early manuscript of 1844 he intimated a third, comedic moment; and to the rhetorical question of what purpose is served by this ironic movement from tragedy through farce to comedy Marx replied: "So that humanity can part from its past *gaily*."[36] This comment introduces the Benjamin remark concerning surrealism as the comedic death of the nineteenth century, and it allows us to interpret it. Surrealism is a metaphorical death of the nineteenth century in the sense that it breaks with it—its dominant values concerning art and politics, subjectivity and sexuality. But surrealism breaks with it through comedy, a rhetorical mode of collective reintegration, so it is also a symbolic working-through of the nineteenth century—of its image sphere of broken political promises, suppressed social movements, frustrated utopian desires.[37] Thus if surrealism repeats images of the nineteenth century, it is to work through them as ciphers of repressed moments: to complete them precisely so that they can be broken with, so that the twentieth century can be awoken from the dream of the nineteenth century (or, as Benjamin says, its spell cast by the commodity) into a transformed twentieth century. In this way the surrealist repetition of historical representations is both critical and comedic. In chapter 3 we saw that surrealism was concerned to work through psychic trauma by means of images that juxtapose different scenes or space-times. Here we may see that it is concerned to work through historical trauma too—and again through dialectical juxtapositions of past and present. In a statement whose paradoxicality attests to the difficulty of this project, Breton once remarked that surrealist collages are *"slits in time"* that produce *"illusions of true recognition"* "where former lives, actual lives, future lives melt together into one life."[38]

To what historical moments do these "slits in time" connect? What are the patterns of reclamation, the periods of attraction? The surrealists often celebrated peripheral or suspect figures in European art, literature, and philosophy, but more than a fetishistic marginality is involved in these enthusiasms, as the recovery of Lautréamont and the rapport with Rimbaud makes clear.[39] In *What Is Surrealism?* (1936) Breton considered this special resonance.

> 1868–75: it is impossible . . . to perceive an epoch so *poetically* rich, so victorious, so revolutionary, and so charged with distant meaning. . . . It is not an idle hope to wish to see the works of Lautréamont and Rimbaud restored to their correct historical background: the coming and the immediate results of the war of 1870. Other and analogous cataclysms could not have failed

to rise out of that military and social cataclysm whose final episode was to be the atrocious crushing of the Paris Commune; the last in date caught many of us at the very age when Lautréamont and Rimbaud found themselves thrown into the preceding one, and by way of revenge has had as its consequence—and this is the new and important fact—the triumph of the Bolshevik Revolution.[40]

Two important points are suggested here. First, Breton poses a general relation, neither causal nor fortuitous, between political and poetic "cataclysms," a relation crucial to the very possibility of "surrealism in the service of the revolution." Second, he claims a specific sense of historical correspondence not only between Lautréamont and Rimbaud and surrealism, but between the Franco-Prussian War and the Commune on the one hand and the First World War and the Bolshevik Revolution on the other. In this vision history does become a slit in time, a hyphen of prior and past moments—a political *Jetztzeit,* as Benjamin and Bloch would say, filled with "the presence of the now."[41] This presence can be seized for radical purposes in art and politics alike, and it is to this double effectivity that surrealism seeks to restore Lautréamont and Rimbaud—in order to set up this past revolutionary epoch in resonance with the present one.[42] Paradoxically this resonance depends on a certain distance: though returned in surrealism, Lautréamont and Rimbaud remain "charged with distant meaning." And it is this charged distance, this auratic dimension,[43] that turns the resonance between these two moments into revolutionary shock, which simultaneously works to blast the prior moment out of its historical continuum and to give the surrealist moment its political depth. In this way the outmoded can become protorevolutionary, the auratic may be made explosive.

These two different moments are times of crisis in more than art and politics. Just as surrealism occurs in the midst of the second technological revolution, so the moment of Lautréamont and Rimbaud punctuates the long economic wave produced by the first technological revolution.[44] During the 1860s and 1870s French capital began to retool toward a monopolistic order; the attendant socioeconomic dislocation was evident in the very transformation of Paris, as the premodern city of the early nineteenth century was Haussmannized into the spectacular city of the late nineteenth century.[45] (As we will see, this process produced the privileged instance of the surrealist outmoded, the condemned Passage de l'Opéra recorded by Aragon.) In this way the surrealists not only looked back to this prior revolutionary moment but also sought to redeploy it at a time when its very traces were threatened with disappearance.

Of course, the surrealist gaze ranges beyond this moment too—wherever "the most important evidence of [the] latent 'mythology'" of bourgeois modernity may be found.[46] Influenced by Aragon, this statement of Benjamin must be supplemented by a remark of Sigfried Giedion, who, influenced in turn by Ernst, wrote that nineteenth-century architecture "had the role of the subconscious" for the surrealists.[47] This connection between psychic charge, architectural form, and social "mythology" is indeed a surrealist insight, one I want to develop now in three test cases of the surrealist outmoded: the passages, the bourgeois interior, and art nouveau architecture as seen respectively by Aragon, Ernst, and Dalí.

These surrealists see these architectures as psychological spaces. For Aragon the passages are "dream houses"—not only as the first stage sets of the phantasmagoria of the commodity, "the ur-landscape of consumption," as Benjamin notes, but also as spaces "that have no outside—like the dream."[48] For Ernst the bourgeois interior is the very figure of the unconscious, the Rimbaudian salon at "the bottom of a lake."[49] Finally, for Dalí art nouveau architectures are so many "desires grown solid," as if the unconscious were hysterically extruded into form.[50] Together, then, these three surrealists suggest a partial archaeology of bourgeois patriarchal subjectivity as fossil-

Photograph of Passage de l'Opéra, 1822–1935.

ized in its nineteenth-century spaces, one that uncovers three stages in its becoming unconscious.

At the same time this partial archaeology registers three stages of a complementary process: the becoming industrial of bourgeois society. While the passages are an early confident example of industrial technique (iron and glass construction), the bourgeois interior is produced as a sanctuary from this industrial world now seen as a site of moral and physical threat. Finally, art nouveau suggests an attempt to bridge the resultant gap between private and public realms, to reconcile the contradictory demands of art and industry, through the production in modern materials of fantastic shapes.[51] In these three outmoded architectures, then, the industrial is first embraced, then repressed, only to return in an uncanny, even phantasmagoric way.

In the process there is a curious mixing of the future and the archaic in these spaces. "In the dream in which every epoch sees in images the epoch which is to succeed it," Benjamin writes, "the latter appears coupled with elements of prehistory."[52] So it is here too: the modern is mixed with the primordial or the infantile as a site of "modern mythology" in the passage of Aragon, of primal fantasy in the bourgeois interiors of Ernst, of "infantile neurosis" in the art nouveau of Dalí.[53] For Benjamin this turn to the prehistoric conveys a utopian desire for the classless, but it may also signify a social withdrawal, perhaps a psychic regression. Ultimately it may be in this opening to a past that is both social and psychic that the surrealist outmoded is most directly related to the uncanny.[54]

The arcades, Aragon writes, were "born towards the end of the romantic era" (P 109), and by the time he wanders through them 100 years later in *Le Paysan de Paris* (1926) they have become romantic ruins, the very image of the surrealist marvelous as the outmoded. In hallucinatory detail Aragon describes one passage, the Passage de l'Opéra, as a "bazaar of the bizarre" (P 114), *unheimlich* home to old shops, objects, and inhabitants. Though often antiquarian, his history is also critical, made urgent by the scheduled destruction of the passage by the Boulevard Haussmann Building Society. The forces arrayed in this "real civil war" (P 40) are clear to Aragon: small tradesmen against big business and corrupt government, the arcades of one era of capitalism against the department stores of another era (he names the Galeries Lafayette specifically). Although "this battle . . . is lost in advance" (P 80), there is still a victory to be gained, for in "these despised transfor-mations" (P 24) there emerges "a modern mythology" (P 19). More than 40 years later in *Je n'ai jamais appris à écrire* Aragon glosses this phrase:

> Having observed that all the mythologies of the past became transformed into romances [*romans*] as soon as people no longer believed in them, I formulated the idea of reversing the process and elaborating a novel [*roman*] that would present itself as a mythology. Naturally, a mythology of the modern.[55]

This mythology is intended not to mystify the modern (as Benjamin thought) but to expose the marvelous in "everyday existence" (P 24). As we saw in chapter 2, the marvelous for Aragon is "the eruption of contra-diction within the real" (P 216), a real that otherwise conceals such contra-diction. In this way the "despised transformations" wrought by capitalism may reveal conflicts *within* its order—between old and new manufactures, architectures, behaviors—and this "asynchronism of desire" (P 66) may in turn be used *against* this order.[56] For not only does such "asynchronism" show capitalism to be never complete (or completely rational), but it also opens it up in such a way that moments repressed in its past can return to disrupt and perhaps transform its present. Such are the implications of the modern mythology of the marvelous, which Aragon elsewhere terms "a dialectical urgency born of another, lost urgency."[57] For Benjamin this "materialistic, anthropological illumination" is the greatest achievement of surrealism,[58] the politics of its aesthetics. It is an illumination that may be glimpsed in collage, which Aragon practices in *Le Paysan* precisely as a juxtaposition of outmoded and modern images.

In his passage Aragon poses as an Odyssean wanderer, but he is less a detached *flâneur* than an active archaeologist. In this capacity he is not apart from his field of investigation, for his juxtapositions provoke not only historical illuminations but also "moral confusions" (P 122). The passage is not only a dream space for Aragon; in a more uncanny register the "disturbingly named *passages*" (P 28) are also both a womb and a tomb, at once maternal (even intrauterine) and chthonic. In this sense the passage is indeed "illuminated by [his] instincts" (P 61), by "the double game of love and death played by *Libido*" (P 47).

Crucial here is that Aragon comes to understand these psychic conflicts in terms of historical contradictions and vice versa. "Our cities are peopled with unrecognized sphinxes" (P 28), he writes, yet if the modern Oedipus "interrogates them in his turn, all that these faceless monsters will grant is that he shall once again plumb his own depths" (P 28). This connection between the historical riddles of the outmoded and the psychic enigmas of the uncanny is essential to Aragon, and it produces the ambivalence of *Le Paysan*. For even as the uncanny enlivens the outmoded, renders it disruptive in the present, it threatens to overwhelm the subject, as it overwhelms Aragon at the conclusion of his passage: "What has become of my poor certainty, that I cherished so, in this great vertigo where consciousness is aware of being nothing more than a stratum of unfathomable depths? I am just one moment of an eternal fall" (P 122–123). This is the fate of the surrealist subject when the uncanny is not recouped.

If Aragon returns to the nineteenth-century passage in *Le Paysan,* Ernst recalls the nineteenth-century interior in his three collage novels, *La Femme*

Max Ernst, collage from *Une Semaine de bonté*, 1934.

100 têtes (1929), *Rêve d'une petite fille qui voulut entrer au carmel* (1930), and *Une Semaine de bonté* (1934). In these texts Ernst collages nineteenth-century illustrations, most from melodramatic novels and salon paintings, some from old goods catalogues and scientific magazines, into elliptical narratives. *La Femme 100 têtes,* which Giedion reads as "a symbolic name for the nineteenth century,"[59] is filled with scenes of violation. Steeped in surrealist anticlericalism, *Rêve d'une petite fille* and *Une Semaine de bonté* are more conventionally scandalous: the first concerns a little girl whose dream of a life devoted to God is turned into a perverse parody of the religious vocation, while the second is a compendium of seven deadly sins, an anti-prayer book or parodic book of hours. The significance of the novels, however, does not reside in these fragmented story lines; it has to do with an implicit mise-en-scène of the unconscious.

Ernst found these outmoded images in the literary equivalent of the flea market—used book stores, magazine stalls along the Seine, and the like. And he deploys them in the novels precisely in the register of the uncanny, as once familiar representations made strange by modern repression. Many of the images are literally *unheimlich*—Victorian homes distanced in time and dislocated by collage. In this way Ernst relates the historically outmoded to the psychically repressed at the very level of representation, specifically of representations residual in surrealist childhoods—that is to say, in the era of the Freudian "discovery" of sexuality and the unconscious.

The novels are punctuated by images of outmoded interiors reworked so as to suggest traumatic tableaux constitutive of subjectivity (e.g., primal scenes and castration fantasies). Implicitly this not only restages these particular scenes in the formation of sexuality and the unconscious, but also returns the Freudian discovery of these forces to its general historical setting: the late Victorian interior.[60] Through the connection between the outmoded and the repressed a visual archaeology of this discovery is thus sketched: just as Aragon saw the arcade as an analogue of the "hitherto forbidden realm" (P 101) of the unconscious, so Ernst proposes another analogue in the interior. But no more than in Aragon is this relation only metaphorical: in the collage novels Ernst suggests historical preconditions of this becoming unconscious of subjectivity.

Many of the sources are overtly melodramatic. Several images in *Une Semaine de bonté* are based on Jules Marey illustrations for *Les Damnées de Paris,* a 1883 novel of murder and mayhem.[61] These illustrations depict *drames de passion,* a woman spied upon by a man, for example, or a scene of a suicide. In his appropriation Ernst relocates these particular scenes in psychic reality through the substitution of surrealist figures of the unconscious: an Easter Island head in the first image, a lion head in the second, and a general becoming animal in both. This transformation only articulates what is implicit in the found illustrations, for melodrama is a genre already given over to the unconscious, a genre in which repressed desires are hysterically expressed. In *Une Semaine de bonté* especially, this melodramatic return of the repressed is registered not only in the becoming-monstrous of the figures but also in the becoming-hysterical of the interiors: images evocative of "perverse" desires (e.g., sodomy, sadomasochism) erupt in these rooms, most often in the spaces of representation—in paintings or mirrors on the walls. Here the mirror as a reflection of perceptual reality, the paradigm of realist painting, becomes a window onto psychic reality, the paradigm of surrealist art.

In short, these stuffed interiors are literally convulsed, but by what exactly? What is the repressed of this architecture, of this epoch, as registered in these rooms? One answer is obvious enough: sexual desire.[62] As if to underscore this symptomatology of the repressed and to complete his archaeology of the unconscious, Ernst concludes the last of his novels, *Une Semaine de bonté,* with images of hysterics derived from the Charcot *Iconographie.*[63] As Ernst well knew, psychoanalysis is pitched on the body of the hysteric: it is where workings of the unconscious were first posited—and where relationships between the image and the body, knowledge and desire, are still often probed. If Ernst connects the uncanny and the outmoded through scenes of the unconscious and the interior, it is here that he does so most precisely, at the site of hysteria—not only the late Victorian home but the Charcot clinic, the analyst couch, wherever the body of the woman is surveyed for symptoms.[64]

The uncanny disruptions of the Ernst interiors also register other types of repressed contents: social contents sedimented, as it were, in this historical space. The bourgeois interior has a special place in critical studies on nineteenth-century culture contemporaneous with the collage novels. In his 1933 dissertation on Kierkegaard, Adorno argued that his notion of an inward realm of spirituality is grounded in an ideological image of the interior, in its status as a refuge from a debased material world: "the immanence of consciousness itself is, as *intérieur,* the dialectical image for the nineteenth century as alienation."[65] This alienation misrecognized as spirituality is evoked in several images in the Ernst collage novels; one image in *La Femme 100 têtes* implies that it is the very precondition of the artist or aesthetician.

In his 1935 exposé "Paris—the Capital of the Nineteenth Century" Benjamin also analyzed the bourgeois interior as a refuge from the reality principle of the workplace. For Benjamin the interior embodies the new ideological division not only between living and working, home and office, but also between private and public, subjective and social. In this private space both the industrial aspects of the work world and the antagonistic aspects of the public realm are repressed—only to return, according to the formula of the uncanny, in displaced fantastic form. For in the bourgeois interior the actual retreat from the social world is compensated by an imaginary embrace of exotic and historical worlds: hence its typical arrangements of different objects in eclectic styles.

> From this [repression of the social] sprang the phantasmagorias of the interior. This represented the universe for the private citizen. In it he assembled the distant in space and in time. His drawing-room was a box in the world-theatre.[66]

That this embrace is illusory is suggested by the other principal characteristic of the interior for Benjamin: its function as a "casing," i.e., a protective shell wherein the bourgeoisie attempts to preserve its private familial traces against the very impermanence that its public capitalist order produces.[67] In his novels Ernst exposes both these aspects of the interior: in some collages he points to the repression that underlies its historical phantasmagoria, while in others he parodies its status as a private casing through a literal fossilization of natural forms. More generally, Ernst not only exposes the interior as a figure of bourgeois subjectivity (in the manner decoded by Adorno), but also opens up the interior to the outside that defines it as such, i.e., to the sexual and cultural others of this subjectivity. In one typical image a middle-class matron gazes in a mirror only to find a primitive head reflected there; meanwhile two praying mantes perform a deadly coitus on her dressing table as a naked young woman roams outside her window.

Neither Adorno nor Benjamin quite capture the "psychic unrest"[68] of the bourgeois interior tapped by Ernst in such collages. This articulation was left to Giedion, for whom the collage novels reveal that the bourgeois interior had failed as a refuge from the industrial world. "These pages of Max Ernst," he writes in his 1948 history *Mechanization Takes Command*, "show how a mechanized environment has affected our subconscious."[69] For Giedion this effect has to do with "the devaluation of symbols" caused by industrial production, a devaluation evident in the bourgeois interior.[70] Such interiors were filled with carpets and drapes, statues and ornaments, all dressed up in historical styles and natural motifs. But this pseudo-aristocratic disguise could not protect the objects, let alone the owners, from industrial production. Such production, Benjamin, Aragon, and Giedion all agree, penetrates these things too, "hollows [them] out," turns them into kitsch; thus alienated, they become ciphers of "wish and anxiety."[71] In his interiors Ernst makes these anxious desires manifest. Many of his images derive from old catalogues of goods and fashions (e.g., *Catalogue de grand magasin du Louvre, Magasin des nouveautés, Attributs de commerce*). The fetishistic shine of these products has long since dulled; what remains are the

Max Ernst, collage from *Une Semaine de bonté*, 1934.

Max Ernst, *La Femme 100 têtes*, 1929: "The monkey who will be a policeman, a catholic, or a broker."

intentions of wish and anxiety with which they were once invested. In his collages Ernst seizes on these traces. As a result the objects of the nineteenth-century bourgeoisie appear there less as ruins than as phantoms—phantoms that for the patriarchal subject are often figured as women.[72]

Ernst thus returns to a moment when mechanical-commodified objects had begun to dominate bourgeois interiors at a time (c. 1930) when such objects and interiors have begun to be outmoded. In these same years Dalí focuses on a somewhat later point in this dialectic of the industrial and the outmoded, specifically on a form then situated somewhere between the modern and the *démodé:* art nouveau architecture. What remains implicit in Aragon and Ernst—the arcade and the interior as spatial analogues of the unconscious, indeed as hysterical expressions of repressed desires—becomes explicit in Dalí:

> No collective effort has produced a dream world so pure and so disturbing as the "Modern Style" buildings, these being, apart from architecture, a true realization in themselves of desires grown solid. Their most violent and cruel automatism pitifully betrays a hatred of reality and a need for seeking refuge in an ideal world, just as it happens in infantile neurosis.[73]

Here Dalí not only relates this architecture to the unconscious, but does so in terms of a withdrawal from social reality—though hardly in the manner of Adorno and Benjamin. For Dalí *celebrates* this withdrawal as a regression, and rather than grasp its historical conditions in industrialization, he reacts "infantilely" against them. For Dalí is determined to see art nouveau as "postmechanical"[74] when in fact it treats the industrial in a fetishistic way:

it uses industrial materials but mostly to mitigate them through idiosyncratic designs, to absorb them into art. If industry rivals art in the arcades near the beginning of the nineteenth century, and if mechanization penetrates the interior during the middle of the century, then art nouveau reveals art "imprisoned by technical advance"[75] at the end of the century.

Its defense against technology is similar to that of the interior: a double tropism to historical styles and natural motifs. Dalí understands this defense as pathological, and this pathology delights him. "In a 'Modern Style' building," he writes in his 1933 *Minotaure* essay "De la beauté terrifiante et comestible, de l'architecture modern'style," "the Gothic metamorphoses into the Hellenic, into the Far Eastern and . . . into the Renaissance . . . all in the 'feeble' time and space, . . . little known and truly vertiginous, which are none other than those of the dream."[76] This historical phantasmagoria in art nouveau is matched by its natural fantasias, its floral motifs forged in iron (e.g., Hector Guimard), its concrete facades in the form of waves (e.g., Antonio Gaudí), and the like. These conceits, compensatory as they are, also delight Dalí, as the images that accompany his text—photographs by Brassaï and Man Ray of Guimard Métro entrances in Paris and Gaudí buildings in Barcelona—attest.

Dalí places his essay on art nouveau architecture in *Minotaure* between his "Involuntary Sculptures" and his "Phenomenon of Ecstasy," the first a series of photographs (made by Brassaï and captioned by Dalí) of trivial things subconsciously molded into strange shapes sometimes reminiscent of art nouveau ornament, the second a short text accompanied by a montage of "ecstatic," mostly female faces and anthropometric ears juxtaposed with an art nouveau detail. Dalí arranges these visual texts in this way to under-score the "automatic" and "hysterical" aspects of art nouveau, perhaps even to suggest that its historicist and natural forms are uncanny as such.[77] However, as with Ernst, the association with hysteria suggests more: that the psychic disturbance registered by Dalí in this style is also rooted in historical contradiction, that this strange architecture expresses, hysterically as it were, a social repression. For Dalí this is the repression of the "sym-

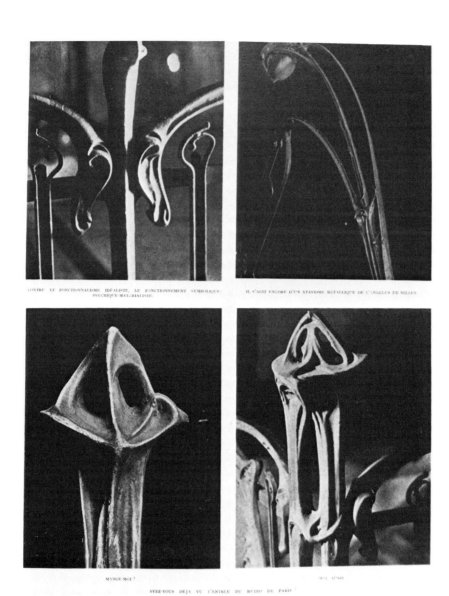

Brassaï, photographs of Paris Métro details, 1933.

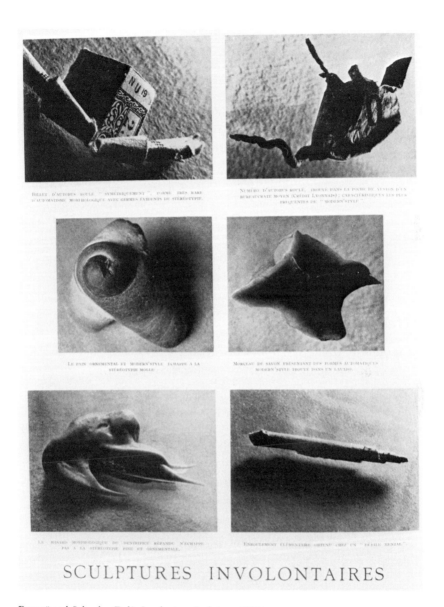

Brassaï and Salvador Dalí, *Involuntary Sculptures*, 1933.

bolic-psychic-materialist function" of art nouveau by the "functionalist ideal" of modernist art and architecture.[78]

But more is at stake here than style, for in art nouveau the contradiction inherent in bourgeois culture—that it becomes ever more technologistic *and* ever more subjectivist—is developed to an extreme point. On the one hand, art nouveau attempts to absorb "technical advance" within the categories of art; thus its use of novel processes like concrete in traditional practices of ornamentation. On the other hand, as Benjamin argues, art nouveau also attempts to mobilize "all the forces of interiority" against such technical advance; thus its insistence on "the mediumistic language of line, in the flower as symbol of . . . naked, vegetable Nature."[79] Dalí intuits this cultural conflict between the technical and the subjective: it is this that he terms the "perversity" of art nouveau. Yet, though interested in its disruptive potential, he delimits its critical effect. For the most part he portrays art nouveau as perverse in order to scandalize functionalist doxa, modernist puritanism, and "intellectualist aesthetics."[80]

In Dalí, then, the outmoded becomes more *outré* than explosive, more anachronistic than "asynchronistic" (again the Aragon term for the outmoded). And in fact he develops a notion of anachronism in his early writing and throughout his artistic practice. In this regard his retrograde techniques complement his simulated regressions (e.g., paranoia, oral sadism, coprophilia). Indeed, this double performance of technical anachronism and psychic atavism is crucial to both his oeuvre and his persona. And it may be what leads him to his flirtations first with fascism and then with fashion. These flirtations are important for us here too, for finally it is in relation to these two formations that the surrealist outmoded must be placed.

In a 1934 text Dalí defines anachronism in terms reminiscent of my account of the surrealist outmoded as a disruptive return of the repressed— as a "sentimental cataclysm," a "traumatic renewal."[81] However, here again his purpose is to outrage vanguardist sensibility more than, as with Aragon and Ernst, to convulse given constructions of history and identity. Dalí sets up anachronism as a process of "uprooted ephemera"[82] in implicit opposition to modernism as a process of continuous innovation. Yet even this incipient critique of modernist art as bound up in commodity production is suspect—not because it is wrong or because it comes from "Avida Dollars," future designer of kitsch jewelry, objets d'art, and window displays,[83] but because anachronism assists commodity innovation in the form of the *démodé* returned as *à la mode,* of the retro recovered as risqué. Today this dynamic informs cultural production both high and low (which distinction it works to dissolve), but in art it was first articulated by Dalí, who effectively displaced the surrealist practice of the outmoded with the surrealistic taste for the *démodé*—with camp, if you like.[84] Rather than an uncanny disruption of the present and a comedic working-through of the past, such Daliesque anachronism "uproots" past forms precisely so as to serve present "ephemera"; rather than a cultural revolution keyed to disjunct modes of production, it abets a compulsive repetition calibrated to smooth cycles of consumption.

The surrealists are aware of this tendency within surrealism, of the outmoded recouped as the retro, of the aura of the old placed in the service of the empathic commodity. As early as 1929 Robert Desnos noted the "pseduo-consecration" that "time or market value confers upon objects."[85] And in a retrospective essay 50 years later Claude Lévi-Strauss, a late associate of the surrealists, described the recuperation of the surrealist outmoded within the very system of exchange that it once critiqued—a transformation that sees the flea market *trouvaille* become the fashion boutique accessory.[86] Dalí exploits this recuperation of "the revolutionary energies of the outmoded" by the frenetic status quo of fashion, and he is often made its scapegoat.

He is also often made the sacrificial victim of another taboo connection—between surrealism and fascism, specifically between the surrealist use of the outmoded and the fascist exploitation of the atavistic.[87] For Dalí not only comes to serve the fashion industry; he also displays a momentary interest in Nazism—in the figures of Hitler, whom he regards as "the perfect image of the great masochist," and the swastika, which he sees as a surrealistic "amalgam of antagonistic tendencies."[88] This interest prompted his

———

first expulsion from surrealism in 1934, which was defensive at least to the degree that Dalí here touched upon a secret sharing in the archaic between surrealism and Nazism.[89] Of course, the Nazis would have disavowed this commonality too; they abhorred regression even as they practiced it (indeed, they charged it to such modernisms as surrealism in the "Entartete Kunst" show and elsewhere). In this context at least, for all its superficial scandalism, the hyperbolic display of regression in Dalí may assume a critical aspect.

As suggested in chapter 4, Benjamin could think the fascist exploitation of the mechanical-commodified in the surrealist milieu in part because surrealism turned this exploitation to dialectically different ends. The same is true of the fascist exploitation of the outmoded or the nonsynchronous: the surrealist use threw the fascist abuse into relief. Here, however, an important difference emerges between Benjamin and Ernst Bloch, fellow critic of fascism and advocate of surrealism. For Benjamin the outmoded became contaminated by its fascist exploitation. For Bloch the outmoded became all the more urgent *because* of fascism, literally in spite of it. And in this regard we may have more to learn from Bloch than from Benjamin.[90]

Bloch discusses the nonsynchronous in his 1935 text *Erbschaft dieser Zeit* (Heritage of Our Times), a text profoundly influenced by surrealism (it includes a section titled "Thinking Surrealisms"). Like Benjamin, Bloch derives the notion from the Marxian concept of the uneven development of productive modes and social formations, and its gist is simple: "Not all people exist in the same Now."[91] The nonsynchronism that most concerns Bloch is the "uncompleted past which has not yet been 'sublated' by capitalism" but which is presently exploited by fascism.[92] For Bloch fascism preys on class fractions displaced by capitalism and/or threatened by communism (e.g., *déclassé* youth, peasants, the petite bourgeoisie), fractions seduced by its "primitive-atavistic 'participation mystique.'"[93] This mystique is nothing other than a concerted regression, through the nonsynchronous, to archaic structures of feeling (as captured in the infamous slogan of "Blood and Soil"), a regression that serves the purposes of blind allegiance to Nazi power. In effect, fascism works to subsume the forces of the outmoded in the form of the atavistic in order to bind its subjects psychically. In this way its ideology seeks "to incorporate the morbid components of all cultural phases."[94]

Bloch does not condemn the atavistic as such; that its power cannot be so dismissed is the very lesson of the Nazis. "The task," he writes, "is to extrapolate the elements of the nonsynchronous contradiction which are capable of antipathy and transformation, that is, those hostile to capitalism and homeless in it, and to refit them to function in a different context."[95] According to Bloch, official Marxism failed in this regard; its principal strategy was to *accelerate* the sublation of the nonsynchronous.[96] As a result it forfeited "the energies of intoxication" to fascism. Now for both Benjamin and Bloch the great merit of surrealism was its move to win these energies "for the revolution."[97] And indeed it is against the fascist abuse of the nonsynchronous, the archaic image of fascist ideology, that the surrealist use of the outmoded, the dialectical image of surrealist art, must finally be posed.[98] Once again surrealism appears as a critical double of fascism, which it anticipates, partially collaborates with, mostly contests.[99] If fascism exploits the uncanny in order to lock both present and future into a tragic repetition of atavistic psychic and social structures, a repetition governed by the death drive,[100] surrealism exploits the uncanny so as to disrupt the present and to open up the future—if not to turn the compulsive return of the repressed into comedic resolution that might somehow free the subject from defusion and death, then at least to divert its forces in a critical intervention into the social and the political.

✦ ✦

The surrealists associated old architecture with the unconscious in part because they understood its outmoding to be its repressing. Aragon implic-

itly charges this repression to moder*nization,* specifically to Haussmanni-
zation. Dalí, on the other hand, explicitly blames this repression on
moder*nism,* specifically on "the functionalist ideal." This charge of a re-
pressive modernism is often reactive (today it is the battle cry of many
antimodernisms that masquerade as postmodernisms), but it does bear a
certain truth, and it does allow us to position surrealism once again as the
dialectical counterpart to such functionalism. (As Benjamin writes, "To
encompass Breton and Le Corbusier, that would mean drawing the spirit
of present-day France like a bow and shooting knowledge to the heart of
the moment.")[101] Functionalism is about *discipline:* it breaks down the domestic body into functions and assigns them to antiseptic spaces; the result
is often a house type with scant allowance for history, sexuality, the unconscious.[102] Surrealism is about *desire:* in order to allow it back into architecture
it fixes on the outmoded and the ornamental, the very forms tabooed in
such functionalism, associated as they became not only with the historical
and the fantastic, but with the infantile and the feminine.[103] In effect, against
"the machine for living in," surrealism presents the house as hysterical body.
In so doing it not only insists that desire cannot be reduced out, but also
reveals that the "distortions" due to its "prohibition" cannot be undone.

This leads to a second point that needs to be developed: the surrealist
gendering of these spaces. I have argued that the forces repressed in modernism often return in surrealism as demonically feminine: why is this guise,
this association of the feminine and the unconscious, so automatic? One can
refer this association to the patriarchal psyche—but only if this psyche is
referred to its social spaces. In its beginnings the pictorial possibilities of
modernism depended on access to the public spaces of modernity, of the
new world of high capitalist business and pleasure. As Griselda Pollock has
argued, such access was mostly denied to bourgeois women, confined as
they largely were to domestic spaces.[104] A system of spatial oppositions thus
developed in bourgeois life—e.g., office and home, public and private,
exterior and interior—that were coded as a gendered opposition of male and
female. (A psychoanalytic account might insist that this opposition is already

given as the master code for all such hierarchical oppositions.) Not only did the interior become identified with women, but interiority became associated with femininity, whether understood as spiritual, emotional, or "hysterical."

Surrealism does nothing to disturb this coding; on the contrary, it appears to exacerbate it. Our three surrealists feminize the passage, the interior, and art nouveau, as they do the unconscious: they hystericize the former as they historicize the latter. But a strange thing happens to this association of the feminine and the unconscious along the way. Historically bourgeois women may be trapped in the interior, but bourgeois men may also retreat there in sanctuary from the exterior, and as they do so they appropriate it as an analogue of their own consciousness (which may retain a feminine coding). Our surrealists expose this appropriation, only to exceed it, for they appropriate these spaces as analogues of their own *unconscious* as well. This hardly permits them to question the old association of the feminine and the unconscious. As we have seen, surrealism *depends* on these associations: convulsive beauty is largely an aestheticization of hysteria, and so on. And yet this appropriation, this aestheticization, is not without its disruptive effects. The feminine subject is objectified through the analogy of surrealist image and hysterical symptom—that much is true. But at the same time the masculine subject is disrupted by this feminine object, this hysterical beauty. In effect, he is rendered hysterical too, as his axes of identification and desire become confused (again, as in the classic question of the hysteric: am I a man or a woman?).[105] As this gender opposition is thereby confused, so symbolically are the social-spatial oppositions with which it is bound up: oppositions of interior versus exterior, unconscious versus reality—all the divides between "inside" and "outside" that surrealism seeks to blur, if not to erase. It is to the psychic underpinnings of this surrealist apprehension of space that I want to turn.

Brassaï, *The Statue of Marshal Ney in the Fog*, 1935.

7
___

A U R A T I C   T R A C E S

At several points in this essay I have suggested that surrealism not only revolves around the return of the repressed in general, but oscillates between two uncanny fantasies in particular, one of maternal plenitude, of a space-time of bodily intimacy and psychic unity before any separation or loss, and another of paternal punishment, of the trauma of such separation or loss. I have also argued that surrealism works to restage these fantasies in order to disrupt the structures of subjectivity and representation that are largely rooted there.

As the surrealists project an uncanny animation onto the world (e.g., in the form of enigmatic signals, objects, and persecutors for Breton, de Chirico, and Ernst), the world, as it were, gazes back upon them, and this gaze also oscillates between the two registers of the benevolent and the castrative, an oscillation that produces different subjective effects and spatial apprehensions. Here I want briefly to think these two types of gazes, effects, and spaces in terms of two concepts that, bound up with the uncanny, are also thought either at the time of surrealism or in its milieu: the Benjamin concept of *aura* and the Freudian concept of *anxiety*.

The connection between anxiety and the uncanny is clear: the first is one effect of the second.[1] Aura and the uncanny are also associated, for just as the uncanny involves the return of a familiar thing made strange through repression, so aura also concerns "a strange web of space and time: the unique appearance of a distance, however close at hand."[2] In some sense, then, aura and anxiety share a point of origin or intersection in the uncanny, a point developed in surrealism.

Freud posed at least two different conceptions of anxiety. He first saw anxiety in almost physiological terms as a discharge of sexual tension by the ego. However, in *Inhibitions, Symptoms and Anxiety* (1926) he posited the ego as the source of anxiety. Here anxiety becomes a homeopathic signal of danger, a repetition of a past trauma in a mitigated mnemic form deployed by the ego to ward away expected trauma or at least to gird for it.[3] In part this account was a riposte to Otto Rank, who in *The Trauma of Birth* (1924) refers all anxiety to this ur-trauma. On the contrary, Freud argues, trauma takes many forms: other separations from the mother, threats of castration, premature initiations into sexuality, even intimations of mortality. Like birth, however, these traumas produce a helplessness *(Hilflosigkeit),* a help-lessness that generates anxiety. According to the psychic law of the com-pulsion to repeat, the anxiety first generated by the helplessness of birth is later repeated in traumatic situations, e.g., in the stirring of sexuality in childhood: "It is a curious thing that early contact with the demands of sexuality should have a similar effect on the ego to that produced by pre-mature contact with the external world."[4] Indeed, it is repeated whenever the subject cannot bind excessive stimuli. These stimuli may be external, exogenic, worldly ("realistic" anxiety), or internal, endogenic, instinctual ("neurotic" anxiety), or both—as in the traumatic situation where the inter-nal is often projected so that it appears external. In effect, then, like the *fort/ da* game, anxiety is a device of repetition triggered by danger in order to mitigate a traumatic situation of perceived loss.[5]

This concept is pertinent to my "traumatic" account of surrealism, for I have read much of its art as so many attempts to abreact trauma, with its primary feeling-tone precisely one of anxiety. On a theoretical level the transformation of trauma into a mnemic symbol is intuited in the surrealist analogy between symptomatization and symbolization. And on a psychic level various oeuvres in surrealism recapitulate different moments of trauma as noted by Freud: the feared separation from the mother (especially in Breton), the traumatic awakening of sexuality (in de Chirico), the shocked recognition of sexual difference (in Ernst), the fantasmatic loss of the penis (in Giacometti), the defusive helplessness before masochistic demands (in Bellmer), and so on. Moreover, the attributes of anxiety are prominent in surrealist experience: e.g., a confusion of inside and outside whereby endogenous or "compulsive" stimuli are projected outward as exogenous or "convulsive" signs, as in convulsive beauty; a relay of repetition and expectation in which past and future, memory and prophecy, cause and effect, are somehow conflated, as in objective chance; and generally a replaying of the loss of a primal love object as an ambiguous defense or working through of trauma, apparent in the work of all the aforementioned surrealists. Finally, the traumas thus parried in surrealism derive not only from individual experience but from capitalist society as well: the excessive stimuli of the city, the becoming machine and/or commodity of the body, and so on.[6] Much of this is evoked in the Bretonian formula "Interpretive delirium begins only when man, ill-prepared, is taken by a sudden fear in the *forest of symbols.*" This formula captures many surrealist notions precisely in terms of anxiety: the "surprise" evoked by de Chirico, the convulsive identity advocated by Ernst, the paranoid-critical method of Dalí, and, more generally, the pose of *disponibilité* before a world of ambiguous signs.[7]

Auratic experiences are no less cultivated in surrealism. Above I noted the similarity of aura as "a unique manifestation of distance" to the uncanny as a return of the repressed, a similarity that suggests in turn that this auratic distance is temporal, i.e., that it involves the perception of a "forgotten human dimension."[8] For Benjamin this dimension seems to encompass at least three registers. One is natural: the aura of an empathic moment of human connection to material things, which Benjamin evokes through images of a hand that traces the line of a mountain range and a recumbent body that receives the shadow of a twig.[9] The surrealists were sensitive to this aura of found natural objects, which they often exhibited. (Breton, Caillois, and Mabille were fascinated in particular by "the language of stones.")[10] Another register is cultural and historical: the aura not only of cultic works of art but also of artisanal objects where the "traces of the practiced hand" are still evident.[11] As noted, this aura is especially active in the surrealist interest in the outmoded. Finally, the third register, which invests the other two with psychic intensity, is subjective: the aura of the memory of a primal relationship to the body, to the *maternal* body—a relationship evoked in *The Invisible Object* but also in all the childhood images that so attracted the surrealists. In surrealism as in Benjamin all three registers are allegorically interwoven: thus the connections, made in *Le Paysan de Paris, Une Semaine de bonté,* and many other visual texts, among natural (or prehistoric) images, historical (or phylogenetic) references, and subjective (or psychic) effects.[12]

Some of these registers are evoked in the fullest description of aura offered by Benjamin:

> Experience of the aura thus rests on the transposition of a response common in human relationships to the relationship between the inanimate or natural object and man. The person we look at, or who feels he is being looked at looks at us in turn. To perceive the aura of an object we look at, means to invest it with the ability to look at us in return. This experience corresponds to the data of the *mémoire involontaire.*[13]

Clearly for Benjamin aura involves a gaze distinct from the anxious look found in de Chirico and Ernst, but two other points should first be noted. Benjamin articulates aura in relation to Marxian and Freudian conceptions of fetishism. Its definition as an empathic "transposition" of a human rapport to a relationship with an object inverts the definition of commodity fetishism as a perverse confusion of the human and the thing, a reification of producers and a personification of products—as if aura were the magical antidote to such fetishism. Whereas in auratic experience the object becomes human, as it were, in commodity fetishism the human becomes objectified, and social relations assume "the fantastic form of a relation between things."[14] Contrary to auratic experience, the human dimension remains forgotten in commodity fetishism; it may be the most profound form of this forgetting. And yet this forgetting is also crucial to aura: it is what renders auratic any outmoded image that retains a human dimension. For when such an image returns to the present it does so as an uncanny reminder of a time before alienation. Such an image looks at us across the distance of this alienation, but, because it is still part of us or we part of it, it can look at us, as it were, in the eye.[15]

The relation of aura to sexual fetishism is also complicated. If aura involves an involuntary memory of a forgotten human dimension, then it may also involve the forgotten figure of the phallic mother. Indeed, the memory of our pre-Oedipal relationship to this figure, of her look exchanged with our own, seems to be the paradigm of the empathic rapport and the reciprocal gaze fundamental to aura (although Benjamin does not say so—in fact, he resists a psychoanalytic frame here).[16] At first glance the unitary body and reciprocal gaze recalled in auratic experience appear quite distinct from the fragmented body and fixed look operative in sexual fetishism. But this first maternal body is precisely lost, forgotten, *repressed,* and it is this repression that produces the uncanny distance or estrangement essential to aura.[17] It is repressed (at least for the little boy privileged by Freud) since the maternal body is the image not only of a lost pre-Oedipal unity but also of a present Oedipal lack, i.e., of castration. Or rather, it represents this castration as soon as the father intervenes between mother and child to concretize its threat, often with a gaze castrative in its import. Upon this threat the maternal body becomes occluded in memory, and the maternal gaze assumes an ambiguity, a *non*reciprocity, an anxiety, that it may never have had before. Benjamin speaks of this strange distance of the auratic object in terms of "inapproachability," which he also calls "a primary quality of the ceremonial image."[18] According to Freud, this inapproachability is also a primary quality of the totemic figure, which, significantly, he regards as the very token of paternal interdiction against incest.[19] To the extent, then, that aura is bound up with a promise of maternal redemption it also recalls a threat of paternal castration; thus its experience, like that of the ceremonial image or totem, is one of desire founded on prohibition, of attraction mixed with repulsion.[20] Both Benjamin and Bretonian surrealists often sought to overcome this ambivalence through feminized images of happiness, but the auratic redemptive-maternal aspect of this feminine imaginary is never quite free from its anxious deathly-erotic aspect.

Thus productive of ambivalence, aura cannot be simply opposed to anxiety, at least as aura is perceived in surrealism.[21] Essentially this perception follows the three Benjamin registers: a concern with natural, historical, and maternal images. In *Le Paysan de Paris* (1926), for example, Aragon writes of "the mystery" of "everyday objects," "the great power" of "certain places," which can be natural (as at the Buttes-Chaumont) or historical (as in the Passage de l'Opéra) but which must recall a "feminine element of the human spirit," a forgotten "language of caresses."[22] In *Nadja* (1928) Breton also finds an aura in particular objects and places (though he tinges them with more anxiety), and here again this empathy with the inanimate is a transposition of a rapport with the human. Thus he writes of Nadja: "When I am near her I am nearer things which are near her" (N 90). This ambivalent aura is also captured in the spatial *Stimmung* imbued by de Chirico with its own gaze, or in "real or imagined articles" endowed by Dalí "with a real life of their own . . . a 'being' entirely independent."[23] As we will see, aura in all its ambivalence is also active in the surrealist reception of tribal works (e.g., the New Guinea mask which, Breton writes in *Nadja*, "I have always loved and feared" [N 122]).

In *L'Amour fou* Breton speaks specifically of aura, which he relates to the intensity of sensation in certain motifs as opposed to the "banality" of repetition in most products.[24] Breton focuses here on a rather eccentric Cézanne painting, descriptively titled *The House of the Hanged Man,* which resonates with an anxious intimation of his own concerning a murder. This association suggests again that aura is somehow involved in trauma, more precisely with the involuntary memory of a traumatic event or repressed condition—that this repression produces the distance or estrangement requisite to auratic experience. Thus, for instance, if Breton feels intimate with things because of his intimacy with Nadja, the force of this intimacy depends paradoxically on the distance effected by repression—the repression of a primal love object. This uncanny dialectic of near and far, of familiar and strange, is evoked by Giacometti in erotic terms in his text on the "objets mobiles et muets" and in Oedipal terms in his allegory of the cave and the rock in "Hier, sables mouvants." In Benjamin this dialectic is thought in terms of vision: "The deeper the remoteness which a glance has to overcome, the stronger will be the spell that is apt to emanate from the gaze."[25] Yet it also governs the perception of aura in the word (as evoked by Karl Kraus: "the closer the look one takes at a word, the greater the distance from which it looks back") as well as in the image (as evoked by the Belgian surrealist Paul Nougé: "the more an image recedes the larger it grows").[26] So, too, it governs the perception of aura in history, such as the period of the Commune, of Lautréamont and Rimbaud, "charged with distant meaning."

Here again aura and anxiety are bound up with one another through the return of the repressed. Throughout surrealism they are thus mixed, as a brief resumé of examples noted elsewhere will attest. Breton describes the affect of objective chance as "a mixture of *panic-provoking* terror and joy" (AF 40), experienced most intensely with the flea market *trouvailles.* Keyed to the maternal body, the slipper spoon and the metal mask are simultaneously auratic and anxious because each promises a restored unity even as it recalls an old loss. A similar mixture of aura and anxiety, of a joyful gaze that seduces and a terrible one that threatens, is active in de Chirico, Ernst,

and Bellmer, in the primal "world of uncanny signs" that they attempt
to navigate in art. And finally, the surrealists also project this ambivalence
on social ciphers such as the automaton-machine and the mannequin-com-
modity as so many figures of desire and death, as well as on outmoded
images, which, through a relation to the things of childhood, also appear
as both redemptive and demonic. In all these ways aura and anxiety are
combined in surrealism, with the energy of the first often used to detonate
a temporal shock, a convulsive history (as Benjamin saw), and the ambivalence of the second often used to provoke a symbolic ambiguity, a convulsive identity (as Ernst advocated).

Ultimately, the relationship between aura and anxiety in surrealism may
be captured best through the Baudelairean reference that runs throughout
its practices—from the de Chirican "world of uncanny signs" to the Bretonian "sudden fear in the *forest of symbols*." I mean the famous lines from
"Correspondances," the *Fleurs du mal* poem so crucial to the Benjamin theory
of aura:

> Nature is a temple whose living pillars
> Sometimes give forth a babel of words;
> Man wends his way through forests of symbols
> Which look at him with their familiar glances.
>
> As long-resounding echoes from afar
> Are mingling in a deep, dark unity,
> Vast as the night or as the orb of day,
> Perfumes, colors, and sounds commingle.[27]

Here the correspondences that constitute aura are those between natural and
maternal glances, prehistoric and psychic echoes—correspondences intuited
by Baudelaire (and Proust), theorized by Freud (and Benjamin), and devel-

oped by the surrealists. The surrealists detected such correspondences in many things, but perhaps most of all in tribal objects, especially from Oceania and the Pacific Northwest coast, which they sometimes considered in the auratic terms of a reciprocal gaze. "New Hebrides sculpture is true," Giacometti once remarked, "and more than true, because it has a gaze. It's not the imitation of an eye, it's purely and simply a gaze."[28] And here Lévi-Strauss writes of a favorite haunt of surrealist emigrés in New York during the war, the Northwest Coast Hall of the American Museum of Natural History:

> Stroll for an hour or two across this hall so thick with 'living pillars'. By way of another correspondence, the words of the poet translate exactly the native term designating the sculptured posts used to support house beams: posts that are not so much things as living beings with 'familiar glances', since in days of doubt and torment, they too let out 'a babel of words,' guide the dweller of the house, advise and comfort him, and show him a way out of his difficulties.[29]

It is significant that Giacometti associates this gaze with truth, and that Lévi-Strauss relates these correspondences to "difficulties." For Benjamin also saw aura both as a mark of genuine experience and as a way to make such experience "crisis-proof."[30] Here again aura is implicitly related to trauma: not only because its effect of involuntary memory requires a temporal distance to overcome, a distance created by loss or repression, but also because it serves as a salve to such loss or repression, to such "difficulties" or "crises."[31] This insight is crucial to modernism from Baudelaire to Breton, at least to the degree that it privileges auratic (or symbolist) correspondences. For the correspondences in question are not only "the primordial ties" that exist between the natural and the human or the mother and the child—these ties, as Breton remarks, "are cut" for all of us.[32] The correspondences also come after the fact as so many attempts to remake such ties in new nonregressive ways.[33] In my reading, this is a primary psychic imperative perhaps of art in general but certainly of this modernist tradition in particular—and it need not be narcissistically redemptive, at least as long as the ties to be remade are understood to be social as well.

The cutting of "the primordial ties," our different separations from the maternal body, the natural world, and so on, are as necessary to aura as they are to anxiety. Indeed, in surrealism as in Baudelaire it is this cutting, this castration, that renders "the forest of symbols" as productive of "sudden fear" as it is of remembered joy, that makes the "familiar glances" as strange as they are familiar. Ultimately, it is this "world of uncanny signs" that is the essential subject of surrealism. It is a world of aura mixed with anxiety, and it is one that Freud referred precisely to the maternal body estranged through paternal interdiction. To cite this line one last time: "In this case, too, the *unheimlich* is what was once *heimisch,* home-like, familiar; the prefix 'un' is the token of repression."[34]

The "familiar glances" that envelop the subject with aura are thus not so distant from the fearsome look that riddles him with anxiety. These two gazes do, however, generate different spaces, at least in surrealism: the first, theorized by Benjamin, is especially evident in Breton, Aragon, and others, while the second, theorized by Lacan, is most marked in de Chirico, Ernst, and others.[35] The anxious space or Lacanian scenario, associated with the fantasy of castration, is familiar to us from chapter 3. In effect, if the subject is dispossessed by a castrative gaze, so too the space ordered around this subject as its point of coherence is disarranged. Typically, in this register of threat, such space is distorted in these surrealist ways: it appears detumescent, even "convalescent,"[36] as often in Dalí and Tanguy; or it appears calcified, even petrified, as often in de Chirico and Ernst. (Perhaps the most characteristic type of surrealist pictorial space is an oxymoronic combination of the two, an impotently rigid space, sometimes anamorphic in effect, as befits the contradictory subject positions of the surrealist subject.)[37] This particular spatiality is paranoid, and in a deferred way it may well have influenced Lacan in *The Four Fundamental Concepts of Psychoanalysis*. In his discussion of the gaze Lacan relies on a text by Roger Caillois, "Mimétisme et psychasthénie légendaire" published in *Minotaure* 7 (1935). There Caillois theorizes a "schizophrenic" dispossession of an organism by its space. "Space seems to be a devouring force," he writes of this schizophrenic subject. "He feels himself becoming space. . . . And he invents spaces of which he is 'the convulsive possession'."[38] This is one extreme of surrealist spatiality.

The other extreme, the auratic space or Benjaminian scenario, associated with the fantasy of maternal intimacy, even of intrauterine existence, is evoked less in images than in texts regarding architectural forms and urban *dérives,* though it is sometimes projected upon nature as well.[39] Highly ambiguous—for death is involved in this reunion with the maternal, this return to the material, as much as life—these spaces are often represented as subterranean or submarine. Thus the typical surrealist portrait, influenced by Baudelaire, of Paris as a "human aquarium" (P 28), a "morass of dreams," where figures of woman and death intermingle.[40] I have noted how Aragon, Ernst, and Dalí register such uncanniness in the "hysterical" architectures of the outmoded passage, the bourgeois interior, and art nouveau structures, but perhaps Breton was most sensitive to this uncanny spatiality. In effect, his texts map a maternal body onto a prehistoric physiognomy of Paris.[41] *L'Amour fou,* for example, designates the Hôtel de Ville as the "cradle" of this maternal city (AF 47), while *La Clé des champs* (1953) describes the Place Dauphine as its "sex."[42] This "profoundly secluded place" (N 80) is rather more uterine in form, but it is not purely auratic for Breton on this account. In fact, its "embrace is over-insistent, and, finally, crushing" (N 83), and while Breton experiences anxiety there, Nadja associates the place directly with death. Thus not even this maternal space is free of the *unheimlich.* "Why is it that the maternal landscape, the *heimisch,* and the familiar become so disquieting?" Hélène Cixous asks. "The answer is less buried than one might suspect. The obliteration of any separation, the realization of the desire which in itself obliterates a limit."[43]

Nevertheless, maternal space remains an ideal for Breton: thus, for instance, the celebration of the Palais idéal of the Facteur Cheval, a photograph of which in *Les Vases communicants* (1932) shows Breton in its very mouth or maw.[44] Two years later, in *Minotaure* 3–4, Tristan Tzara made this ideal programmatic. For Tzara (who lived in a house with indoor pool designed by Adolf Loos) functionalist architecture denies "the dwelling place"—a denial that he refers to its "aesthetics of castration."[45] Explicitly Tzara opposes the castrative to the intrauterine, for against such "self-punitive aggressiveness" he calls for an architecture of "prenatal comfort" sensitive to the ur-forms of the home—cave and yurt, cradle and tomb.[46] However, this program is more a conscious appeal than an uncanny intuition. And as such it figures maternal space in the regressively simple terms of *heimisch* enclosure rather than in the psychically difficult terms of *unheimlich* passage.

This other vision remains proper to the original *flâneurs* of surrealism, Breton and Aragon, as they wander through Paris—Paris understood *in toto* here as a passage. Sometimes these *flâneurs* identify with Odysseus lured by "sirens," sometimes with Oedipus confronted by "sphinxes" (P 37, 28), but finally the mythological model of these surrealists is Theseus in the labyrinth, a Theseus more involved with his double, the Minotaur, than with his other, Ariadne.[47] Aragon writes of a "double game" of love and death, of the redemptive and the demonic, which, played out in the passage, renders it at once a dream space and a "glass coffin" (P 47, 61).[48] For the most part these surrealists are able to hold these ambivalent terms in tension precisely in passage, through wandering. And it is in the labyrinth produced by such wandering that the contradictory gazes between which surrealism oscillates are at least momentarily suspended. For as both interior and exterior the labyrinth simultaneously envelops the subject in a maternal embrace and threatens him with a paranoid perspective.[49] In this spatial trope

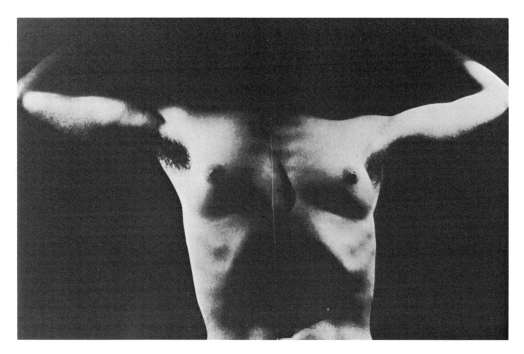

Man Ray, Untitled, 1933.

cherished by the surrealists, refinding a lost home is one with facing a deathly end: the two terms communicate in the labyrinth; the labyrinth *is* their communication.[50]

Finally, it is in this metaphorical space of the unconscious that several of the riddles fundamental to surrealism are formed: the ambiguous role of sexuality in life and death drives; the search for an object that is never recovered so much as lost again and again; the attempt to found an identity, an art, on fantasies that upset rather than ground these terms; and the passage through Oedipal questions of desire and identification in which the subject moves back and forth between fantastic imagos of the maternal and the paternal. In surrealism there are a few repeated images that appear arrested before such contradictions—images so familiar that we may forget how strange they are (or is it vice versa?), images such as the automaton-writer and the mannequin-muse, the persecuting father and the praying mantis. But below these images is one figure in particular, one that in the labyrinth of surrealist intimations of desire and death not only condenses maternal and paternal imagos, pre-Oedipal and Oedipal states, but also connects the psychic involvements of surrealism to its mythological, historical, and contemporary interests; and that figure is the Minotaur.

Max Ernst, *Health through Sports,* c. 1920.

BEYOND THE SURREALISM PRINCIPLE?

And what about surrealism today, exploited as it is by academic and cultural industries alike? When the Minotaur returns as Batman, what remains of the surreal? And what about the uncanny—does it have a historicity too?

Along the way I have tended toward other questions, often to do with the sexual politics of surrealism. Bound up as it is with the Freudian uncanny in castration anxiety, is the surreal a masculinist domain? Are women excluded from it as practitioners precisely to the degree that they are made to represent it as figures? What happens when the surrealists identify with these figures? Is there a genuine troubling of masculine identity, or merely an appropriation of positions ambiguously associated with the feminine (e.g., the hysteric, the masochist)? I have argued that these figures are crucial to the shift in surrealism away from a sublimatory practice of the beautiful. But is its desublimatory strategy of the sublime any real alternative to other modernisms that transgress the image of the female body—or is it the grim epitome of this persistent imaginary?[1] In this same register of doubt I want to conclude with a few different questions regarding the historical limits of surrealism.

Breton hoped that the surreal would become the real, that surrealism would overcome this opposition with liberatory effects for all. But might it be that the reverse has occurred, that in the postmodern world of advanced capitalism the real has become the surreal, that our forest of symbols is less disruptive in its uncanniness than disciplinary in its delirium? Surrealism sought to overcome two oppositions above all: waking and dreaming, self and other. Yet already in the 1920s the surrealists could glimpse the dissolution of the first opposition in the dream-spaces of Paris. And today, in the phantasmagoria of the postmodern city, this dissolution seems complete—but with its liberatory effects reversed. The same could be argued about the second opposition of self and other. The surrealist ideal of convulsive identity was subversive, at least in relation to a fixed bourgeois ego. But what was a critical loss of self then might be an everyday condition of asubjectivity now. Remember that Roger Caillois described the schizophrenic apprehension of space as a "convulsive possession" that seems to devour the subject. For many critics this particular psychological condition—whereby the subject is opened raw to its outside—is today a general social diagnostic. Certainly the reaction to this condition—whereby the subject becomes armored against all such openings—is apparent enough in both personal regimens and political movements.[2]

All these putative transformations in subjectivity and spatiality are familiar ideologemes of the discourse on postmodernism. If such cultural periodization is to be persuasive, it is important to consider the place of surrealism in its tracing. Already over 40 years ago Breton suggested one account of this place: "The sickness that the world manifests today differs from that manifested during the 1920s. . . . The spirit was then threatened by *congealing* [*figement*] whereas today it is threatened by *dissolution*."[3] Here Breton implies that surrealism arose to break up a "congealing" in subjective and social relations, to release these relations into liberatory flows, only to see this breakup recouped, these liberatory flows recoded as "dissolution." On this reading if surrealism was in the service of the revolution in the first moment, it was in the service of "revolutionary" capitalism in the second. Perhaps surrealism always depended on the very rationality that it opposed—its practice of juxtaposition first prepared by the equivalences of

capitalist exchange and now exceeded by them. "The pervasiveness of Surrealism is proof enough of its success," J. G. Ballard, one of the few artists
to extend surrealism creatively, wrote 25 years ago. "It is now the *outer*
world which will have to be eroticized and quantified."[4] But is this not
largely achieved? And in what sense should it be deemed a success?

❦ ❦

This belief that capitalism no longer has an outside may be the greatest
postmodern ideologeme of all, the one that subtends the other claims about
the eclipse of this space, the end of that narrative. But is it not clear that
this postmodern sense of an end is a narrative of its own, one that often
projects different pasts-that-never-were (e.g., a fixed bourgeois ego, a truly
transgressive avant-garde) in such a way that might hinder alternative fu-
tures-that-could-be? With this caution in mind one could reply to the contemporary eclipse of the uncanny that as long as there is repression there
will be its uncanny return. And one might argue against the postmodern
"realization" of the surreal that the capitalist dream world is nowhere so
consistent or so complete. In short, one could insist that surrealism is not
entirely outmoded.

I noted that for Benjamin the outmoded as well as the auratic became
contaminated by fascism, and that this nudged him away from his advocacy
of surrealism. Obscenely easy though it is to say now, this was in part a
mistake, at least to the extent that it conceded the powers of the archaic to
the other side. It was also a deformation of his own theory, for criticality
lies not in mechanical reproduction and technical innovation as such but in
the dialectical articulation of such values with the auratic and the outmoded.
In effect, Benjamin reduced out this dialectic even as he defined it. And this
mistake was repeated in the dominant leftist discourse on postmodernist art
50 years later—in its total embrace of the photographic, the textual, the
anti-auratic. To be fair, this position (my own) was provoked by the most
forced resurrection of the pseudo-auratic since historical fascism, i.e., all

those Frankenstein monsters—postmodern architecture, neo-expressionism, art photography, and the like—cooked up in the laboratories of market, media, museum, and academy. But this technologistic bias was also advanced in systemic analyses of postmodern culture. As one result, not only was the auratic tabooed in advanced art but the outmoded was declared obsolete in advanced capitalism. Fredric Jameson: "The postmodern must be characterized as a situation in which the survival, the residue, the hold-over, the archaic, has finally been swept away without a trace."[5] Jean Baudrillard: "Today, when functionalism has graduated from the isolated object to the system, . . . surrealism can only survive as folklore."[6] Yet whose "postmodern" do they mean? Indeed, whose "today"?

The outmoded is problematic not because it is now recouped or effaced but because it is too bound up in a singular logic of historical development. The same is true of most versions of the postmodern. And yet this is also the source of the power of both terms, for it is precisely the tensions among productive modes, social relations, and cultural modes that the outmoded can expose and the postmodern can describe. Today, however, these tensions must be understood nonsynchronously, indeed "multitopically" as well. For just as all people do not live in the same now, so too do these different nows occupy different spaces. And it is precisely these different space-times that can be invoked critically in the present—such is one project of multiculturalism at its nonidentitarian best. But so too can these differences be treated phobically, as the many reactions against such nonidentitarian multiculturalism also attest. In this regard the old opposition of surrealism and fascism has in part returned. Uncannily?

One final remark. The power of the outmoded depends on the utopian as well as the nonsynchronous. Both are evoked by Breton in his definition of surrealist juxtaposition as a "slit in time" that produces an "illusion of true recognition" "where former lives, actual lives, future lives melt together in one life."[7] From a psychoanalytical perspective such overcoming is entirely too redemptive: repression cannot be so easily undone, the uncanny recouped, the death drive redirected. I have argued that surrealism struggles precisely at this point: it seeks to redeem what can only be riven—at least at the level of the individual, which is where surrealism, for all its ambition, mostly remained. But such overcoming is not impossible in the utopian dimension, i.e., at the level of the collective. For Benjamin this utopian dimension could be glimpsed not only in the outmoded but in the *démodé* as well. At the end of his brief meditation on the outmoded he asks, enigmatically enough, "What form do you suppose a life would take that was determined at a decisive moment precisely by the street song last on everyone's lips?"[8] This may be an image of a commodification of consciousness, of so many consumerist automatons of a culture industry on the rise. But, however distorted, is it not also an image of a collectivity that is a body too, ready for "collective bodily innervation"? There will be other revolutions, and to win the energies of intoxication for new movements is not an outmoded task.

NOTES

PREFACE

1

I should say straightaway that for the most part my subject is the Bretonian group of male surrealists in Paris from 1919 to 1937.

2

This description (if not this evaluation) seems about right to me. See the scant remarks in such Clement Greenberg texts as "Towards a Newer Laocoon" (1940) and "Surrealist Painting" (1944–45), in *Clement Greenberg: The Collected Essays and Criticism,* vol. 1, ed. John O'Brian (Chicago, 1986).

3

See, for example, Peter Bürger, *Theorie der Avantgarde* (Frankfurt, 1974), translated by Michael Shaw as *Theory of the Avant-Garde* (Minneapolis, 1984). Although Bürger hardly neglects surrealism, he tends to conflate it with dada.

4

Two morals might be drawn from this historical tropism. Formalist and neo-avant-garde positions are not directly opposed (both see modernism in objectivist terms); and every new insight into past art is attended by a concomitant blindness. For a review of the historical sympathies of the minimalists see Maurice Tuchman, "The

Russian Avant-Garde and the Contemporary Artist," in Stephanie Barron and Maurice Tuchman, eds., *The Avant-Garde in Russia 1910–1930* (Los Angeles, 1980), pp. 118–121. Surrealism was also taboo due to its involvement in fashion and advertisement: directly in the case of Man Ray, Dalí, Magritte, etc., indirectly through the appropriation of many of its devices.

5

A principal exception is the work of Rosalind Krauss: see her "Giacometti," in William Rubin, ed., *"Primitivism" in 20th-Century Art: Affinity of the Tribal and the Modern,* vol. 2 (New York, 1984), pp. 503–534; "Photography in the Service of Surrealism" and "Corpus Delicti," in *L'Amour fou: Photography & Surrealism* (Washington and New York, 1985), pp. 15–114; and "The Master's Bedroom," *Representations* 28 (Fall 1989), pp. 55–76. Krauss has long contested the accounts centered on official Bretonian surrealism with an advocacy of dissident Bataillean surrealism. I assume this distinction, but my reading also cuts across it.

6

This turn must be critical given the heterosexist bias of many surrealists, especially Breton (this petit-bourgeois prudery is paraded, with little sense of self-contradiction, in "Recherches sur la sexualité," *La Révolution surréaliste* 12 [March 15, 1928], pp. 32–40). And yet the sexual politics of surrealism are not as prejudicial, nor its subject positions as fixed, as one may think—or so I will suggest.

7

For more on this problematic see my "L'Amour faux," *Art in America* (January 1986), and "Signs Taken for Wonders," *Art in America* (June 1986).

8

Even as we resist continued attacks, we should be alert to the ways that the advocacy of this countermodernism has become an orthodoxy of its own.

9

For more on the mirror stage in relation to surrealism (and fascism), see my "Armor Fou," *October* 56 (Spring 1991).

10

Among others, Krauss has considered the Freud/Lacan connection in surrealism; Susan Buck-Morss has addressed the Marx/Benjamin axis in *The Origin of Negative Dialectics: Theodor W. Adorno, Walter Benjamin and the Frankfurt Institute* (New York,

1977), pp. 124–129, and *The Dialectics of Seeing: Walter Benjamin and the Arcades Project* (Cambridge 1989), passim; and James Clifford has noted the Mauss/Bataille association in *The Predicament of Culture: Twentieth Century Ethnography, Literature, and Art* (Cambridge, 1988), pp. 117–151.

11

Louis Aragon, *La Peinture au défi,* Galerie Goemans catalogue (Paris, 1930). Max Ernst, "Au-delà de la peinture," *Cahiers d'art* 2, nos. 6–7 (1936). As we will see, for neither figure could painting engage contradiction, psychic or social, as adequately as collage.

12

André Breton, "Le Surréalisme et la peinture," *La Révolution surréaliste* 4 (July 1925), pp. 26–30. Developed by Breton in texts first collected in *Le Surréalisme et la peinture* (Paris, 1928), this opposition was reinvented by William Rubin in *Dada, Surrealism, and Their Heritage* (New York, 1968). For a deconstruction of this opposition see Krauss, "The Photographic Conditions of Surrealism," *October* 19 (Winter 1981), pp. 3–34.

13

Max Morise, "Les Yeux enchantés," *La Révolution surréaliste* 1 (December 1, 1924), p. 27. Over the years this criticism was rehearsed by surrealists (e.g., Ernst) and critics (e.g., Theodor Adorno). Although Breton later favored the automatist mode of painting, he too recognized its contradictory aspect. More recently J.-B. Pontalis has questioned the unconscious presupposed in this definition ("un inconscient déjà figurable et déjà mis en mots") in "Les Vases non communicants," *La Nouvelle revue française* 302 (March 1, 1978), p. 32.

14

Pierre Naville, "Beaux Arts," *La Révolution surréaliste* 3 (April 15, 1925), p. 27. Challenges like this led Breton to seize editorship of *La Révolution surréaliste* from Naville.

15

See *Situationist International Anthology,* ed. and trans. Ken Knabb (Berkeley, 1981), pp. 1–2, 18–20, 41–42, 115–116, 171–172. Also see Peter Wollen, "From Breton to Situationism," *New Left Review* 174 (March/April 1989), pp. 67–95. Critical though it was of surrealism, situationism developed both Bretonian and Bataillean aspects.

16

I discuss a third master term of surrealism, paranoia, in chapter 3, but not according to the "paranoiac-critical method" of Dalí. More work needs to be done on this subject, especially on the exchange between Dalí and Lacan.

17

However simplistic, my cautions about such methods should at least be straightforward. Some social art histories tend to fall back into a premodernist model of representation: e.g., as if class were somewhere there to be painted, or as if social conflict were somehow registered in aesthetic rupture. Meanwhile, some semiotic art histories tend to the obverse: i.e., in the desire to unfix meaning, they sometimes overlook its historical overdetermination.

18

The notion of the outmoded is developed by Benjamin from Marx, who suggests (before the fact, as it were) an uncanny compulsion to repeat at work in history. See Jeffrey Mehlman, *Revolution and Repetition: Marx/Hugo/Balzac* (Berkeley, 1977), pp. 5–41; and Ned Lukacher, *Primal Scenes: Literature, Philosophy, Psychoanalysis* (Ithaca, 1986), pp. 236–274. In chapter 6 I argue that the surrealists push the uncanny in this direction.

Freud thinks "the primitive" in relation to the uncanny, e.g., in *Totem and Taboo* (1913), a crucial precedent of "The Uncanny" (1919). Here again the surrealists push the uncanny in this direction, but I cannot develop the argument here. The problem of surrealist primitivism is very complicated. Though counterracist, it retains primitivist assumptions, especially in the association between the primitive and the primal, whether understood as infantile or neurotic (Bretonian surrealists) or regressive or base (Bataillean surrealists). I intend to explore this association, endemic as it is in modernism, in a future book.

19

My use of the latter two is often opportunistic. Lacan, for example, dismisses the phylogenetic dimension crucial to the Freudian uncanny: "The unconscious is neither primordial nor instinctual; what it knows about the elementary is no more than the elements of the signifier" ("The Agency of the Letter in the Unconscious or Reason since Freud," in *Écrits,* trans. Alan Sheridan [New York, 1977], p. 170). His relationship to surrealism requires further study; here I stick mostly to Freud for historical reasons.

20

The same is true of critics of surrealism. For example, Jean Clair discusses the uncanny in relation to Giorgio de Chirico in "Metafisica et unheimlichkeit" (in *Les Réalismes 1919–39* [Paris, 1981], pp. 27–32) but refuses to relate it to surrealism. Krauss develops the concept seriously, in "Corpus Delicti" and "The Master's Bedroom," but it is not central to her analyses.

21

Breton, "Second manifesto du Surréalisme," *La Révolution surréaliste* 12 (December 15, 1929); translated by Richard Seaver and Helen R. Lane in *Manifestoes of Surrealism* (Ann Arbor, 1972), pp. 123–124.

22

Breton, *L'Amour fou* (Paris, 1937); translated by Mary Ann Caws as *Mad Love* (Lincoln, 1987), p. 15.

23

This remark might be glossed with another by Benjamin on Proust: "He lay on his bed racked with homesickness, homesick for the world, a world distorted in the state of resemblance, a world in which the true surrealist face of existence breaks through" ("The Image of Proust" [1929], in *Illuminations,* ed. Hannah Arendt, trans. Harry Zohn [New York, 1969], p. 205).

1
_____

BEYOND THE PLEASURE PRINCIPLE?

1

André Breton and Louis Aragon, "Le cinquantenaire de l'hystérie," *La Révolution surréaliste* 11 (March 15, 1928). The only Freud text to appear in the strictly surrealist journals was an excerpt, in *La Révolution surréaliste* 9–10 (October 1, 1927), from *The Question of Lay Analysis* (1926).

2

My brief account of the surrealist encounter with psychoanalysis is indebted to Elisabeth Roudinesco, *La Bataille de cent ans: Histoire de la psychanalyse en France,* vol. 2 (Paris, 1986), pp. 19–49; now translated by Jeffrey Mehlman as *Jacques Lacan & Co.: A History of Psychoanalysis in France, 1925–1985* (Chicago, 1990). In her reading,

French doctors resisted psychoanalysis in part to protect the national school of psychology (which went so far as to proclaim a Gallic unconscious). Thus for Roudinesco the importance of the surrealists: they opened up an artistic channel at a time when the medical channel was jammed. However, I question her implication that surrealism was simply "in the service of psychoanalysis."

3

Breton annotated the Régis and Hesnard *Précis de psychiatrie* (1914); he may also have known the 1906 Maeder summary as well as the 1920 anthology *Origine et développement de la psychanalyse*. (Translation was not a problem for Ernst, the other surrealist most involved in psychoanalysis, who first read Freud before the war as a psychology student at the University of Bonn.) For dates of French translations see Roudinesco, *La Bataille,* vol. 1, appendix.

4

The visit is recounted in "Interview de professeur Freud à Vienne" (*Littérature* n.s. 1 [March 1922]), and the accusation is made in *Les Vases communicants* (1932), to which Freud replied in three letters. (Breton also accused Freud of failure to acknowledge a theoretical predecessor on dreams, but this misunderstanding stemmed from a translation oversight.)

5

Freud moved away from hypnotic techniques in order to break with the cathartic method of Breuer. For a complication of this inaugural break see Mikkel Borch-Jacobsen, "Hypnosis in Psychoanalysis," *Representations* 27 (Summer 1989), pp. 92–110.

6

Note his famous remark to Stefan Zweig that the surrealists were "absolute (let us say 95 percent, like alcohol) cranks" (*Letters of Sigmund Freud 1873–1939,* ed. Ernst L. Freud, trans. Tania and James Stern [New York, 1960], p. 449). The best text regarding the differences between Freud and Breton on dreams is J.-B. Pontalis, "Les Vases non communicants," *La Nouvelle revue française* 302 (March 1, 1978), pp. 26–45.

7

Bataille is rather more his opposite. I take up this triangulation in chapter 4. Freud and Breton do seem to agree that art involves a working-over of trauma (see chapter 3), but this is not quite clear even to them.

8

Breton, "Manifesto," in *Manifestoes of Surrealism,* trans. Richard Seaver and Helen R. Lane (Ann Arbor, 1972), p. 26. Janet published his *L'Automatisme psychologique* in 1893. That the term is so derived from Janet was confirmed by Philippe Soupault in the 1976 Gallimard edition of *Les Champs magnétiques.*

9

Breton, *Nadja* (Paris, 1928), trans. Richard Howard (New York, 1960), p. 139. The letter was published in *La Révolution surréaliste* 3 (April 15, 1925).

10

Breton also attacked psychiatry to deflect his responsibility for the disintegration of Nadja. But the Société Médico-Psychologique was provoked, and it was this counterattack, published in the *Annales Médico-Psychologiques,* that Breton excerpted in the "Second Manifesto," where he also counter-counterattacked, as he did in "La Médecine mentale devant le surréalisme," *Le Surréalisme au service de la révolution* 2 (October 1930). More work should be done on the surrealist influence on the antipsychiatric movements of the 1950s and 1960s.

11

Janet as quoted by Jean Starobinski, "Freud, Breton, Myers," *L'Arc* 34 (special issue on Freud, 1968), p. 49. Hardly unique to Janet, automatism was a pervasive concern of the *psychologie nouvelle* of the late nineteenth century. See Jan Goldstein, *Console and Classify: The French Psychiatric Profession in the Nineteenth Century* (Cambridge, 1987).

12

Starobinski suggests as much in "Freud, Breton, Myers," pp. 50–51. In this transvaluation of automatism Breton turned to its spiritualist traditions, in particular the "gothic psychology" of F. W. H. Myers and Théodore Flournoy (he also drew on Alfred Maury, Hervey de Saint-Denys, and Helene Smith). This surrealist fascination with the occult has long embarrassed critics (including Walter Benjamin), yet it is important here for it suggests an interest in uncanny phenomena conceived outside the Freudian formulation.

13

Breton, "Le Message automatique," *Minotaure* 3–4 (December 14, 1933); translated as "The Automatic Message" in Breton, *What Is Surrealism? Selected Writings,* ed. Franklin Rosemont (New York, 1978), pp. 97–109; here pp. 105, 109. His conception

---

of the unconscious may be influenced by the "subliminal ego" of Myers. In any case, Breton is much more romantic than Freud about "the primitive" and the child.

14

Ibid., p. 98.

15

Breton noted the interference of "conscious elements" as early as "Entrée des médiums" (*Littérature* n.s. 6, November 1922). By the next year he had discouraged not only automatic writing but also hypnotic sessions and dream recitals, and the *époque des sommeils* wound down. Contradictory valuations of automatism persisted, but in the "Second Manifesto" (1930) and in "Le Message Automatique" (1933) he deemed automatism *"une infortune continue."*

16

See Breton, "Max Ernst" (1920), in Max Ernst, *Beyond Painting* (New York, 1948), p. 177; and Ernst, "Instantaneous Identity" (1936), in *Beyond Painting,* p. 13. Breton writes here of Ernst collages that, when exhibited in Paris in May 1921, had an enormous impact on emergent surrealists. I discuss this decentering further in chapter 3.

17

Breton, *Surrealism and Painting,* trans. Simon Watson Taylor (New York, 1972), p. 68. Significantly he refers this state to "the pleasure principle alone"—as if in defense against any principle *beyond* this one.

18

Breton, "The Automatic Message," p. 105; "Preface," *La Révolution surréaliste* 1 (December 1, 1924). *La Révolution surréaliste* 3 (April 15, 1925) opens with an image of a mannequin in armor.

19

This figure is also at variance with Freudian tropes of the unconscious, e.g., the "mystic writing pad."

20

Breton, "The Automatic Message," p. 98.

21

One might also read this line in a Lacanian way, as Roland Barthes does here: "Automatism . . . is not rooted at all in the 'spontaneous', the 'savage', the 'pure', the 'profound', the 'subversive', but originates on the contrary from the 'strictly coded': what is mechanical can make only the Other speak, and the Other is always *consistent*" ("The Surrealists Overlooked the Body" [1975], in *The Grain of the Voice,* trans. Linda Coverdale [New York, 1985], p. 244).

22

Lacan translates "the compulsion to repeat" *(Wiederholungszwang)* as *"automatisme de répétition."* So too he develops the term *automaton* from Aristotle as the very figure of repetition. (See his *Les quatres concepts fondamentaux de psychanalyse* [Paris, 1973]; translated by Alan Sheridan as *The Four Fundamental Concepts of Psychoanalysis* [New York, 1977], pp. 53–64, 67.) This translation may elide the Freudian distinction between "compulsion" and "automatism," made in order to separate psychoanalysis from hypnotism specifically and from French psychology generally. However, my argument is that the surrealists also elided this distinction: i.e., that in "French" automatism they intuited a "Freudian" compulsion, but resisted the recognition.

23

Freud, "The Uncanny," in *Studies in Parapsychology,* ed. Philip Rieff (New York, 1963), p. 54.

24

Ibid., pp. 21–30. Among French equivalents Freud offers *inquiétant* and *lugubre*— words that appear in surrealist titles, especially those of de Chirico and Dalí.

25

Ibid., p. 51.

26

Ibid., p. 55. For Freud infantile and primitive states are "not always sharply distinguishable" (p. 55): in his phylogenetic thought the first recapitulates the second, while the second preserves the first. This implicit association of the infantile, "the primitive," and the insane is made in many modernisms, surrealism included. The surrealists may articulate this ideological trio differently (we too, they say, are children, "primitive," and mad), but they never *dis*articulate it.

27

Ibid., pp. 40–50. Freud first notes the uncanniness of these beliefs in *Totem and Taboo* (1913; translated into French in 1923).

28

The evil eye is discussed by anthropologist Marcel Griaule in "Mauvais oeil," *Documents* 4 (1929), p. 218, and by Kurt Seligmann in "The Evil Eye," *View* 1 (June

1942), pp. 46–48; other surrealists (e.g., Bataille, Desnos) also wrote about its fascination. As we will see, surrealist painting and writing often engage the psychic effects of the gaze theorized by Lacan in *The Four Fundamental Concepts of Psychoanalysis* ("The Gaze as *Objet petit a*"). The deferred influence of surrealism on this text should be considered.

29

Ibid., p. 40. Freud here acknowledges the Otto Rank text on "Der Doppelgänger" published in *Imago* in 1914.

30

This is why Freud discusses the E. T. A. Hoffmann story "The Sandman" at such length in "The Uncanny"—not only because it involves uncanny figures (e.g., Olympia, "the automatic doll," who is neither live nor dead) but also because it reenacts the Oedipus complex through uncanny doubles that threaten the protagonist Nathaniel with death. In the story Nathaniel confuses the fantasmatic figure of the Sandman with the horrific figure of Coppelius/Coppella; both represent the bad castrative father for him. Significantly, in these uncanny figures the fear of castration returns as an anxiety about blindness. I return to the Freudian account of this story in chapter 3. Among the most provocative of the many recent texts on "The Uncanny" are Neil Hertz, "Freud and the Sandman," in Josué Harari, ed., *Textual Strategies: Perspectives in Post-Structuralist Criticism* (Ithaca, 1979), pp. 296–321, Hélène Cixous, "Fiction and Its Phantoms: A Reading of Freud's *Das Unheimliche*," in *New Literary History* 7 (Spring 1976), pp. 525–548, and Jacques Derrida, "The Double Session" (1972) and "To Speculate—on 'Freud'" (1980), in *A Derrida Reader*, ed. Peggy Kamuf (New York, 1991).

31

Ibid., p. 44.

32

Freud understood trauma differently at different times. After he renounced the seduction theory of hysteria in 1897, he did not focus on the subject again until he was confronted by the traumatic neuroses produced by the war. Important for my account is that the surrealists were interested in both these traumatic instances, i.e., hysteria and shock, and like Freud they were always ambiguous as to its agency— i.e., whether trauma concerned internal or external stimuli or both. I discuss both positions further in chapter 2.

33

Freud, *Beyond the Pleasure Principle,* trans. James Strachey (New York, 1961), p. 9. This example also points to the compensatory function of representation. For the Lacanian gloss on the *fort/da* game see "The Function and Field of Speech and Language in Psychoanalysis," in *Écrits: A Selection,* trans. Alan Sheridan (New York, 1977), pp. 30–113, and *The Four Fundamental Concepts,* pp. 62–63. One of the most provocative analyses is that of Samuel Weber, *The Legend of Freud* (Minneapolis, 1982), pp. 95–99, 137–139.

34

Freud, *Beyond the Pleasure Principle,* p. 61. Freud distinguishes among *Schreck* or fright, *Furcht* or fear, and *Angst* or anxiety as follows: in a state of fear the object of danger is known; in anxiety the object is not known but the danger is expected; in fright there is no such warning or preparation—the subject is shocked.

35

Ibid., p. 23. According to Freud, this "shield," both physiological and psychological, filters external excitation into the organism, for "*protection against* stimuli is an almost more important function than *reception of* stimuli" (p. 21). For a gloss on this term see Jean Laplanche and J.-B. Pontalis, *The Language of Psychoanalysis,* trans. Donald Nicholson-Smith (New York, 1973), pp. 357–358.

36

Ibid., pp. 30, 32. As is well known, the standard English translates *Trieb* as "instinct," which suggests a biologism not stipulated in the original. However, in this instance Freud does stress such a basis. The nineteenth-century science out of which this theory developed is now obsolete, but its test lies less in scientific truth than in psychological explanation. Freud: "The theory of the instincts is so to say our mythology. Instincts are mythical entities, magnificent in their indefiniteness" (*New Introductory Lectures on Psychoanalysis* [1933], trans. James Strachey [London, 1964], p. 84). On the scientific bases of psychoanalysis see Frank J. Sulloway, *Freud, Biologist of the Mind* (New York, 1979).

37

Freud, *An Outline of Psychoanalysis* (1938), trans. James Strachey (New York, 1949), p. 5.

38

Freud, *Civilization and Its Discontents* (1930), trans. James Strachey (New York, 1961), pp. 73–77. In *The Ego and the Id* (1923; trans. James Strachey [New York, 1960])

Freud had already stated that "the two classes of instincts are fused, blended, and mingled with each other." In *The Freudian Body* (Berkeley, 1986), Leo Bersani argues the shattering inextricability of the two, the sexual and the (auto)destructive.

39

This is essentially the argument of Gilles Deleuze in *Masochism,* trans. Jean McNeil (New York, 1989), pp. 103–121. In Lacan this "dissolution" becomes a fantasy of the body in pieces *(corps morcelé)* projected back in time before the development of the ego image.

40

See Jacques Derrida, *La Carte postale: De Socrate à Freud et au-delà* (Paris, 1980); also see Jacqueline Rose, "Where Does the Misery Come From? Psychoanalysis, Feminism, and the Event," in Richard Feldstein and Judith Roof, eds., *Feminism and Psychoanalysis* (Ithaca, 1989).

41

Freud, *Beyond the Pleasure Principle,* p. 57.

42

Freud, *Instincts and Their Vicissitudes* (1915), in *A General Selection from the Works of Sigmund Freud* (New York, 1957), ed. John Rickman, p. 74.

43

Ibid., p. 77. For Freud drives are always active; only aims can be passive. Again, my resumé of these texts is necessarily schematic.

44

Freud, "The Economic Problem of Masochism" (1924), in *General Psychological Theory,* ed. Philip Rieff (New York, 1963), p. 194. Of course, to speak of a "subject" here is not quite accurate.

45

Not incidentally, Sade was recovered by the surrealists, Marcel Heine in particular, who published several Sade texts with annotations in *Le Surréalisme au service de la révolution* 2, 4, and 5 (October 1930, December 1931, and May 15, 1933). Enthusiasm for Sade cut across all factions.

46

The "Preface" to *La Révolution surréaliste* 1 (December 1, 1924) reads in part: "Any discovery changing the nature, the destination of an object or a phenomenon constitutes a surrealist fact."

47

See Freud, "Fetishism" (1927), in *On Sexuality* (New York, 1977), ed. Angela Richards, pp. 356–357. For the revision that the female object represents a loss or "castration" preexistent in the male subject, see Kaja Silverman, *The Acoustic Mirror: The Female Voice in Psychoanalysis and Cinema* (Bloomington, 1988), pp. 1–22, and my "The Art of Fetishism," in Emily Apter and William Pietz, eds., *Fetishism as a Cultural Discourse* (Ithaca, 1993).

48

As performed, for example, by Xavière Gauthier in *Surréalisme et sexualité* (Paris, 1971) and by Whitney Chadwick in several books and articles.

49

Some made good on this interest: e.g., Jacques Vaché, the dadaesque dandy who so influenced the young Breton; Jacques Rigaut, who also wrote on suicide; René Crevel, who died in despair of any surrealist-communist *rapprochement;* and Oscar Dominguez. In *Jacques Lacan & Co.* Roudinesco also mentions "the Surrealist cult of suicide." And she adds: "The Surrealists were not 'influenced' by the publication in German of *Beyond the Pleasure Principle,* which would be translated into French in 1927. . . . And yet the love of death . . . constituted an advantageous terrain for the implantation of the Freudian notion of the death instinct" (p. 15). Advantageous for others, perhaps, but ambiguous for the (Bretonian) surrealists.

50

La Révolution surréaliste 2 (January 15, 1925), p. 11.

51

"The inorganic precedes life. Scarcely born, the organism strains to neutralize all excitation in order to reestablish this previous condition" ("Les Mobiles inconscients de suicide," *La Révolution surrealiste* 12 [December 15, 1929], p. 41). Although "The Economic Problem of Masochism" was translated by 1928, Frois-Wittmann retains the theoretical primacy of sadism: "The desire of the ego for its own extinction can only come of a turning round of sadism on the ego . . ." (p. 41).

52

Frois-Wittmann, "L'Art moderne et le principe du plaisir," *Minotaure* 3–4 (December 14, 1933), pp. 79–80.

53

Political Freudians faced a similar problem at the same time. In "The Masochistic Character," Wilhelm Riech contested the theory as a biologization of destruction that obviated "critique of the social order," a challenge that Freud dismissed. And in "A Critique of the Death Instinct" Otto Fenichel also questioned its psychoanalytical bases: e.g., its contradiction of other definitions of the instincts, its ambiguity regarding (de)fusion, its assumption of a primary masochism. See Reich, *Character Analysis* (1933; New York, 1949), pp. 214, 225; and Fenichel, *The Collected Papers of Otto Fenichel,* ed. Hanna Fenichel and David Rapaport (New York, 1953), vol. 1, pp. 363–372.

54

Program to *L'Age d'or* (Paris, November 1930), n.p. By this time Breton must have read *Beyond the Pleasure Principle* and/or *The Ego and the Id,* which rehearses the theory of the two drives, and/or a summary (again, both were translated by 1927).

55

In his 1929 text on suicide Frois-Wittmann also associated the death drive with the decadence of ruling classes.

56

In Breton this defense takes excessive forms: his fascination with Fourier (concepts of attraction, natural regeneration, sexual liberation, and cosmic humanism), with myths of androgyny, with analogical thought, etc. The "philosophical" analyses of surrealism reiterate this metaphysics rather than deconstruct it: e.g., Michel Carrouges, *André Breton et les données fondamentales du surréalisme* (Paris, 1950), and Ferdinand Alquié, *Philosophie du surréalisme* (Paris, 1955).

57

But then how fully is *psychoanalysis* in this service? It too may be cross-examined. If surrealism is self-contradictory, at odds with itself, so too is psychoanalysis—and often in the same ways.

58

Breton, cited in Roudinesco, *Jacques Lacan & Co.,* p. 32 This is typical of Breton, as is this response from Bataille: "Too many fucking idealists." For his critique of Bretonian idealism see "The 'Old Mole' and the Prefix *Sur*" (1929–30?), in *Visions of Excess,* trans. Allan Stoekl et al. (Minneapolis, 1985), pp. 32–44, and chapter 4 below. Breton attended the catalytic lectures on Hegel given by Alexandre Kojève in the 1930s, though not as assiduously as Bataille (or, for that matter, Lacan).

59

This statement appeared on the cover of *La Révolution surréaliste* 1. Of course, it is this humanism that (post)structuralist thought cannot abide. Barthes: "It's always this idea of origins, of depth, of primitiveness, in short of *nature,* that bothers me in Surrealist discourse" ("The Surrealists Overlooked the Body," p. 244).

60

This tension recurs with a difference on the left in the 1960s–between a Marcusean liberationism and a Lacanian skepticism.

61

It is around these questions that official Bretonian and dissident Bataillean surrealisms differ most dramatically. As we will see, while the first poses desire as a synthetic force against the defusion of death, the second regards both desire and death as an ecstatic return to the continuity shattered by life (see *L'Erotisme* [Paris, 1957] in particular, where Bataille often agrees with *Beyond the Pleasure Principle* [without mention of it]). And while Bretonian surrealism seeks to reconcile such oppositions as life and death idealistically in the surreal, Bataillean surrealism works to destructure them materialistically in the *informe*—to contest Hegelian sublation with heterological abjection. Thus it is to be expected that Bretonian surrealists would resist the ramifications of the death drive, and Bataillean surrealists would develop, even exacerbate them. Finally, however, the opposition is not so simple, for at times the fatal attraction of the uncanny cuts across it.

2

Compulsive Beauty

1

Discussed by other surrealists both early (e.g., Aragon, whom I engage briefly below) and late (e.g., Pierre Mabille), the marvelous is most significant in Breton. I refer to these editions of the novels: *Nadja* (Paris, 1928), trans. Richard Howard (New York, 1960), hereafter cited in the text as N; *Les Vases communicants* (Paris, 1932; 1955), VC hereafter; and *L'Amour fou* (Paris, 1937), trans. Mary Ann Caws (*Mad Love,* Lincoln, 1987), AF hereafter.

2

On the medieval marvelous see Jacques Le Goff, *L'Imaginaire médiéval* (Paris, 1980), pp. 17–39; also see Michael Camille, *The Gothic Idol* (Cambridge, 1989), p. 244. In "Le Merveilleux contre le mystère" Breton privileges "pure and simple surrender to the marvelous" over "mystery sought for its own sake" (*Minotaure* 9 [October 1936], pp. 25–31).

3

Concerned with taboo and transgression, the repressed and its return, gothic literature addressed the uncanny long before Freud. For two provocative Lacanian readings of the uncanny in this context see Mladen Dolar, "'I Shall Be with You on Your Wedding-Night': Lacan and the Uncanny," and Joan Copjec, "Vampires, Breast-Feeding, and Anxiety," *October* 58 (Fall 1991).

4

Sometimes, as I suggest in chapter 5, the surrealists see these processes not as opposed but as dialectical: rationalization as irrationalizing.

5

Louis Aragon, *La Révolution surréaliste* 3 (April 15, 1925), p. 30. This aphorism is repeated in *Le Paysan de Paris* (Paris, 1926), translated by Simon Watson Taylor as *Paris Peasant* (London, 1971), p. 217.

6

Aragon, "La Peinture au défi" (Paris, 1930); partially translated by Lucy R. Lippard as "Challenge to Painting," in Lippard, ed., *Surrealists on Art* (Englewood Cliffs, N.J., 1970), here pp. 37–38. It is here that Aragon thinks the marvelous as "negation." For Michel Leiris too the marvelous is a "rupture of relations, intense disorder" ("A Propos de 'Musée des Sorciers,'" *Documents* 2 [1929], p. 109). This notion, in which the marvelous as a tabulation of wondrous objects is recast as a rupture in the modern order of things, is operative in many surrealist assemblages, tableaux, and collages.

7

Walter Benjamin, "Surrealism: The Last Snapshot of the Intelligentsia" (1929), in *Reflections,* ed. Peter Demetz, trans. Edmund Jephcott (New York, 1978), p. 179. Benjamin is at pains to distinguish this surrealist "inspiration" from spiritualist versions.

8

Breton, "Max Ernst," in Max Ernst, *Beyond Painting* (New York, 1948), p. 177.

9

Breton, "The Manifesto of Surrealism" (1924), in *Manifestoes of Surrealism,* trans. Richard Seaver and Helen R. Lane (Ann Arbor, 1972), p. 15; hereafter cited in the text as M.

10

Again "The Uncanny" was not translated until 1933, or several years after the articulation of the marvelous and convulsive beauty in the "Manifesto" and *Nadja*. However, Breton did publish parts of *L'Amour fou* in 1934 and 1935 ("La beauté sera convulsive" and "La nuit de tournesol" in *Minotaure* 5 and 7 [February 1934 and June 1935], "Equation de l'objet trouvé" in *Documents 34* [June 1934]), and we know from a 1936 postscript that he had read *The Ego and the Id* (1923), which contains a short chapter on "The Two Classes of Instincts," in the 1927 translation that included *Beyond the Pleasure Principle*. Breton may have read this text too by the time of *L'Amour fou;* he may also have read *Civilization and Its Discontents,* which, translated in 1934, glosses the death drive. However, what he read when is less important than his relation to Freud on this matter, his approach-and-swerve. For a typology that opposes the marvelous and the uncanny see Tzvetan Todorov, *Introduction à la littérature fantastique* (Paris, 1970).

11

I develop this relation in chapter 5.

12

Breton places these two found objects under the magic-circumstantial, but they are also veiled-erotic.

13

The Brassaï and Man Ray photographs appeared in *Minotaure* 3–4 (December 1933); the former illustrated the Dalí text "Sculptures involontaires" (see chapter 6), the latter the Tzara text "D'un certain automatisme du goût."

14

Although these examples mostly concern inorganic substances in organic guises rather than animate forms returned to inanimate states, the uncanniness resides in the *confusion* of the two conditions. In "Mimétisme et psychasthénie légendaire" (*Minotaure* 7 [June 1935]), Roger Caillois thinks this confusion in relation to natural mimicry, which promotes a dissolution of the distinction between organism and environment. The human parallel is a loss of self, a "convulsive possession" akin to schizophrenia, which for Caillois is evoked in surrealist art (Dalí in particular). Significantly he relates this convulsive possession to the death drive—or to a similar "instinct of renunciation" that works "alongside the instinct of self-preservation."

This text may have influenced Breton; certainly it influenced Lacan, who returned to it in his discussion of the gaze 30 years later in *The Four Fundamental Concepts of Psychoanalysis*. This discussion might be productively read "through" surrealism (see chapter 7).

15

And to do so, again, for the patriarchal subject only?

16

Withheld from *L'Amour fou* without explanation, the image appeared in a short text by Benjamin Péret titled "La Nature dévore le progrès et le dépasse" in *Minotaure* 10 (Winter 1937). With its title and date this text reads as a gloss on the fixed-explosive, and Péret describes several related images: e.g., a telegraph wire cut in a jungle, a pistol "murdered" by flowers, a rifle "crushed" by a snake. In his allegory the locomotive and the forest are first adversaries, then lovers. "Then begins the slow absorption."

17

See Freud, *Civilization and Its Discontents* (1930), trans. James Strachey (New York, 1961), pp. 73–77, and chapter 1 above.

18

Leo Bersani and Ulysse Dutoit, *The Forms of Violence: Narrative in Assyrian Art and Modern Culture* (New York, 1985), p. 34. Bersani and Dutoit remark "the terror of motion in the apparently uncontrolled motions of sado-masochistic sexuality."

19

In "The Photographic Conditions of Surrealism" and "Corpus Delicti," Krauss delineates two further principles: doubling and the *informe*. The first is uncanny as such; the second, pledged to the de-definition of form, is uncannily suggestive of the death drive. In this regard it may also be seen as complementary to the veiled-erotic in Breton—or to natural mimicry in Caillois.

20

Roland Barthes, *Camera Lucida*, trans. Richard Howard (New York, 1981). Brassaï is quoted to this effect in Lawrence Durrell, "Introduction," *Brassaï* (New York, 1968), p. 14.

21

Barthes, *Camera Lucida*, pp. 14–15.

22

Ibid., p. 96. Significantly, Barthes alludes to the Lacanian term for trauma, *tuché,* "the encounter with the real" that is always missed. See *The Four Fundamental Concepts of Psychoanalysis,* trans. Alan Sheridan (New York, 1978), pp. 53–54, and below.

23

Immanuel Kant, *The Critique of Judgement,* section 26, in David Simpson, ed., *German Aesthetic and Literary Criticism* (Cambridge, 1984), p. 47.

24

When Kant writes of the "delight in terror" provoked by the natural sublime, he refers to "threatening rocks, thunder clouds . . ., volcanoes . . ., hurricanes . . ., the boundless ocean . . ., the high waterfall of some mighty river" (ibid., p. 53), all so many tropes of the fragmentary and the fluid, i.e., of a fantasmatic feminine body that threatens to overwhelm the patriarchal subject—an overwhelming that is both desired and feared. For a provocative discussion of this overwhelming, see Victor Burgin, "Geometry and Abjection," in John Tagg, ed., *The Cultural Politics of "Postmodernism"* (Binghamton, 1989).

25

Breton, *Entretiens* (Paris, 1952), pp. 140–141.

26

This last statement refers to dreams, but in *Les Vases communicants* Breton relates objective chance to dreamwork, its manifestations to the primary process of condensation, displacement, substitution, revision (also see AF 32). Is it appropriate to call this chance? It is hardly dadaist chance. Indeed, in surrealism as in Freud there is no simple chance.

27

Here I amend the Caws translation slightly. Again, what Breton calls objective chance Freud calls uncanny: "The most remarkable coincidences of desire and fulfilment, the most mysterious recurrence of similar experiences in a particular place or on a particular date, the most deceptive sights and suspicious noises . . ." ("The Uncanny," in *Studies in Parapsychology,* ed. Philip Rieff [New York, 1963], p. 54.

28

The Ernst quotation is from *Beyond Painting,* p. 8. The original Breton phrase is *temoin hagard. Temoin* suggests an external event, while *hagard,* which Richard Howard aptly translates as "agonized," suggests a psychic origin. I return to this projection, essential as it is to surrealist pictoriality, in chapter 3.

29

Freud, *Beyond the Pleasure Principle* (1920), trans. James Strachey (New York, 1961), p. 29. Freud first discussed this repetition in its relation to resistance and transference in "Recollection, Repetition and Working Through" (1914). A most symptomatic character in this regard is Nadja.

30

Or rather, "extimate." For the relation between Lacanian *extimité* and Freudian uncanniness see Dolar, "'I Shall Be with You on Your Wedding-Night,'" and Copjec, "Vampires, Breast-Feeding, and Anxiety."

31

Freud, *Inhibitions, Symptoms and Anxiety* (1926), trans. James Strachey (New York, 1961). In his prior model anxiety was regarded as an effect of a sexual excitation that could not be mastered. As an internal process, anxiety is also triggered when the ego comes under attack by the drives. I discuss surrealist anxiety further in chapter 7.

32

In *Le Surréalisme* (Paris, 1984) Jacqueline Chénieux-Gendron reads objective chance as an empty sign completed by a later event, but this account, though often insightful, mostly rehearses surrealist self-understanding in semiotic terms. In chapter 3 I argue that the repetition of trauma—a trauma that need not be real to be psychically effective—structures the most important surrealist oeuvres.

33

Freud, *Beyond the Pleasure Principle*, p. 15.

34

Two sets of events suggestive of this fate compulsion intrigued the Bretonian surrealists particularly: the 1914 de Chirico portrait of Apollinaire with a bandaged head painted *before* he was wounded in the war, and the 1931 Victor Brauner *Self-Portrait with a Gouged Eye* painted *before* his eye was blinded in a 1938 fight. For a discussion of the latter see Pierre Mabille, "L'Oeil du peintre," *Minotaure* 12–13 (May 1939).

35

Benjamin, "Paris—the Capital of the Nineteenth Century" (1935), in *Charles Baudelaire: A Lyric Poet in the Era of High Capitalism*, trans. Harry Zohn (London, 1973), p. 166. I might have selected as well the two uncanny tribal objects illustrated in

Nadja, which Breton also regards ambivalently ("I have always loved and feared" [N 122]).

36

Freud: "The obsessional act is *ostensibly* [i.e., consciously] a protection against the prohibited act; but actually [i.e., unconsciously], in our view, it is a repetition of it" (*Totem and Taboo* [1913], trans. James Strachey [New York, 1950], p. 12; translated into French in 1924). In *The Ego and the Id* Freud argues "the marked emergence of the death instinct" in obsessional neurosis (p. 32).

37

Like *Dora: Fragment of an Analysis of a Case of Hysteria* (1905), *Nadja* is a case history of a failed cure: although Breton understands her transferential desire, he does not fully grasp his countertransferential desire. As we will see, in the same year as *Nadja* Breton defined hysteria as a "reciprocal seduction," which seems to implicate this other desire. In *Nadja,* however, he resists this recognition, and then blames psychiatry for his failing of Nadja.

38

In *L'Amour fou* Suzanne Musard is associated with the ambiguous token of death, the flea market mask, and Jacqueline Lamba with the move way from such enthrallment. In *Nadja* Breton addressed the former thus: "All I know is that this substitution of persons stops with you" (N 158). In *L'Amour fou* he both recognizes and disavows the impossibility of this closure of metonymic desire, in a tortured catechism addressed to the latter: "Because you are unique, you can't help being for me always another, another you" (AF 81). The prototype of this object of desire is discussed below.

39

This *dérive* passes from Les Halles to the Hôtel de Ville by the Tour Saint-Jacques to the Quai aux Fleurs.

40

The alternate titles all but announce a link between (lost) object and mother.

41

Breton plays on "the phonic ambiguity of the world 'glassy'" (AF 33), which combines the *verre* of the fetishistic glass slipper with the *vair* of the fetishistic ermine fur (see Caws note 6, AF 126). Meanwhile, Giacometti often uses the spoon as an emblem of woman (e.g., *Spoon Woman* [1927]). In the Lacanian formulation the slipper spoon is perhaps a *point de capiton,* a stitching or buttoning of desire that gives way. At times Breton exploits this metonymic slide of desire; at other times he attempts to arrest it, as he does here.

42

"The *objet a* is something from which the subject, in order to constitute itself, has separated itself off as organ. This serves as a symbol of the lack, that is to say, of the phallus, not as such but in so for as it is lacking. It must, therefore, be an object that is, firstly, separable and, secondly, that has some relation to the lack" (*The Four Fundamental Concepts of Psychoanalysis,* p. 103). Lacan speaks of the *objet a* as a primal separation, a self-mutilation; the "little a" signals that it is barely other *(autre),* i.e., barely detached, from the subject (as one example he offers the spool from the *fort/da* game [p. 62]).

43

As with surrealist chance (see note 26), the surrealist object must be distinguished from its dadaist precedent. According to Duchamp, the readymade is "based on a reaction of visual indifference . . . a complete anesthesia" ("Apropos of 'Readymades'" [1961/66], in *Salt Seller: The Essential Writings of Marcel Duchamp,* ed. Michel Sanouillet and Elmer Peterson [London, 1975], p. 141). The surrealist object, on the other hand, is "the only one deemed indispensable" (Breton, "Quelle sorte d'espoir mettez-vous dans l'amour?," *La Révolution surréaliste* 12 [December 15, 1929]). If the subject selects the readymade, the surrealist object selects the subject: he is always already marked by it.

44

Freud, *Three Essays on the Theory of Sexuality,* trans. James Strachey, in *On Sexuality,* ed. Angela Richards (London, 1953), p. 144. Translated into French in 1923, this crucial text includes an early account of fetishism, but it is not known when Breton read it. If he did, he probably did so by 1936.

45

Ibid. In the special issue of *Cahiers d'Art* on the surrealist object (1936) Marcel Jean seems to echo Freud: "The found object is always a rediscovered object. . . ." He also suggests its implication in a sadomasochistic sexuality: "Exalted by sexual desire, it implies, opposed to a fixation (as in painting or sculpture), a potential motion of a great poetic violence. . . ." See "Arrivée de la Belle Époque," in Marcel Jean, ed., *The Autobiography of Surrealism* (New York, 1980), p. 304.

46

The beginnings of fantasy and sexuality are thus bound up with one another—an origin that, I argue in chapter 3, surrealist aesthetics seeks to (re)construct. "The first wishing," Freud writes, "seems to have been a hallucinatory cathecting of the memory of satisfaction." On the relationship of need and desire see Jean Laplanche, *Life and Death in Psychoanalysis,* trans. Jeffrey Mehlman (Baltimore, 1976), pp. 8–34; on the relationship of fantasy and sexuality see Laplanche and J.-B. Pontalis, "Fantasy and the Origins of Sexuality" (1964), in *Formations of Fantasy,* ed. V. Burgin, J. Donald, and C. Kaplan (London, 1986), pp. 5–34. They write of this "mythical moment of disjunction between the pacification of need and the fulfilment of desire, between the two stages represented by real experience and its hallucinatory revival, between the object that satisfies and the sign which describes both the object and its absence: a mythical moment at which hunger and sexuality meet in a common origin" (p. 25). This is the place to note how many surrealist objects—from the Breton spoon to various Dalí assemblages to the Oppenheim cup—involve a marked orality: receptacles of food and sense, which, already a part of us, always feel amputated from us as objects. Dalí in particular fantasized a cannibalistic incorporation of the object, whereby it is variously preserved, destroyed, assimilated.

47

An account of *The Invisible Object* was written before the sculpture was made in a poem by Paul Eluard from *Capitale de la douleur* (Paris, 1926), which reads in part: "The shape of your hands is chimerical/And your love resembles my lost desire,/O sighs of amber, dreams, glances./But you were not always with me. My memory/ Is still obscured, having seen you coming/And going. Time uses words, as love does."

48

I develop this further in chapter 3.

49

Elisabeth Roudinesco argues that Lacan reasserted the distinction between desire and need blurred in the French reception of Freud (see *La Bataille de cent ans,* vol. 2 [Paris, 1986]; translated by Jeffrey Mehlman as *Jacques Lacan & Co.* [Chicago, 1990], p. 146). My suggestion is that Breton did so too. In *Les Vases communicants* (1932; trans. Mary Ann Caws as *Communicating Vessels* [Lincoln, 1990]) he stresses that desire is "haphazard" ("the least object . . . is able to represent anything"), that motility is its "essence" (pp. 108–109, 130).

50

Guy Rosolato, "L'Amour fou," manuscript. Also see J.-B. Pontalis, "Les Vases non communicants," *La Nouvelle revue française* 302 (March 1, 1978), pp. 26–45.

51

On this point see the Pontalis introduction to Xavière Gautier, *Surréalisme et sexualité* (Paris, 1971).

52

As does the Giacometti *Head* (1934), which seems to conflate maternal gaze and death mask—as if this gaze were frozen as a *memento mori*.

53

In the Belgian journal *Documents 34* (June 1934), under the title "Equation de l'objet trouvé."

54

As suggested, both must be seen in relation to the lost object, to the metonymic *mise-en-abime* of desire. Breton insists that the mask arrested this displacement for Giacometti, as he insists that the spoon effected a closure for him, but the only possible arrest is in death, desire for which the mask and the spoon also figure. This is what makes the mask in particular so cruel a riddle: an image of a longing for the mother conflated with an evocation of the drive toward death.

55

For the Strachey translation of this passage see *The Ego and the Id* (New York, 1961), pp. 30–31. This passage also glosses the association of sexual and self-preservative drives and the relation between binding and defusion.

56

Trauma and repetition are fundamental to both modernist art and psychoanalytical theory; surrealism describes this commonality, but it extends far beyond this one movement. In "On Some Motifs in Baudelaire" (1939) Benjamin draws directly on *Beyond the Pleasure Principle* to think the significance of modern shock for the aesthetic of "involuntary memory" from Baudelaire to Proust, an aesthetic that surrealism develops (in *Illuminations*, ed. Hannah Arendt, trans. Harry Zohn [New York, 1969]). And in *The Four Fundamental Concepts of Psychoanalysis* Lacan discusses trauma and repetition in terms of *tuché* and *automaton*, Aristotelian terms that he uses respectively to think trauma as "the encounter with the real" and repetition as "the return, the coming-back, the insistence of the signs" (pp. 53–54). This encounter, this trauma, is both always "missed" and ever repeated because it is never recognized by the subject as such: "What is repeated, in fact, is always something that occurs—the expression tells us quite a lot about its relation to the *tuché*—*as if by chance*." This is precisely the formula of objective chance.

57

Aragon describes this experience, in terms prophetic of objective chance, in *Une Vague de rêves* (Paris, 1928): "Then I grasp within myself the occasional, I grasp suddenly how to go beyond myself: the occasional is myself. . . . It is at this point perhaps that there would be grandeur in death."

58

On shock in the nineteenth century see Wolfgang Schivelbusch, *The Railway Journey: The Industrialization of Time and Space in the 19th Century,* trans. Anselm Hollo (New York, 1977), pp. 129–149.

59

This conjunction has a precedent in Baudelaire, who thinks his "sublime" aesthetic in terms of both shock ("every sublime thought is accompanied by a more or less violent nervous shock which has its repercussion in the very core of the brain") and hysteria. See "The Painter of Modern Life" in *The Painter of Modern Life and Other Essays,* trans. and ed. Jonathan Mayne (London, 1964), p. 8, and below.

60

Breton and Aragon, "Le Cinquantenaire de l'hystérie," *La Révolution surréaliste* 11 (March 15, 1928), 20–22. Subsequent references are to this text.

61

Pierre Janet, *L'État mental des hystériques* (Paris, 1894), pp. 40–47.

62

Sigmund Freud and Josef Breuer, "On the Psychical Mechanism of Hysterical Phenomena: Preliminary Communication" (1893), in *Studies on Hysteria,* trans. James and Alix Strachey (London, 1955), p. 63.

63

Freud (with Josef Breuer), "On the Psychical Mechanism of Hysterical Phenomena" (1892), in *Early Psychoanalytical Writings,* ed. Philip Rieff (New York, 1963), p. 40.

64

His ideas may have influenced the Breton/Eluard text *L'Immaculée conception* (Paris, 1930), which simulates certain mental disorders.

65

In one way the surrealists respecularize hysteria, and so run counter to the epochal shift from the visual theater of Charcot to the talking cure of Freud (both paradigms, however, rest on the figure of woman). In another way the surrealists move away from a physical model of hysteria as conversion of psychic conflict to a semiotic model of hysteria as a "forest of signs" related to traumatic fantasy. In this regard the surrealists, like Freud, fall between the organic conception of hysteria of Charcot and the semiotic conception of Lacan. See Monique David-Ménard, *Hysteria from Freud to Lacan: Body and Language in Psychoanalysis,* trans. Catherine Porter (Ithaca, 1989), and Georges Didi-Huberman, *L'Invention de l'hystérie* (Paris, 1982).

66

Here Dalí seems to play on Charcot, devotee of hysteria and art nouveau alike, a connection to which I return in chapter 6. Through the anthropometric set of ears (often used in physiognomic classifications of criminals and prostitutes) Dalí also seems to invoke the discourse of degeneration in which the hysteric as constitutionally flawed was long placed. But what exactly does this work do to these connections, these classifications?

67

Freud, *Totem and Taboo,* p. 73. Apart from the *Nouvelle iconographie de la Salpêtrière,* relevant texts by Charcot (with Paul Richet) include *Les Démoniaques dans l'art* (1887) and *Les Difformes et les malades dans l'art* (1889). On this research see Debora L. Silverman, *Art Nouveau in Fin-de-Siècle France* (Berkeley, 1989), pp. 91–106.

68

See Jan Goldstein, "The Uses of Male Hysteria: Medical and Literary Discourse in Nineteenth-Century France," *Representations* 34 (Spring 1991), 134–165. I am indebted to Goldstein here, but there is much other new literature on this subject as well: e.g., Martha Noel Evans, *Fits & Starts: A Genealogy of Hysteria in Modern France* (Ithaca, 1991), and Jo Anna Isaak, "'What's Love Got to Do, Got to Do with It?' Woman as the Glitch in the Postmodern Record," *American Imago* 48, no. 3 (Fall 1991).

69

Baudelaire, *Intimate Journals,* trans. Christopher Isherwood (San Francisco, 1983), p. 96 (translation modified).

70

Goldstein, "The Uses of Male Hysteria," p. 156.

71

Roudinesco, *Jacques Lacan & Co.,* pp. 20–21. The phrase "female ecstatic" is hers.

72

One might argue the same thing about my own association of the surreal and the uncanny. On a more obvious level I have also excluded the woman surrealists from my analysis, but I am not convinced that they treated the figure of women in a radically different way.

3

_____

CONVULSIVE IDENTITY

1

Might the modernist obsession with originality in part stem from a resisted recognition of its impossibility? Might it be due not only to the historical lateness of the artist and the capitalist proliferation of the image, but to the inexorable repetition operative in psychic life? The postmodernist critique of modernist originality has missed this point almost entirely: too often it has sentenced modernism on the charge of a mastery that was sought obsessively precisely because it could not be possessed actually.

2

To repeat the remark from "The Uncanny" (1919): "'Love is a homesickness,' and whenever a man dreams of a place or a country and says to himself, still in the dream, 'this place is familiar to me, I have been here before,' we may interpret the place as being his mother's genitals or her body. In this case, too, the *unheimlich* is what was once *heimisch,* homelike, familiar; the prefix 'un' is the token of repression" (*Studies in Parapsychology,* ed. Philip Rieff [New York, 1963], p. 51).

3

Freud: "Here we have an instance of a memory exciting an affect which it had not excited as an experience, because in the meantime the changes produced by puberty

_____

had made possible a new understanding of what was remembered. Now this case is typical of repression in hysteria. We invariably find that a memory is repressed which has only become a trauma *after the event*. The reason for this state of things is the retardation of puberty as compared with the remainder of the individual's development" ("Project for a Scientific Psychology" [1895], in *The Origins of Psychoanalysis,* trans. James Strachey [New York, 1954], p. 413). Also see Jean Laplanche and J.-B. Pontalis, *The Language of Psychoanalysis,* trans. Donald Nicholson-Smith (New York, 1973), pp. 111–114.

Dominick LaCapra and Peter Brooks (among others) have discussed the ramifications of this concept for historical and literary studies; it is time art historians did the same. Among other possibilities "deferred action" allows one to complicate readings of influence, to think the effectivity of the present on the past, and to mitigate the teleological determination of dominant narratives of Western (especially modern) art. See LaCapra, *Soundings in Critical Theory* (Ithaca, 1989), pp. 30–66; Brooks, *Reading for the Plot: Design and Intention in Narrative* (New York, 1984), pp. 264–285; and my "Postmodernism in Parallax," *October* 63 (Winter 1992).

4

Freud, *On the History of the Psychoanalytical Movement* (1914), trans. Joan Rivière (New York, 1963), p. 52. This revision led to his recognition first of infantile sexuality and then of the Oedipus complex.

Inasmuch as these fantasies bear on sexual origins, they are also involved in the vagaries of sublimation. In this regard they are especially pertinent to artistic origins. See Jean Laplanche and J.-B. Pontalis, "Fantasy and the Origins of Sexuality" (1964), in *Formations of Fantasy,* ed. V. Burgin, J. Donald, and C. Kaplan (London, 1986), p. 25. I am indebted to this important text throughout this chapter. Also helpful are Ned Lukacher, *Primal Scenes* (Ithaca, 1986), and Elizabeth Cowie, "Fantasia," *m/f* 9 (1984), reprinted in P. Adams and E. Cowie, eds., *The Woman in Question: m/f* (Cambridge, 1990).

5

For many, this recourse to hereditary narratives remains the most problematic aspect of the theory. In "From the History of an Infantile Neurosis" (1918) Freud argues that under the pressure of the inherited schema the Wolf Man came to imagine his father as castrative despite his "negative Oedipus complex," i.e., despite his love for him (see note 25). The cases of de Chirico and Ernst offer parallels in this regard.

6

Laplanche and Pontalis, "Fantasy and the Origins of Sexuality," p. 26. On mobile identifications, see especially "A Child Is Being Beaten" (1919; French trans. 1933).

7

As noted in chapter 2, Ernst wrote of the artist as a passive "spectator" and Breton as an "agonized witness" in *Nadja*. Before them de Chirico wrote of the artist as a "surprised" viewer in "Meditations of a Painter" (1912; trans. in James Thrall Soby, *Giorgio de Chirico* [New York, 1955]). The helpless child in fright before a traumatic event may be the prototype of the "ill-prepared" surrealist "taken by a sudden fear in the *forest of symbols*" (Breton, *L'Amour fou*, translated by Mary Ann Caws as *Mad Love* [Lincoln, 1987], p. 15; hereafter cited in the text as AF). I return to this in chapter 7.

8

Breton, *Manifestoes of Surrealism*, trans. Richard Seaver and Helen R. Lane (Ann Arbor, 1972), p. 21. Breton considers this the ur-image of his automatist writing.

9

Breton, *Surrealism and Painting*, trans. Simon Watson Taylor (New York, 1972), p. 4; SP hereafter in the text.

10

Of the "Manifesto" image Breton writes: "Here again it is not a matter of drawing, *but simply of tracing.*" The image seems to point to a trauma, perhaps the residue of a primal fantasy of castration, that Breton cannot "incorporate . . . into . . . poetic construction" (*Manifestoes of Surrealism*, pp. 21–22). The *L'Amour fou* metaphor also suggests a "tracing" of trauma, which Breton typically projects from the past to the future: "This grid exists. Every life contains those homogenous patterns of facts, whose surface is cracked or cloudy. Each person has only to stare at them fixedly in order to read his own future. Let him enter the whirlwind; let him retrace the events which have seemed to him fleeting and obscure among all others, which have torn him apart" (AF 87).

11

Theodor W. Adorno, "Looking Back on Surrealism" (1954), in *Notes to Literature*, vol. 1, trans. Shierry Weber Nicholsen (New York, 1991), p. 89. Between the lines this reads as an objection, long after the fact, to the surrealist influence on Benjamin.

See Susan Buck-Morss, *The Origin of Negative Dialectics: Theodor W. Adorno, Walter Benjamin and the Frankfurt Institute* (New York, 1977), pp. 124–129.

12

Max Ernst, *Beyond Painting* (New York, 1948), p. 20; hereafter cited in the text as BP.

13

Laplanche and Pontalis, "Fantasy and the Origins of Sexuality," p. 10.

14

Dalí and Bellmer are also likely candidates for analysis in terms of primal fantasy. In "L'Ane pourri" Dalí wrote of the "traumatic nature of images [*simulacres*]" evocative of both "desire" and "terror" (*Le Surréalisme au service de la révolution*, July 1930). I discuss Bellmer in chapter 4.

15

The primal scene was mentioned as early as *The Interpretation of Dreams* (1900; French trans. 1926). The idea of primal fantasies was sketched in "The Sexual Enlightenment of Children" (1907) and "Family Romances" (1908), and the fantasy of seduction was elaborated in *Leonardo da Vinci and a Memory of His Childhood* (1910; French trans. 1927). But the typology of the fantasies was not fully developed until "A Case of Paranoia Running Counter to the Psychoanalytic Theory of the Disease" (1915; French trans. 1935) and "From the History of an Infantile Neurosis" (1914/18; French trans. 1935).

The de Chirico texts that I cite below date from 1912–1913, 1919, and 1924, and the relevant works begin in 1910. The Ernst texts date from 1927, 1933, and 1942, and the relevant works from 1919. Both Giacometti texts and works are from the early 1930s. Ernst had begun to read Freud as early as 1911, and he would have known some of the relevant Freud texts, certainly *Leonardo*. (On this point see Werner Spies, *Max Ernst, Loplop: The Artist in the Person* [New York, 1983], pp. 101–109.) It is unlikely that the others knew of the relevant concepts; the critical literature is silent on the subject.

16

See Jean Laplanche, *New Foundations for Psychoanalysis*, trans. David Macey (London, 1989). "The *enigma* is in itself a *seduction* and its mechanisms are unconscious. It was not for nothing that the Sphinx appeared outside the gates of Thebes before Oedipus's drama began" (p. 127).

17

As will soon be clear, in "surprise" I want to hear "shock," and in "enigma" "seduction." The texts from 1911–1915, written in Paris, remained in the collection of Jean Paulhan and Paul Eluard; the texts from 1919 were published in *Valori plastici*. Translated extracts can be found in Soby, *Giorgio de Chirico;* in Marcel Jean, ed., *The Autobiography of Surrealism* (New York, 1980), pp. 3–10; and in Herschel B. Chipp, ed., *Theories of Modern Art* (Berkeley, 1968), pp. 397–402, 446–453.

18

De Chirico, in Jean, p. 6. De Chirico did not rehearse the Freudian uncanny, yet his art is populated by its avatars—mannequins, doubles, spectral father figures, most of which he introduced into the surrealist repertoire. In "Metafisica et unheimlichkeit" (*Les Réalismes 1919–39* [Paris, 1981]), Jean Clair notes the contemporaneity of "On Metaphysical Art" and "The Uncanny."

19

De Chirico, in Jean, pp. 5–6.

20

De Chirico, "On Metaphysical Art" (1919), in Chipp, p. 448.

21

The latter, once owned by Breton, was a talisman of the surrealists, some of whom speculated about its sexual implications in *Le Surréalisme au service de la révolution* 6 (May 15, 1933).

22

De Chirico, "Meditations of a Painter" (1912), in Chipp, pp. 397–398.

23

This identification is supported here by the further association with Dante, "father" of Italian culture. (In the 1933 questionnaire devoted to the 1914 *Enigma* Eluard identifies the statue as the father.)

24

De Chirico, "Meditations," in Chipp, p. 398. *Stimmung* (atmosphere) is another privileged de Chirican term, borrowed from Nietzsche.

25

"The more complete Oedipus complex . . . is twofold, positive and negative, and is due to the bisexuality originally present in children: that is to say, a boy has not merely an ambivalent attitude towards his father and an affectionate object-choice towards his mother, but at the same time he also behaves like a girl and displays an affectionate feminine attitude to his father and a corresponding jealousy and hostility towards his mother" (*The Ego and the Id* [1923], trans. James Strachey and Joan Rivière [New York, 1962], p. 23).

26

De Chirico, "Meditations," in Chipp, p. 400.

27

De Chirico, "Mystery and Creation" (1913), in Chipp, p. 402. "At that moment it seemed to me that I had already seen this palace, or that this palace had once, somewhere, already existed . . ." (in Jean, p. 9).

28

This structure is similar to that of the famous dream in "From the History of an Infantile Neurosis," the *locus classicus* of the primal scene, where the look of the young Wolf Man is returned as the staring of wolves.

29

It is as if de Chirico pictorializes what Lacan theorizes about "the scopic field": "Everything is articulated between two terms that act in an antinomic way—on the side of things, there is the gaze, that is to say, things look at me, and yet I see them" (*The Four Fundamental Concepts of Psychoanalysis,* trans. Alan Sheridan [New York, 1977], p. 109). De Chirico was interested in Renaissance treatises on perspective, especially *Tutte le opere d'architettura* of Sebastiano Serlio (1537–1575), which he seems to have used (see William Rubin, "De Chirico and Modernism," in Rubin, ed., *De Chirico* [New York, 1982], pp. 58–61). However, his partial rehabilitation of perspective, like that of Duchamp, destabilizes it. Not only does de Chirico rework it in psychic rather than realist terms, but he also stresses its paranoid aspect (i.e., the sense that the viewer is watched in turn). For a discussion of this aspect in Sartre and Lacan see Norman Bryson, "The Gaze in the Expanded Field," *Vision and Visuality,* ed. Hal Foster (Seattle, 1988).

30

De Chirico, "Meditations," in Chipp, p. 400. In *The Seer* (1916) it is as if the "seer" that constructs the pictorial space within the picture also represents it in its Medusan effects—both blind and blinding, fragmented and fragmenting.

31

Freud, *Introductory Lectures on Psycho-Analysis* (1916–1917), trans. James Strachey (New York, 1966), p. 371. This is Freud in his phylogenetic mode: "It seems to me quite possible that all the things that are told to us today in analysis as phantasy—the seduction of children, the inflaming of sexual excitement by observing parental intercourse, the threat of castration (or rather castration itself)—were once real occurrences in the primaeval times of the human family, and that children in their phantasies are simply filling in the gaps in individual truth with pre-historic truth."

32

Breton, "Giorgia de Chirico," *Littérature* 11 (January 1920), and *Les Pas perdus* (Paris, 1924), p. 145.

33

De Chirico, "On Metaphysical Art," in Chipp, p. 451.

34

Ibid., p. 452. Of interest in relation to de Chirico is that Weininger, a Jewish anti-Semite, misogynist, and suicide, proposed a fundamental bisexuality—as did Fleiss and Freud in very different ways. See Frank J. Sulloway, *Freud, Biologist of the Mind* (New York, 1979), pp. 223–229.

35

Like the texts concerning primal fantasies, the Freud texts on these subjects are roughly contemporaneous with the de Chirico oeuvre, not prior to it.

36

This problematic account runs roughly as follows. For Freud libido passes from autoerotism through narcissism to object-love. A first love object of the male infant is a narcissistic one, his own body; a first outer love object is a homosexual one, a body with the same genitals, his father. When the child intuits the stake of this love object—that he must be castrated in order to receive it—he sublimates his homosexual desire. Later, if frustrated, he may regress to this point in his passage—the paranoiac past sublimated homosexuality to narcissism. For Freud this point of fixation suggests the motive of the paranoiac: he regresses to narcissism as a defense against homosexual desire. And this defense often takes the form of projection—of an excessive recon-struction of the world. Such reconstruction is necessary to the paranoiac because he regards his withdrawal from the world as its end. Thus "the delusion-formation, which we take to be a pathological product, is in reality an attempt at recovery, a process of reconstruction" ("Psychoanalytic Notes on an Auto-biographical Account of a Case of Paranoia" [1911], in *Three Case Histories,* ed. Philip Rieff [New York, 1963], p. 174).

37

As we will see, it is marked in Ernst, and it becomes programmatic with Dalí, who was also influenced by two 1933 texts on the subject by Lacan, "Le Problème du style et la conception psychiatrique des formes paranoïaques de l'expérience" and "Motifs du crime paranoïaque: le crime des soeurs Papin," published in *Minotaure* 1 and 3–4.

38

Freud, "The Uncanny," pp. 38–39. The association in Freud of "passive" with "feminine" is obviously problematic, as it is in surrealism. However, as we will see, it is disturbed in Ernst and, to a lesser extent, in Giacometti.

39

The most famous incarnation of this "dissociated complex" of the son may be in *Pietà*, where the figure of the mustachioed father is also derived from de Chirico.

40

This paternal loss was compounded by cultural dislocations, and de Chirico may have associated the two. In this way compulsive repetitions of certain emblems (e.g., the train) may also involve attempts to work through paternal loss. (In a 1913 drawing titled *Joy* the train appears as a toy.)

41

Freud, "Mourning and Melancholia" (1917), in *General Psychological Theory*, ed. Philip Rieff (New York: Collier Books, 1957), p. 166.

42

Ibid., p. 172. This is how Freud understands the "self-torment of melancholics": as "sadistic tendencies" toward the object "turned around upon the self." "Thus the shadow of the object fell upon the ego, so that the latter could henceforth be criticized by a special mental faculty like an object, like the forsaken object" (p. 170). This is suggestive in relation to de Chirican shadows, which, detached from naturalistic purpose, seem to "fall" in a related way on his fragmented ego-surrogates.

43

Breton, "Le Surréalisme et la peinture," *La Révolution surréaliste* 7 (June 15, 1926). Breton reproduced many de Chirico works in this journal, even though their classicist program was announced as early as 1919 (e.g., in "The Return to Craft").

44

Pursuit of profit alone did not drive these repetitions. If *The Disquieting Muses* represents the first moment when de Chirico still inflects the uncanny return of the repressed (*unheimlich* is often translated *inquiétant*), its repetitions represent the second moment when he is overcome by its compulsive mechanism. In this light the reprise of this image by Andy Warhol (1982) is especially appropriate: the contemporary master of deathly repetition repeats the image in the modernist canon most emblematic of the compulsion to repeat.

45

Freud, *The Ego and the Id*, p. 43.

46

De Chirico, *La Révolution surréaliste* 1 (December 1, 1924). In *Hebdomeros*, his 1929 novel that recaptured some surrealist favor, this glance returns—in the body of a woman: "All at once, Hebdomeros saw that this woman had his father's eyes; and *he understood*. . . . 'Oh Hebdomeros,' she said, 'I am Immortality. . . .'" (*Hebdomeros*, trans. Margaret Crosland [New York, 1988], p. 132).

47

Besides the title text, *Beyond Painting* includes a draft of this text ("Comment on force l'inspiration," *Le Surréalisme au service de la révolution* 6 [1933]) as well as a psycho-autobiography ("Some Data on the Youth of M.E. as Told by Himself," *View* [April 1942]). "Visions de demi-sommeil" appeared in the same issue (*La Révolution surréaliste* 9/10 [October 1, 1927]) as an extract from *The Question of Lay Analysis* (1926).

48

Ernst: "Certainly little Max took pleasure in being afraid of these visions and later delivered himself voluntarily to provoke hallucinations of the same kind" (BP 28).

49

Ernst: "When someone would ask him: 'What is your favorite occupation?' he regularly answered, 'Looking'. An analogous obsession conducted Max Ernst later to search for and discover some technical possibilities of drawing and painting, directly connected with the processes of inspiration and revelation (frottage, collage, decalcomania, etc.)" (BP 28). Interestingly, his father was a teacher of the deaf and dumb.

50

As is well known, Freud worked from a mistranslation of "vulture" for "kite," which renders most of his mythological speculations spurious. See, among other texts,

Meyer Schapiro, "Leonardo and Freud: An Art Historical Study," *Journal of the History of Ideas* 17 (1956), pp. 147–178.

51

In one image in his 1934 collage-novel *Une Semaine de bonté* Ernst seems to quote the Leonardo fantasy directly.

52

Leo Bersani, *The Freudian Body: Psychoanalysis and Art* (New York, 1986), p. 43. His provocative discussion of *Leonardo* is pertinent to Ernst, as is that of Laplanche in "To Situate Sublimation," *October* 28 (Spring 1984), pp. 7–26. Laplanche is especially insightful about the theoretical slippages between repression and sublimation in *Leonardo*.

53

Freud, *Instincts and Their Vicissitudes,* in *General Psychological Theory,* p. 96. The best discussion of these processes is Jean Laplanche, *Life and Death in Psychoanalysis* (1970), trans. Jeffrey Mehlman (Baltimore, 1976), pp. 85–102.

54

My italics. The dadaist Ernst sought to decenter the authorial subject in several ways: anonymous collaborations (the Fatagagas with Grünwald and Arp), the use of found materials and automatist techniques, etc. Here Ernst derives the term "principle of identity" from Breton, who in turn used it regarding the early dadaist collages (see *Beyond Painting,* p. 177). For Breton too these collages "disturb us within our memory."

55

These couplings need not be collages per se; as Ernst once remarked, "Ce n'est pas la colle qui fait le collage" (*Cahiers d'Art* [1937], p. 31). Some (e.g., *The Master's Bedroom*) are overpaintings on found illustrations, a concealing-that-reveals that suggests a further connection between psychic and technical operations. For a related analysis of this work see Rosalind Krauss, "The Master's Bedroom," *Representations* 28 (Fall 1989).

Two other collages of 1920 evoke such a traumatic experience, only to relate it to military-industrial shock. In the first (untitled) work, part of a female body is coupled with part of a biplane, while a wounded soldier is carried from the field; in the second (*The Swan Is Very Peaceful*), three putti displaced from a nativity onto a triplane gaze upon a swan identified with a rape. In both works images of peace and war, sex and death, are collided, and it is precisely in this collision, which appears to be temporal as well as spatial, that the trauma of these scenes is registered (as if in accordance with the Freudian formula of *Nachträglichkeit*). See my "Armor Fou," *October* 56 (Spring 1991).

56

Freud: "In fact, the child is not getting rid of his father but exalting him" ("Family Romances," in *The Sexual Enlightenment of Children,* ed. Philip Rieff [New York, 1963], p. 45). In "Some Data" Ernst writes that he ran away as a child, only to be taken by "pilgrims" as Christ—a story that at least appeased his father, who painted him in this guise. Such godly fantasies are classically paranoid (as Ernst may have known through the Schreber case). They are reworked (suggestively in relation to *Leonardo*) in *The Virgin Spanking the Child Jesus in Front of Three Witnesses: André Breton, Paul Eluard, and Max Ernst* (1926). In *Subversive Intent: Gender, Politics, and the Avant-Garde* (Cambridge, 1990) Susan Suleiman reads this painting through "A Child Is Being Beaten" in a way commensurate with my account.

57

This is hardly without interest. Particularly in his collage novels, *La Femme 100 têtes* (1929), *Rêve d'une petite fille qui voulut entrer au carmel* (1930), and *Une Semaine de bonté* (1934), Ernst contrives primal scenes, castration fantasies, paranoid projections, and other such fantasmatic scenarios. "These archaic moments of disturbed visual representation," Jacqueline Rose writes, "these troubled scenes, which expressed and unsettled our groping knowledge in the past, can now be used as theoretical prototypes to unsettle our certainties again" (*Sexuality in the Field of Vision* [London, 1987], p. 227). This is what Ernst attempts, 50 years before the feminist art that concerns Rose, in the best of these collages. "They are reminiscences of my first books," Ernst told Sigfried Giedion, "a resurgence of childhood memories" (*Mechanization Takes Command* [New York, 1948], p. 363). This is true materially as well, for many of his collages were made from late nineteenth-century school primers (especially, in the early collages, the Kölner Lehrmittel-Anstalt), illustrated novels, catalogues, and popular magazines. I discuss his use of the outmoded in chapter 6.

58

Freud thinks fetishism in relation to the castration and Oedipus complexes in the 1920s, the classic period of surrealism, in such texts as "Some Psychical Consequences of the Anatomical Distinction between the Sexes" (1925) and "Fetishism" (1927). In

---

a very early text on Giacometti (1929) Michel Leiris reads his objects in terms of a curative fetishism, one that treats "that affective ambivalence, that tender sphinx we nourish, more or less secretly, at our core," in a way that questions not only sexual identities but also cultural conventions, "our moral, logical and social imperatives." Leiris nonetheless sees this ambivalence in traumatic terms as "when abruptly the outside seems to respond to a call we send it from within." See "Alberto Giacometti," *Documents* 1, no. 4 (1929), pp. 209–210, trans. James Clifford in *Sulphur* 15 (1986), pp. 38–40.

59

Alberto Giacometti, "Le Palais de quatre heures," *Minotaure* 3–4 (December 1933), p. 46.

60

These objects were produced by others "so I could see them all done, like a projection" ("Entretien avec Alberto Giacometti," in Charles Charbonnier, *Le Monologue du peintre* [Paris, 1959], p. 156.

61

Giacometti, "Le Palais," p. 46. The quotations in the next paragraph are from this text.

62

Giacometti was sometimes suspected of such scripting, in this work in particular. See Reinhold Hohl, *Alberto Giacometti* (London, 1972).

63

In the same issue Dalí credits "the object of symbolic function" to Giacometti (specifically his *Suspended Ball*), which he relates to "clearly characterized erotic fantasies and desires." See "Objets surréalistes," *Le Surréalisme au service de la révolution* 3 (December 1931).

64

Giacometti, "Objets mobiles et muets," pp. 18–19. In a later text, "Le Rêve, le sphinx et la mort de T." (*Labyrinthe* 22–23 [December 15, 1946], pp. 12–13), Giacometti again alludes to the action of memories related in content but distant in time.

65

Giacometti, "Hier, sables mouvants," *Le Surréalisme au service de la révolution* 5 (May 15, 1933), p. 44.

66

Here the passage in "The Uncanny" concerning the maternal body might be recalled (see note 2). Giacometti was very close to his mother Annetta throughout his life, and in his memory it is in fact his father who shows him the cave.

67

Giacometti, "Hier, sables mouvants," p. 44. As experienced in this memory, the uncanny has an auratic aspect, which figures the desire of the mother, as here with the cave, and an anxious aspect, which signals the risk if this desire is acted upon, as here with the rock. A related connection between the uncanny and the auratic, crucial to surrealism, is noted in Miriam Hansen, "Benjamin, Cinema and Experience: 'The Blue Flower in the Land of Technology,'" *New German Critique* 40 (Winter 1987). I discuss the connection further in chapter 7.

68

See "Splitting of the Ego in the Defensive Process" (1938), *in Sexuality and the Psychology of Love,* ed. Philip Rieff (New York, 1963), p. 221. In other texts Freud alters the sequence of these "events" but insists on the necessity of both.

69

I borrow this term from Rosalind Krauss, who addresses a similar question through the Bataillean concept of *alteration.* See her "Giacometti," in William Rubin, ed., *"Primitivism" in 20th Century Art,* vol. 2 (New York, 1984), pp. 503–533. For a formalist analysis of the objects discussed here see Michael Brenson, "The Early Work of Alberto Giacometti: 1925–1935" (Ph.D. dissertation, Johns Hopkins University, 1974).

70

Many feminists have focused on this blind spot, Naomi Schor, Mary Kelly, and Emily Apter prominent among them. The formulation is even more problematic for gay men and lesbians: according to Freud, fetishism is one way to "fend off" homosexuality, and lesbians outstrip fetishists in their disavowal of castration ("Fetishism," *On Sexuality,* p. 352; "Some Psychical Consequences," pp. 336–337).

71

Giacometti, "Letter to Pierre Matisse" (1947), in *Alberto Giacometti,* ed. Peter Selz (New York, 1961), p. 22.

72

Among other things it is able, when dead, to "imitate" death. See Caillois, "Le Mante religieuse," *Minotaure* 5 (February 1934), and Krauss, "Giacometti," pp. 517–

518; also see William Pressley, "The Praying Mantis in Surrealist Art," *Art Bulletin* (December 1973), pp. 600–615. Freud: "These creatures die in the act of reproduction because, after Eros has been eliminated through the process of satisfaction, the death instinct has a free hand for accomplishing its purposes" (*The Ego and the Id,* p. 37).

73

This was recognized by Dalí and recounted by Maurice Nadeau: "This emotion has nothing to do with satisfaction, rather with irritation, the kind provoked by the disturbing perception of a *lack*" (*The History of Surrealism* [1944], trans. Richard Howard [New York, 1965], p. 188). Together the objects are hellish in an almost Dantean way, as if the medieval image of damnation and the psychoanalytical conception of desire were here made one.

74

See Krauss, "Giacometti," pp. 512–514.

75

Ibid. Krauss likens this to the series of ocular forms in *Histoire de l'oeil* (1928), or rather to the Roland Barthes reading of Bataille. See Barthes, "La Métaphore de l'oeil," *Critique* 196 (August–September 1963).

76

Are these terms relevant here to a feminine subject as well? Or is the castration anxiety that seems to deform this object that of a masculine subject alone?

77

These little spikes also allude to "tribal fetishes," and both *Disagreeable Objects* are associated with Oceanic objects (see Krauss, "Giacometti," p. 522): the first with a Marquesan ear ornament, the second with an Easter Island club in the shape of a fish. Moreover, the subtitle of the first, "to be disposed of," suggests not only the ambivalence but also the transience of the tribal ritual object. And the drawing of the second in "Objets mobiles et muets" includes a hand that barely touches it—as in the *prohibition* against touching that Freud regarded as essential to the totem, a taboo that belies a *desire* to touch . . . the penis. In fact, all these objects both attract and repel a tactile impulse. See *Totem and Taboo* (1913; French trans. 1924), trans. James Strachey (New York, 1950).

Giacometti termed some pieces "objets sans base," i.e., objects without a base and/or without value (see Brenson, "The Early Work," p. 168). For Krauss these works perform a rotation to the horizontal crucial to postwar object making. Could this turn to the ground, this double tropism to *bassesse* and baselessness, be partly permitted by a turn to the materiality, to the structure, of the "tribal fetish"?

78

Freud, "Some Psychical Consequences," p. 336.

79

This might be read into *Woman with Her Throat Cut,* partly inspired as it was by a memory of Michel Leiris, "the most painful of all my childhood memories," recounted in *L'Age d'Homme* (1939; trans. by Richard Howard as *Manhood* [San Francisco, 1984], pp. 64–65): "From this moment on I can remember nothing except the sudden assault of the surgeon, who plunged some kind of sharp instrument into my throat, the pain that I felt, and the scream—like that of a slaughtered animal—that I uttered."

80

Giacometti, "Letter to Pierre Matisse." According to Marcel Jean, Giacometti repudiated his surrealist work as so much "masturbation" (cited in Brenson, "The Early Work," p. 190).

81

For Lacan on metaphor and symptom see "The Agency of the Letter in the Unconscious, or Reason since Freud," *Écrits,* trans. Alan Sheridan (New York, 1977), p. 166. For his revisionary relation to the surrealist definition of the image as juxtaposition see pp. 156–157.

82

Compare this more sanguine formulation of the relation between fantasy and art offered by Sarah Kofman as a gloss on Freud: "The work of art is not the projection of a fantasy, but, on the contrary, a substitute which makes possible its structuring after the fact, allowing the artist to free himself from it. The art work is the originary inscription of the analytic method" (*The Childhood of Art,* trans. Winifred Woodhull [New York, 1988], p. 85).

83

On this "tragic" restoration in the early 1920s and its "farcical" repetition in the late 1970s, see Benjamin H. D. Buchloh, "Figures of Authority, Ciphers of Regression," *October* 16 (Spring 1981), pp. 39–68.

84

Michel Foucault, *This Is Not a Pipe* (1963), trans. Richard Miller (Berkeley, 1984).

85

Ibid., p. 16. Also see *Death and the Labyrinth: The World of Raymond Roussel* (1963), trans. Charles Ruas (New York, 1986). For Foucault, Roussel (whom the surrealists of course embraced) performs a transformation in writing complementary to that of Magritte in art. In his 1962 seminar Lacan used the "window paintings" of Magritte to illustrate the structure of fantasy.

86

See my "The Crux of Minimalism," in *Individuals,* ed. Howard Singerman (Los Angeles, 1986). As Deleuze writes, "Between the destruction which conserves and perpetuates the established order of representations, models, and copies, and the destruction of models and copies which sets up a creative chaos, there is a great difference" ("Plato and the Simulacrum," *October* 27 [Winter 1983], p. 56). This "chaos," however, may have its own function in the social field of advanced capitalism—where the delirious and the disciplinary are not mutually exclusive.

87

Deleuze, "Plato and the Simulacrum," p. 49.

88

Ibid.

89

As Deleuze writes of Proust, *"The essential thing in involuntary memory is not resemblance, nor even identity, which are merely conditions, but the internalized difference, which becomes immanent.* It is in this sense that reminiscence is the analogue of art, and involuntary memory the analogue of a metaphor" (*Proust and Signs* [1964], trans. Richard Howard [New York, 1972], p. 59; italics in the original). It may be more accurate to think the surrealist image through this Proustian problematic than through the usual references to Lautréamont, Pierre Reverdy, etc.; certainly Benjamin seems to have thought so. For more on the connections between Freud on trauma, Benjamin on the image, and Deleuze on difference and repetition, see J. Hillis Miller, *Fiction and Repetition* (Cambridge, 1982), pp. 1–21. Also see Cynthia Chase, "Oedipal Textuality: Reading Freud's Reading of *Oedipus*," *Diacritics* 9, no. 1 (Spring 1979), pp. 54–68.

4

Fatal Attraction

1

For biographical information as well as critical analysis see Peter Webb (with Robert Short), *Hans Bellmer* (London, 1985).

2

Bellmer was struck by the 1932 Max Reinhardt production of Offenbach's *Tales of Hoffmann*.

3

Bellmer: "People like me only admit with reluctance the realization that it is those things about which we know nothing that lodge themselves all too firmly in the memory" (cited in Webb, *Hans Bellmer*).

4

Hans Bellmer, *Die Puppe* (Karlsruhe, 1934); unless otherwise noted, all quotations are from this text. I have also drawn on the French translation that Bellmer labored over with Robert Valençay (*La Poupée,* Paris, 1936, n.p.). *Sulfur 26* (Spring 1990) includes an English translation by Peter Chametzky, Susan Felleman, and Jochen Schindler, as well as a reading of the dolls by Therese Lichtenstein that also raises the problem of sadomasochism.

5

Although the doll was already established in the surrealist image repertoire, this publication spurred the use of mannequins by many other surrealists.

6

See Rosalind Krauss, "Corpus Delicti," in *L'Amour fou: Photography and Surrealism* (Washington and New York, 1985), p. 86; also see my "L'Amour faux," *Art in America* (January 1986). Freud briefly discusses such multiplication in relation to the threat of castration in "Medusa's Head" (1922).

7

Bellmer, *Petite anatomie de l'inconscient physique, ou l'Anatomie de l'image* (Paris, 1957), n.p. This text was mostly written during World War II, part of which Bellmer spent interned, along with Ernst, as a German alien in France.

8

The first doll suggests an obsessive fragmentation of a female figure, while the second suggests its compulsive recombination.

9

Cited in Peter Webb, *The Erotic Arts* (Boston, 1975), p. 370. The second doll is "a series of endless anagrams" (Bellmer, *Obliques* [Paris, 1975], p. 109).

10

Roland Barthes, "La Métaphore de l'oeil, *Critique* 196 (August–September 1963). Bellmer illustrated an edition of *Histoire de l'oeil*.

11

Susan Suleiman critiques this Barthesian account on the grounds that its celebration of linguistic violation obscures the narrative of sexual violation—a tendency typical for her of the *Tel Quel* celebration of *écriture*. See her *Subversive Intent* (Harvard, 1990), pp. 72–87.

12

Freud describes how Hans, frustrated by nonanswers to his questions about birth, took "the analysis into his own hands" and, in a "brilliant symptomatic act," ripped open a doll (in *The Sexual Enlightenment of Children,* ed. Philip Rieff [New York, 1963], p. 125). In his *poupées* it is as if this other Hans rehearses sexual curiosity in defiance of its repression or sublimation. Incidentally, in a way somewhat proleptic of Freud, Baudelaire saw this desire of children to "see the soul of their toys" as a "first metaphysical tendency," whose failure is "the beginning of melancholy and gloom" ("A Philosophy of Toys" [1853], in *The Painter of Modern Life and Other Essays,* trans. and ed. Jonathan Mayne [London, 1964], pp. 202–203).

13

Freud, "Some Psychical Consequences of the Anatomical Distinction between the Sexes" (1925), in *On Sexuality,* ed. Angela Richards (Harmondsworth, 1977), p. 336.

14

The second doll appears more fetishistic-scopophilic, its structure one of ambivalence, a recognition-disavowal of castration; while the first doll appears more sadistic-voyeuristic, concerned to reveal, even to persecute, such castration. Bellmer: "I admire de Sade very much, especially his idea that violence towards the loved one can tell us more about the anatomy of desire than the simple act of love" (cited in Webb, *The Erotic Arts,* p. 369).

15

Bellmer, *La Poupée*. An illustration in *Die Puppe* connects this mechanism directly to voyeurism; it shows a disembodied eye, a "conscious gaze [as the text has it] plundering their charms." Paul Foss writes of the second doll: "What is this 'thing' or composite of things but the gaze pulled to pieces by the eyes, an open combinatory of spatial visions?" ("Eyes, Fetishism, and the Gaze," *Art & Text* 20 [1986], p. 37). This remark holds for many of the drawings as well.

16

On this shattering of the subject in sexuality see Leo Bersani, *The Freudian Body: Psychoanalysis and Art* (New York, 1986), pp. 29–50.

17

For Bellmer this "erotic liberation" (Webb, *Hans Bellmer*, p. 34) is that of the dolls as well: a "breaking down [of] the wall separating woman and her image" *(Petite anatomie)*. Of course, in some feminist theory it is precisely this presumed proximity of the woman to her image that is problematic. See Mary Anne Doane, "Film and the Masquerade—Theorising the Female Spectator," *Screen* 23, no. 3–4 (September/October 1982).

18

Bellmer cited in Webb, *Hans Bellmer*, p. 38.

19

Bellmer in the exhibition catalogue for "Le Surréalisme en 1947" at the Galerie Maeght (Paris, 1947).

20

On the sadomasochistic basis of sexuality see Jean Laplanche, *Life and Death in Psychoanalysis,* trans. Jeffrey Mehlman (Baltimore, 1976), pp. 85–102, and Bersani, *The Freudian Body,* pp. 29–50. Laplanche traces three related routes through this tangled terrain depending on which moment in the Freudian corpus is privileged.

21

See Freud, "The Economic Problem in Masochism" (1924). For the use of this concept in the problematization of masculinity, see in particular the recent work of Kaja Silverman, especially her "Masochism and Male Subjectivity," *Camera Obscura* 17 (May 1988), pp. 31–67.

22

Bellmer cited in Webb, *Hans Bellmer*, p. 177.

23

Such a masochistic identification is also suggested by another origin story about the *poupées:* that they were partly inspired by the ravaged Christ of the Grünewald altarpiece in Isenheim.

24

For an extended analysis of these conceptions see my "Armor Fou," *October* 56 (Spring 1991).

25

Freud, *The Ego and the Id,* trans. James Strachey (London, 1960), p. 35. Also see Melanie Klein, "Infantile Anxiety Situations Reflected in a Work of Art and in the Creative Process" (1929), in *The Selected Melanie Klein,* ed. Juliet Mitchell (Harmondsworth, 1986).

26

As sexual, indeed perverse, as low, indeed base, these drives are associated with cultural types, which are thus placed outside the process of sublimation, of civilization, either as its other or as its object: in developmental terms the association is made with the child and "the primitive," in sexual and social terms with the woman (always resistant to civilization in Freud), the proletarian, the Jew, and so on. In this patently Euro-bourgeois projection, these types are then regarded ambivalently—as vulgar and vicious but also as vigorous and vital. In the first "conservative" instance (sublimation proper) the vulgar low is refined into the sophisticated high, while in the second "progressive" instance (countersublimation may be the more accurate term) the etiolated high is reinvigorated by the carnal low. However opposed, both these instances posit a low sexual term to be elevated, indeed sublated, into a high civilization one. For preliminary investigations of this ideological system see my "Armor Fou," *October* 56 (Spring 1991), and "'Primitive' Scenes," *Critical Inquiry* (Autumn 1993).

27

In "Recherches sur la sexualité" (*La Révolution surréaliste* 12 [March 15, 1928]) Breton admits only to a little fetishism, while he abominates other practices, especially homosexuality (the discussion included early Bretonian surrealists, e.g., Aragon, Boiffard, Morse, Naville, Péret, Queneau, Man Ray, Tanguy). Is it too facile to suggest that this homophobia is defensive? Much work needs to be done on the homosocial basis of such avant-gardes as the surrealists.

28

Breton disputes Freud before the fact, as it were, since he could not have read *Civilization and Its Discontents* (1930) at the time, which was translated only in 1934. He may have celebrated transgression in his *L'Age d'or* text in part to outflank Bataille. The relation between the sublime and sublimation is a leitmotif of much recent criticism, often articulated in response to the work of Jean-François Lyotard.

29

Breton, *Manifestoes of Surrealism,* trans. Richard Seaver and Helen R. Lane (Ann Arbor, 1972), pp. 123–124; hereafter cited in the text as M.

30

Georges Bataille, *Literature and Evil* (1957), trans. Alastair Hamilton (London, 1973), p. 15; *The Tears of Eros* (1961), trans. Peter Connor (San Francisco, 1989), p. 207; *Erotism* (1957), trans. Mary Dalwood (San Francisco, 1986); *Story of the Eye* (1928), trans. Joachim Neugroschel (New York, 1977), p. 38. The best account of Bataillean thought (to which I am indebted here) is that of Denis Hollier, *La Prise de la Concorde* (Paris, 1974), translated by Betsy Wing as *Against Architecture* (Cambridge, 1989). On these matters in particular see pp. 104–112.

31

Breton: "By their very nature those individuals who are drawn to Surrealism are especially interested in the Freudian concept . . . I mean the definition of the phenomenon known as sublimation." In a note he opposes this directly to regression (M 160). On this point, then, Elisabeth Roudinesco is only partly correct when she writes that "Breton reversed the [Freudian] problematic, rejected sublimation, and situated art in a morbid machination" (*Jacques Lacan & Co.,* trans. Jeffrey Mehlman [Chicago, 1990], p. 16).

32

On this reaction-formation (which suffuses the "Second Manifesto" and several other Breton texts besides), see Freud, "Character and Anal Erotism" (1908), in *On Sexuality*. This text also includes a discussion of sublimation, but, again, not in clear distinction from reaction-formation.

33

Bataille, "The 'Old Mole' and the Prefix *Sur* in the Words *Surhomme* and *Surrealist*" (1929–1930?), in *Visions of Excess: Selected Writings, 1927–1939,* trans. and ed. Allan Stoekl (Minneapolis, 1985), p. 42; hereafter cited in the text as V.

34

Bataille, "L'Esprit moderne et le jeu des transpositions," *Documents* 8 (1930). Hollier glosses this Bataillean project in this way: "Awaken perverse desire to counter neurotic cultural sublimation" (*Against Architecture*, p. 112).

35

Bataille, "L'Art primitif," *Documents* 7 (1930).

36

See Bataille, "Sacrificial Mutilation and the Severed Ear of Vincent van Gogh," in *Visions of Excess*.

37

Bataille, "L'Art primitif."

38

Bellmer: "I agree with Georges Bataille that eroticism relates to a knowledge of evil and the inevitability of death" (cited in Webb, *The Erotic Arts,* p. 369).

39

For example, in a Hegelian mode Bataille speaks of the "agony of the discontinuous creature" (*Erotism,* p. 140; hereafter cited in the text as E).

40

Although Bataille nowhere cites *Beyond the Pleasure Principle* in *Erotism,* it is difficult not to hear an echo of the death drive theory there: eroticism as a return to the continuity of death, a transgressive move that is also entropic. (Implicitly Bataille "corrects" Freud: the death drive is not general to life but specific to humans.)

41

Such is the fascist type outlined by Klaus Theweleit in *Male Fantasies* (1977–1978), 2 vols., trans. S. Conway, E. Carter, and C. Turner (Minneapolis, 1987–1989).

42

Of course, this distinction is not so clear: as is often argued of pornography, representations and fantasies can be performative too.

43

Walter Benjamin, *Passagen-Werk,* ed. Rolf Tiedemann (Frankfurt, 1982), pp. 465–466. Contrast Bellmer: "I want to reveal scandalously the interior that will always remain hidden and sensed behind the successive layers of a human structure and its lost unknowns" *(Petite anatomie).*

44

Theodor W. Adorno and Max Horkheimer, *Dialectic of Enlightenment* (1944), trans. John Cumming (New York, 1972), p. 235. "Those who extolled the body above all else," they add, "the gymnasts and scouts, always had the closest affinity with killing, just as the lovers of nature are close to the hunter." Adorno and Horkheimer also touch upon the masochistic aspect of this sadism.

45

Jean Brun, "Désir et réalité dans l'oeuvre de Hans Bellmer," in Bellmer, *Obliques;* also cited in Christian Jelenski, *Les Dessins de Hans Bellmer* (Paris, 1966), p. 7. That behind the fantasm of the castrative woman avenged in the dolls lurks the figure of a castrative father is suggested by the fact that they were partly inspired by *The Tales of Hoffmann.* For Freud, who, again, glosses one such tale ("The Sandman") in "The Uncanny," associations of castration and fetishism cluster around the doll Olympia (or in the operetta Coppellia), but behind her lurks Coppellius, the evil father figure. More generally in Freud, the threat of castration may be posed for the male subject by the female body, but it is only guaranteed, as it were, by the paternal figure (see "Splitting of the Ego in the Defensive Process" [1938], in *On Sexuality*).

46

From a 1964 letter from Bellmer to Herta Hausmann cited in Webb, *Hans Bellmer,* p. 162.

47

Janine Chasseguet-Smirgel, *Creativity and Perversion* (New York, 1984), p. 2. My understanding of this Bellmerian perversion—which is close to Bataillean eroticism— is influenced by this text, which also includes a brief discussion of Bellmer (pp. 20– 22). Bellmer: "To an extent [the dolls] represented an attempt to reject the horrors of adult life as it was, in favour of a return to the wonders of childhood" (cited in Webb, *Hans Bellmer,* p. 34).

48

Chasseguet-Smirgel, *Creativity and Perversion,* p. 78.

49

Theweleit, *Male Fantasies,* vol. 1, p. 418.

50

The effects of the trauma of the World War I dead and wounded on the postwar imagination of the body are not yet fully appreciated. This damaged body is magically restored in some classicisms, aggressively prostheticized in others. In some postwar modernisms it seems repressed; in others—i.e., surrealism—this repressed damaged male body seems to return as an uncanny dismembered female body. For an account of parts of this problematic, see Kenneth E. Silver, *Esprit de Corps: The Art of the Parisian Avant-Garde and the First World War, 1914–1925* (Princeton, 1989).

51

Bellmer: "It is a question of the peculiar hermaphrodite interconnection between the male and the female principles in which the female structure predominates. What is always vital is that the image of the woman must have been 'lived' (experienced) by the man in his own body before it can be 'seen' by the man" *(Petite anatomie)*. In *Petite anatomie* Bellmer discusses what his dolls and drawings perform: different displacements and superimpositions of male and female organs and limbs, sometimes in difficult articulations, sometimes in dangerous dissolutions.

52

J. Benjamin and A. Rabinbach, "Foreword", in Theweleit, *Male Fantasies,* vol. 2, p. xix.

53

Bellmer: "If the origin of my work is scandalous, it is because, for me, the world is a scandal" (cited in Webb, *Hans Bellmer,* p. 42).

54

For an extended review of these problems see my "Armor Fou."

55

Susan Suleiman: "Why is it a woman who embodies most fully the paradoxical combination of pleasure and anguish that characterizes transgression?" *(Subversive Intent,* pp. 82–83). This points to a double bind noted in chapter 2: that attacks on sublimatory beauty as figured by the feminine may simply lead to a desublimatory sublime that it also figured by the feminine.

56

Bellmer: "Man in that which I appear, I am woman in my physiological horizon, in my amorous vocation" (cited in Webb, *Hans Bellmer,* p. 143).

5

Exquisite Corpses

1

Walter Benjamin, "Surrealism: The Last Snapshot of the European Intelligentsia" (1929), in *Reflections: Essays, Aphorisms, Autobiographical Writings,* ed. Peter Demetz, trans. Edmund Jephcott (New York, 1978), p. 181; and "Paris—the Capital of the Nineteenth Century" (1935), in *Charles Baudelaire: A Lyric Poet in the Age of High Capitalism,* trans. Harry Zohn and Quintin Hoare (London, 1973), p. 176.

2

This is possible because of the liminal status of each to the other: "The impression of the old-fashioned can only come to be where, in a certain way, it is effected by the most contemporary" (Benjamin, *Das Paggagen-Werk,* ed. Rolf Tiedemann [Frankfurt am Main, 1982], p. 118; hereafter cited in the text as PW). Conversely: "All these products [i.e., the outmoded] are on the point of entering the market as commodities. But they still linger on the threshold" (Benjamin, "Paris—the Capital of the Nineteenth Century," p. 176). On this point also see Susan Buck-Morss, *The Dialectics of Seeing* (Cambridge, 1989), pp. 67, 116.

3

E.g.: "Capital is dead labour which, vampire-like, lives only by sucking up living labour, and lives the more, the more labour it sucks" (*Capital,* vol. 1, trans. Ben Fowkes [New York, 1977], p. 342). An extraordinary anthology of this demonic reception was assembled by Humphrey Jennings, an English associate of the surrealists, in *Pandaemonium: The Coming of the Machine as Seen by Contemporary Observers, 1660–1886,* ed. Mary-Lou Jennings and Charles Madge (New York, 1985). This infernal reading of the machine is the dialectical other of its utopian reception, which surrealism, unlike contemporary machinist modernisms, rejected. For an account of a demonic reception of the commodity outside Europe, see Michael T. Taussig, *The Devil and Commodity Fetishism in South America* (Chapel Hill, 1980).

4

Of course, the surrealists do not have a monopoly on these figures; e.g., they inherit some from dada and share others with Neue Sachlichkeit.

5

In a letter of February 29, 1940, Adorno related aura to this "forgotten human residue in things," and in his reply of May 7, 1940, Benjamin questioned this reformulation. See the important essay by Miriam Hansen, "Benjamin, Cinema and Experience: 'The Blue Flower in the Land of Technology,'" *New German Critique* 40 (Winter 1987). Also see Marleen Stoessel, *Aura, das vergessene Menschliche: Zu Sprache und Erfahrung bei Walter Benjamin* (Munich, 1983), as well as Fredric Jameson, *Marxism and Form* (Princeton, 1971), pp. 95–106. I return to this question in chapter 6.

6

Benjamin, "On Some Motifs in Baudelaire" (1939), in *Illuminations,* ed. Hannah Arendt, trans. Harry Zohn (New York, 1969), p. 194.

7

André Breton, "Introduction sur le peu de la réalité" (1924), translated as "Introduction to the Discourse on the Paucity of Reality," in *What Is Surrealism? Selected Writings,* ed. Franklin Rosemont (New York, 1978), here p. 26.

8

Ibid. Breton sees such objects as "gifts"—which suggests a whole other form of exchange than that of commodities. The great Marcel Mauss essay on the gift, *Essai sur le don, forme archaïque de l'échange,* so important to Bataillean surrealists, was published in 1925.

9

See Breton, "Crise de l'objet," *Cahiers d'Art* (Paris, 1936). However, even by this time, with the famous exhibition at the Charles Ratton Gallery and the special issue of *Cahiers d'Art,* the surrealist object had begun to be both commercialized and academicized.

10

Sigmund Freud, "The Uncanny" (1919), in *Studies in Parapsychology,* ed. Philip Rieff (New York, 1963), p. 31.

11

Freud is somewhat critical of the first notion advanced by E. Jentsch in a paper titled "Zur Psychologie des Unheimlichen," but this critique mostly serves to open up his own conception, in which the indistinction between the animate and the inanimate remains important precisely as an uncanny reminder of compulsion and death.

12

This might hold for the uncanny in gothic literature too. For a provocative account of Frankenstein as a figure of the dismembered worker and Dracula as a figure of vampirish capital, see Franco Moretti, "Dialectic of Fear," in *Signs Taken for Wonders* (London, 1983).

13

Marx, *Capital,* vol. 1, p. 165.

14

See ibid., pp. 544–564, especially pp. 548–549. On the paradigm shift from the eighteenth-century machine to the nineteenth-century motor, see the important work of Anson Rabinbach, *The Human Motor* (New York, 1990), especially pp. 56–61.

15

Satire often mocks the human through its reduction to the mechanical. In *Le Rire* (1900) Bergson relates the comic to a substitution of the artificial for the natural, to a mechanization of life. In his book on jokes (1905) Freud relates this mechanization to psychic automatism: the comic has to do with its uncovering. Both observations point to the satirical aspect of the surrealist critique of the mechanical-commodified. (A 1929 issue of *Variétés* edited by Breton and Aragon included a translation of the 1928 Freud essay on humor.)

16

Péret, "Au paradis des fantômes," *Minotaure* 3–4 (December 14, 1933), p. 35. Most of the images are drawn from *Le Monde des automates: Étude historique et technique* (Paris, 1928) by Edouard Gelis and Alfred Chapuis, a compilation that may attest to a more general interest in this subject at the time.

17

Ibid. For the conceptual differences between the automaton and the robot see Jean Baudrillard, *Simulations* (New York, 1983). One is tempted to suggest a genealogy of such figures—from the automaton or machine-as-(wo)man, to the human motor or Taylorist robot, to the cyborg or biotech changeling of our own time.

18

Descartes, *The Meditations Concerning First Philosophy*, VI, in *Descartes: Philosophical Essays*, trans. Laurence J. Lafleur (Indianapolis, 1964), p. 138. An important difference between Descartes in *Description du corps humain* (1648), say, and La Mettrie in *L'Homme machine* is that the first still posits a creator "behind" the body while the second does not. In this brief summary I am indebted to the aforementioned text of Rabinbach, as well as to Hugh Kenner, *The Counterfeiters* (Garden City, N.Y., 1973), and Andreas Huyssen, "The Vamp and the Machine: Fritz Lang's *Metropolis*," in *After the Great Divide* (Bloomington, 1986).

19

Michel Foucault, *Discipline and Punish*, trans. Alan Sheridan (New York, 1977), p. 136. "Not the automaton, but the concept of counterfeitable man, was the age's characterizing achievement," Kenner argues. "On such a man—man only empirically known—rationality is impressed from all directions, from his language, from his work, from his machines. He is installed not amidst a Creation but in a system: in many systems, simultaneous systems" (*The Counterfeiters*, p. 27).

20

For Ure see *The Philosophy of Manufactures* (London, 1835), where he describes the ideal factory as "a vast automaton composed of various mechanical and intellectual organs" (p. 13). For Marx, who uses the same trope in an opposite polemic, see *Capital,* vol. 1, chs. 14 and 15. In 1911 Frederick Taylor writes in *Principles of Scientific Management* (New York, 1967): "The first impression is that this makes [the worker] a mere automaton" (p. 125).

21

Huyssen, "The Vamp and the Machine," p. 70. Again, I am indebted to Huyssen here.

22

This formula no doubt elides a third term, the proletarian masses, the threat of which may be associated in the psyche of the bourgeois male, in a classic instance of overdetermination, with machine and woman alike.

23

Here see Huyssen, "Mass Culture as Woman," also in *After the Great Divide,* pp. 44–62. Glossed in pop, this association only persists, indeed intensifies, throughout the twentieth century.

24

For example, in a short text, "L'Ombre de l'inventeur," Aragon describes his "feeling of panic" before the annual displays of technical inventions at the Concours Lépine (to which he nonetheless compulsively returns), and urges that this uncanniness be simulated in objects that "escape all reasoning" (*La Révolution surréaliste* 1 [December 1, 1924]).

25

Whereas the ragpicker marked "where the limit of human misery lay," the prostitute posed provocative questions concerning sexuality and class, objectification and exploitation (Benjamin, "The Paris of the Second Empire in Baudelaire," in *Baudelaire,* p. 19). On these identifications, see Susan Buck-Morss, "The Flâneur, the Sandwichman and the Whore: The Politics of Loitering," *New German Critique* 39 (Fall 1986), pp. 99–140. Such identifications presuppose access to the public spaces of modernity, access largely limited to male artists of a certain class. For this critique see Griselda Pollock, "Modernity and the Spaces of Femininity," in *Vision and Difference: Femininity, Feminism, and Histories of Art* (London, 1988). The literature on the figure of the prostitute in nineteenth-century art and literature is enormous. Among the best recent texts are T. J. Clark, *The Painting of Modern Life* (New York, 1984); Alain Corbin, *Women for Hire: Prostitution and Sexuality in France after 1850* (Cambridge, 1992); Charles Bernheimer, *Figures of Ill Repute: Representing Prostitution in Nineteenth-Century France* (Cambridge, 1991); and Hollis Clayson, *Painted Love: Prostitution in French Art of the Imperial Era* (New Haven, 1991).

26

"The refuse concerns both," Benjamin writes, and both emerge at a time "when the new industrial processes had given refuse a certain value" ("The Paris of the Second Empire," pp. 80, 19). Are postmodernist *pasticheurs* any different from modernist *bricoleurs* in this ambiguous recuperation of cultural materials cast aside by capitalist society?

27

Benjamin, "Paris—the Capital of the Nineteenth Century," pp. 170–171. In "The Paris of the Second Empire" Benjamin quotes an early Baudelaire poem addressed to a prostitute: "Pour avoir des souliers, elle a vendu son âme;/ Mais le bon Dieu rirait si, près de cette infâme,/ Je trenchais du tartufe et singeais la hauteur,/ Moi qui vends ma pensée et qui veux être auteur" (p. 34). Such identifications are especially problematic when they efface the sexual specificity of prostitution, and/or reduce its exploitation to that of labor. Here Benjamin is preceded by Marx, e.g.: "Prostitution is only a *specific* expression of the *universal* prostitution of the worker" ("Economic and Philosophical Manuscripts" [1844], in *Early Writings,* ed. R. B. Bottomore [New York, 1964], p. 156.

28

Louis Aragon, *Le Paysan de Paris* (Paris, 1926), translated by Simon Watson Taylor as *Paris Peasant* (London, 1971), p. 66; Breton, *Nadja* (Paris, 1928), trans. Richard Howard (New York, 1960), p. 152. Breton saw this figure at the Musée Grevin, a wax museum haunted by the surrealists. In this gaze he seems to intuit a connection between desire and threat, sexuality and death.

29

See Michel Carrouges, *Les Machines célibataires* (Paris, 1954); also Harald Szeemann, ed., *Junggesellenmaschinen/Les Machines célibataires* (Venice, 1975). Here the important precedents are more immediate than Baudelaire and Manet—Duchamp and Picabia above all, but also Roussel, Jarry, Lautréamont, Verne, and Villiers de l'Isle-Adam.

There are at least two complements of these figures in other art of the 1920s and 1930s, the clown and the puppet, which Benjamin Buchloh has read in allegorical terms: "If the first icon appears in the context of the carnival and the circus as masquerades of alienation from present history, the second appears on the stage set of reification" ("Figures of Authority, Ciphers of Regression," *October* 16 [Spring 1981], p. 53.

30

Benjamin, "Paris—the Capital of the Nineteenth Century," p. 166. On this point see Rey Chow, "Benjamin's Love Affair with Death," *New German Critique* 48 (Fall 1989): "The figure of woman . . . is the ultimate figure of death. The beauty of woman is the surreal beauty of an organ which is severed, embellished, and only thus 'enlivened'. In the *elaborate* way in which the prostitute is invested with attention, a process of *labor* is involved: that of re-organizing the dis-organ-ized" (p. 85).

31

In a capitalist society nothing is automatically safe from commodity status: in order to be exchanged, objects, images, even people must be processed through a code of equivalence, of indifference. This indifference is apparent in art by the moment of Baudelaire and Manet at least; it is central to the modernism of each. For even as the artist was delivered up to the market during this time, he also began to recoup its disruptions—to turn its new sensorium into new rhetorical figures and formal procedures. By the moment of surrealism, however, the (ir)rationality of the market could no longer be mediated only within given forms of art. And the (ir)rational juxtapositions of surrealist images and objects might be seen as partial attempts to come to terms with this new capitalist (sur)reality. Of course, the modern subversion of subject matter cannot be reduced to this economic process, but neither can it be seen apart from it, as the surrealists knew. For example, in *La Révolution surréaliste* 12 (December 12, 1929) André Thirion published a short text "Note sur l'argent" that argued the abstractive power of money as "instrument de bouleversements inouïs des conditions d'existence de l'homme" (p. 24).

32

This is one reason why many surrealists saw Grandville (1803–1847) as a precursor, the great illustrator who, 100 years before surrealism, used animal-human combinations and inversions to reflect on the mechanization of art and the commodification of society under capitalism. "Grandville's fantasies transmitted commodity-character onto the universe," Benjamin writes in "Paris—the Capital of the Nineteenth Century" (p. 166). Also see Buck-Morss, *The Dialectics of Seeing,* pp. 154–155.

33

Some of the artists were surrealists or surrealist associates (e.g., the Belgian E. L. T. Mesens, André Kertesz); others were not (e.g., Germaine Krull, Herbert Bayer). Edited by P.-G. van Hecke, *Variétés* published on fashion, movies, and sports as well as on art, poetry, and prose—all as so many entertainments.

34

The surrealists often performed this reversal (e.g., "La Vérité sur les colonies," a surrealist counterexhibition to the infamous Colonial Exhibition of 1931, included a display of Western folk objects labeled "Fétiches européens"). Indeed, beyond Marx and Freud they made fetishism a positive value. Its privitivist associations, however, were not recoded; on the contrary.

35

For Benjamin the sandwichman is "the last incarnation" of the flâneur—a human become commodity who, like the prostitute, "takes the concept of being-for-sale itself for a walk" (PW 562). Again see Buck-Morss, "The Flâneur, the Sandwichman and the Whore," p. 107.

36

In the play a race of robots produced as cheap labor seize their factory, overwhelm their makers, and eventually destroy humankind. The allegory of the satire is clear; the politics are less so.

37

The gas mask is "the only truly authentic modern mask," Georges Limbour remarked, precisely because it threatens to make us all "ghosts in absolutely identical masks with no semblance of a human trait" ("Eschyle, le carnaval et les civilisés," *Documents* 2, 2nd year [1930], pp. 97–102; translated in *October* 60 [Spring 1992]).

38

This sociologization may seem ridiculous to the psychoanalytically rigorous, but Freud admitted its possibility in the sense that he protested against it—especially any biographical or historical contextualization of the death drive.

39

For Carrouges, the essential function of the bachelor machine is "to transform life into a mechanism of death" (*Junggesellenmaschinen/Les Machines célibataires,* p. 21). In the surrealist coupling of the machine and the commodity, the sewing machine and the umbrella, the automaton and the mannequin, the bachelor machine may assume its uncanniest form.

40

On parody in Paris dada see Buchloh, "Parody and Pastiche in Picabia, Pop and Polke," *Artforum* (March 1982), pp. 28–34.

41

Popova quoted in Christina Lodder, *Russian Constructivism* (New Haven, 1983), p. 173.

42

See Fernand Léger, "The Machine Aesthetic: The Manufactured Object, the Artist and the Artisan" (1924), in *Functions of Painting,* ed. Edward F. Fry, trans. Alexandra Anderson (New York, 1973), pp. 52–61.

43

Léger, "The Origins of Painting" (1913) and "The Spectacle: Light, Color, Moving Image, Object-Spectacle," in *Functions of Painting,* pp. 10, 37, 35, 36. His own film *Ballet mécanique* (1924), a celebration of machine vision, montages fragmented female bodies with machine parts: "The thighs of fifty girls, rotating in disciplined formation, shown as a close-up—that is beautiful and *that is objectivity*" (Léger, "Ballet mécanique" [c. 1924], in *Functions,* p. 51). His interest in the mechanical-commodified extended to its perceptual effects (if not, obviously enough, to its gendered ones).

44

"To encompass Breton and Le Corbusier," Benjamin writes in the *Passagen-Werk,* "that would mean drawing the spirit of present-day France like a bow and shooting knowledge to the heart of the moment" (Konvolut N 1a, 5; translated by Leigh Hafrey and Richard Sieburth as "N [Theoretics of Knowledge; Theory of Progress]," *The Philosophical Forum* 15, no. 1–2 [Fall/Winter 1983–1984], p. 4). Again this map is partial; there are several other absent terms, such as the different fascist attitudes to the machine, specifically the armoring of the body embraced by Marinetti, Wyndham Lewis, Jünger, and many others, discussed in chapter 4.

45

Roger Caillois, "Spécification de la poésie," *Le Surréalisme au service de la révolution* 5 (May 15, 1933). The surrealists detected this modern dialectic of reason and unreason in the everyday object, "the irrational knowledge" of which they examined collectively in texts, inquiries, and exhibitions (see, for example, "Recherches expérimentales," *Le Surréalisme au service de la révolution 6* [May 15, 1933]).

46

Jean Baudrillard, "Design and Environment, or How Political Economy Escalates into Cyberblitz," in *For a Critique of the Political Economy of the Sign,* ed. Charles Levin (St. Louis, 1981), p. 194. Conversely, if it takes up the modern object after it has become purely functional, it pushes this functionality to an irrational extreme—once again to release its "subjectivity."

47

Theodor Adorno, "Looking Back on Surrealism" (1954), in *Notes to Literature,* vol. 1, trans. Shierry Weber Nicholsen (New York, 1991), pp. 89–90.

48

In *Mechanization Takes Command: A Contribution to Anonymous History* (London, 1948), Sigfried Giedion, a friend of the surrealists, dates "the time of full mechanization" to 1918–1939, a period that surrealism spans; "around 1920, mechanization involves the 'domestic sphere' as well" (p. 42). This says nothing of the culture of spectacle that Guy Debord also dates to this period (e.g., the profusion of radio and advertising, the development of sound film and television). For a useful overview of these developments see James R. Beniger, *The Control Revolution: Technological and Economic Origins of the Information Society* (Harvard, 1986).

49

Georg Lukács, "Reification and the Consciousness of the Proletariat," *History and Class Consciousness,* trans. Rodney Livingstone (Cambridge, 1971), pp. 91–92. "In the first place, the mathematical analysis of work-processes denotes a break with the organic, irrational and qualitatively determined unity of the product. . . . In the second place, this fragmentation of the object of production necessarily entails the fragmentation of its subject" (pp. 88–90). Modernist art history has still not developed the insights of this significant, problematic text—especially its remarks on "the contemplative stance" produced in the industrial process, which, according to Lukács, "reduces space and time to a common denominator and degrades time to the dimension of space."

50

Benjamin, "On Some Motifs in Baudelaire," p. 175.

51

Giedion, *Mechanization Takes Command,* p. 42.

52

Ibid., p. 8.

53

Michel Beaud, *A History of Capitalism,* trans. Tom Dickman and Anny Lefebvre (New York, 1983), p. 148. I draw most of the information in this paragraph from this text.

54

E.g., revolts in Tunisia in 1920–1921 and in Morocco in 1925–1926, which the surrealists openly supported (see "La Révolution d'abord et toujours," *La Révolution surréaliste* 5 [October 15, 1925]; at Yen Bay and in Indochina in 1930–1931.

55

Merrheim and other French labor activists as quoted by Beaud, *A History of Capitalism,* p. 147. Of course, the capitalist position was that only through such technologization could the conflict between labor and capital be resolved.

56

Marx, *Capital,* vol. 1, p. 527.

57

Henry L. Gantt, another important advocate of scientific management, in a 1910 statement cited in Harry Braverman, *Labor and Monopoly Capital* (New York, 1974), p. 171. Braverman characterizes Taylor as an "obsessive-compulsive personality" (p. 92). The surrealists would have loved it!

58

Lukács, "Reification and the Consciousness of the Proletariat," p. 89; his italics.

59

Benjamin, letter of December 9, 1938 (to Adorno), in *Aesthetics and Politics,* trans. and ed. Rodney Livingstone et al. (London, 1977), p. 140; Adorno and Horkheimer, *Dialectic of Enlightenment* (1944), trans. John Cumming (New York, 1972), p. 137. In "The Automatic Message" (1933) Breton writes: "such curiosity testifies, at least for the first part of the century, to a general need of the sensibility" (in *What Is Surrealism?,* ed. Franklin Rosemont [New York, 1978], p. 100).

60

In "Le Cadavre exquis, son exaltation" (Galerie Nina Dausset, Paris, 1948), Breton remarks that the effect of exquisite corpse drawings was "to bring anthropomorphism to its climax." Is this to imply that the human form is somehow achieved only if it becomes disarranged—that it climaxes only if it comes, is corpsed, or is recombined like some machine? Might all these possibilities somehow converge in such bachelor machines?

61

This gendered ambivalence, this sexed oscillation between technophilia and technophobia, is still very evident today.

6

OUTMODED SPACES

1

For a critique of this redemptive impulse see Leo Bersani, *The Culture of Redemption* (Cambridge, 1990), especially his chastening remarks on Benjamin, pp. 48–63.

2

Adorno regarded surrealist art as reified, fetishistic, undialectical, and Brecht argued that it does "not return back again from estrangement." At times Benjamin also worried about his "fatal proximity" to surrealism. See Susan Buck-Morss, *The Origin of Negative Dialectics: Theodor W. Adorno, Walter Benjamin and the Frankfurt Institute* (New York, 1977), p. 128.

3

Walter Benjamin, "Surrealism: The Last Snapshot of the European Intelligentsia" (1929), in *Reflections,* ed. Peter Demetz, trans. Edmund Jephcott (New York, 1978), pp. 181–182. Benjamin thought of his Arcades Project, the *Passagen-Werk,* as "the philosophical utilization of surrealism" in which "the montage principle [is carried] over into history" (*Passagen-Werk,* ed. Rolf Tiedemann [Frankfurt am Main, 1982], p. 575; hereafter cited as PW).

4

Miriam Hansen, "Benjamin, Cinema and Experience: 'The Blue Flower in the Land of Technology,'" *New German Critique* 40 (Winter 1987), p. 194.

5

Benjamin: "Every generation experiences the fashion of the most recent past as the most thorough anti-aphrodisiac that can be imagined" (PW 130). There are many instances of the surrealist *démodé;* two convenient examples are found in *Minotaure* 3–4 (December 14, 1933), a celebration by Dalí of art nouveau and an assemblage by Eluard of naughty postcards from the turn of the century. Both fly in the face of a vanguardist modernism.

6

On this issue see (among others) Maurice Nadeau, *Histoire du surréalisme* (1944), translated by Richard Howard as *The History of Surrealism* (New York, 1965), pp. 127–182, and Herbert S. Gershman, *The Surrealist Revolution in France* (Ann Arbor, 1969), pp. 80–116.

7

André Breton, *Nadja* (Paris, 1928), trans. Richard Howard (New York, 1960), p. 52. The outmoded has a historicity too; in *L'Amour fou* Breton speaks of "the constant and deep transformation of the flea market" (*Mad Love,* trans. Mary Ann Caws [Lincoln, 1987], p. 26; hereafter cited in the text as AF).

8

Here the outmoded must be distinguished from the readymade: the first is chosen out of desire, the second in putative indifference; the first confronts the hierarchies of art synchronically, the second diachronically. (On a related distinction between surrealist and dadaist objects see chapter 2.)

9

This is not to suggest that these objects cannot be recuperated in turn.

10

Walter Benjamin, "Paris—the Capital of the Nineteenth Century," in *Charles Baudelaire: A Lyric Poet in the Era of High Capitalism,* trans. Harry Zohn and Quintin Hoare (London, 1973), p. 176; translation modified.

11

Benjamin, PW 572. For a translation of Konvolut N ("N [Theoretics of Knowledge; Theory of Progress]") see *Philosophical Forum* 15, no. 1–2 (Fall/Winter 1983–84), here p. 3.

12

See Adorno, "Looking Back on Surrealism," in *Notes to Literature,* vol. 1, ed. Rolf Tiedemann, trans. Shierry Weber Nicholsen (New York, 1991), p. 222.

13

Benjamin, "Surrealism," p. 182.

14

Benjamin, "Theses on the Philosophy of History," in *Illuminations*, ed. Hannah Arendt, trans. Harry Zohn (New York, 1969), p. 261. This idea of destitution recouped as nihilism may be glossed in a prior thesis, which states that the revolutionary strength of the working class is "nourished by the image of enslaved ancestors rather than that of liberated grandchildren" (p. 260).

15

For the nonsynchronous see Ernst Bloch, *Heritage of Our Times*, trans. Neville and Stephan Plaice (Berkeley, 1991). Its most important section (written in May 1932) was translated by Mark Ritter as "Nonsynchronism and the Obligation to Its Dialectics," *New German Critique* 11 (September 1977); on occasion I use this translation. The diverse notions of the outmoded (Benjamin), the nonsynchronous (Bloch), the residual and the emergent (Raymond Williams), and cultural revolution (Fredric Jameson) all elaborate on the historical dynamic sketched by Marx in "Preface" to *A Contribution to the Critique of Political Economy* (1859).

16

Breton, "Manifesto of Surrealism" (1924), in *Manifestoes of Surrealism*, trans. Richard Seaver and Helen R. Lane (Ann Arbor, 1969), p. 16. The term "image sphere" appears in the 1928 Benjamin text on surrealism.

17

"Aragon persistently remains in the realm of dreams, but we want here to find the constellation of waking. . . . Of course, that can only happen through the awakening of a knowledge of the past that is not yet conscious" (PW 571–572; "N [Theoretics of Knowledge]," pp. 2–3). Here Benjamin defends against surrealist influence, for his image of history as a dialectic of dreaming and waking is thoroughly surrealist.

18

Breton, *Surrealism and Painting*, trans. Simon Watson Taylor (New York, 1972).

19

Benjamin, PW 1214. Also see Susan Buck-Morss, *The Dialectics of Seeing: Walter Benjamin and the Arcades Project* (Cambridge, 1989), p. 261.

20

Benjamin, "On Some Motifs in Baudelaire," in *Illuminations*, p. 186. As I will suggest in chapter 7, the Benjaminian definition of aura recalls the Marxian definition of commodity fetishism precisely in order to oppose the alienated distance of the latter with the maternal intimacy of the former. See Marleen Stoessel, *Aura, das vergessene Menschliche: Zu Sprache und Erfahrung bei Walter Benjamin* (Munich, 1983), as well as Hansen, "Benjamin, Cinema and Experience." Fredric Jameson: "Thus what prepares these [outmoded] products to receive the investment of psychic energy characteristic of their use by Surrealism is precisely the half-sketched, uneffaced mark of human labor, of the human gesture, on them; they are still frozen gesture, not yet completely separated from subjectivity, and remain therefore as mysterious and expressive as the human body itself" (*Marxism and Form* [Princeton, 1971], p. 104).

21

The paradigm of the surrealist object in both its psychic-uncanny and social-outmoded registers might be the old toy (which some surrealists did collect). "The toys of all cultures were products, initially, of a cottage industry," Benjamin writes in a short text inspired by his brief 1926–1927 Moscow trip. "The spirit from which these products emanate—the entire process of their production and not merely its result—is alive for the child in the toy, and he naturally understands a primitively produced object much better than one deriving from a complicated industrial process" ("Russian Toys," in *Moscow Diary*, ed. Gary Smith [Cambridge, 1987]). Implicitly here again Benjamin opposes the magic of the toy to the fetishism of the commodity.

22

Roland Barthes, *Camera Lucida*, trans. Richard Howard (New York, 1981), p. 65.

23

Adorno, "Looking Back on Surrealism," p. 90.

24

Ernst Mandel, *Late Capitalism*, trans. Joris de Bres (London, 1975), pp. 120–121.

25

See Benjamin on the Aragon passage quoted below in PW 1215; also quoted in Buck-Morss, *The Origin of Negative Dialectics*, p. 159. Of course, the notion that a historical formation is known only at the moment of its eclipse runs throughout Hegel, Marx, and Benjamin.

26

Louis Aragon, *Le Paysan de Paris* (Paris, 1926), translated by Simon Watson Taylor as *Paris Peasant* (London, 1971), pp. 28–29; hereafter cited as P. This observation is hardly unique to Aragon in the surrealist milieu; in *Paris de nuit* (1933) Brassaï sees it as a basis of his photographic project: "Could I otherwise have torn these few images from the strange Parisian nights of the thirties before they sink into nothingness?"

27

Charles Baudelaire, "The Painter of Modern Life," in *The Painter of Modern Life and Other Essays*, trans. and ed. Jonathan Mayne (London, 1964), p. 13.

28

As suggested in chapter 5, just as the mechanical-commodified produces the out-moded, the outmoded articulates the mechanical-commodified. To Benjamin this was the purpose of the "ritual elements" that Baudelaire mixed with the modern effects in his poetry: to fathom the very loss of such structures of feeling ("On Some Motifs in Baudelaire," p. 181). This, too, is one of the functions of the surrealist outmoded: to register the psychic penetration of the mechanical-commodified in social life—and to resist it. "It is important to strengthen at all costs," Breton writes in "The Crisis of the Object" (1936), "the defenses that can resist the invasion of the feeling world by things men use more out of habit than necessity" ("Crise de l'objet," *Cahiers d'Art* 1–2 [Paris, 1936]).

29

Benjamin Péret, "Ruines: ruine des ruines," *Minotaure* 12–13 (May 1939), p. 58. In a sense Péret here extrapolates his concept of nature as an uncanny process of death rather than life (intimated in his short text "La Nature devore le progrès et le dépasse" published in *Minotaure* 10 [Winter 1937] and discussed in chapter 2).

30

Benjamin, "Paris—the Capital of the Nineteenth Century," p. 176; translation mod-ified. Benjamin refers this ruination to "the convulsions of the commodity economy." Might this lead to another form of convulsive beauty?

31

On this trope in Benjamin see Buck-Morss, *The Dialectics of Seeing*, pp. 58–77.

32

Albert Speer, quoted in Paul Virilio, *War and Cinema: the Logistics of Perception*, trans. Patrick Camiller (London, 1989), p. 55. Also see Speer, *Inside the Third Reich*, trans. Richard and Clara Winston (New York, 1970), pp. 66, 185. I return to the relation between surrealist and fascist (ab)uses of history below.

33

In the sense proposed by Fredric Jameson as "that moment in which the coexistence of various modes of production becomes visibly antagonistic, their contradictions moving to the very center of political, social, and historical life." See *The Political Unconscious: Narrative as a Socially Symbolic Act* (Ithaca, 1981), pp. 95–98.

34

Benjamin, PW 584; "N [Theoretics of Knowledge]," p. 13.

35

Marx, *The Eighteenth Brumaire of Louis Bonaparte*, in *Political Writings*, vol. 2 ("Surveys from Exile"), ed. David Fernbach (New York, 1974), p. 146. The attribution to Hegel is much disputed.

36

Marx, introduction to "Contribution to the Critique of Hegel's Philosophy of Right," as quoted by Benjamin, PW 583; "N [Theoretics of Knowledge]," p. 13.

37

On comedy as a rhetorical form see Northrop Frye, *Anatomy of Criticisms* (Princeton, 1957), pp. 163–185, and as a historical trope see Hayden White, *Metahistory: The Historical Imagination in Nineteenth-Century Europe* (Baltimore, 1973), pp. 94–97, 115–123, 167–169.

38

Breton, foreword to *La Femme 100 têtes* (1929). This definition of the surrealist image is close to the Benjaminian definition of the dialectical image: "It isn't that the past casts its light on the present or the present casts its light on the past; rather, an image is that in which the past and the now flash into a constellation. In other words, image is dialectic at a standstill" (PW 576–577; "N [Theoretics of Knowledge]," p. 7; also see PW 595/N, p. 24). However, the Bretonian definition, pledged to reconciliation, is hardly as dialectical.

39

Most of these enthusiasms hardly appear radical today: they revise the canon within given definitions of art, literature, and philosophy that are broadened but not breached, and they do not contest it at all in the name of oppressed subjects. Nevertheless, these lists surely struck contemporaries of surrealism as perverse historical fixations. The two principal lists are "Erutarettil" (or *Littérature* backwards) published in *Littérature* 11–12 (October 1923) and "Lisez/Ne Lisez Pas" printed on a 1931 catalogue of José Corti publications. (Other examples include the inquiry "Qui sont les meilleurs romanciers et poets méconnus de 1895 à 1914?" in *L'Éclair* [September 23, 1923], the list published by Ernst in *Beyond Painting*, as well as the pantheon noted in "Manifesto of Surrealism" [1924].) Some of the elect are to be expected: Sade, Hegel, Marx, Freud (who is sometimes replaced by Charcot), etc. More suggestive are the literary favorites, in particular the romantics, English gothics (e.g., Mathew Gregory Lewis, Ann Radcliffe, Edward Young), Poe, Baudelaire, Nerval, and, above all, Lautréamont and Rimbaud. Like the preferred artists of the surrealists (e.g., Bosch, Grünewald, Piranesi, Uccello, Fuseli, Goya, Moreau, Böcklin), most of these figures are taken as precursors of the fantastic, i.e., of a project to which (as noted) surrealism is committed: the reenchantment of a rationalized world.

40

Breton, *What Is Surrealism? Selected Writings,* ed. Franklin Rosemont (New York, 1978), p. 112–113.

41

"History is the subject of a structure whose site is not homogeneous empty time, but time filled by the presence of the now [*Jetztzeit*]" (Benjamin, "Theses on the Philosophy of History," p. 261). Another thesis allows us to think the Freudian concept of *Nachträglichkeit* or deferred action, associated with the surrealist concept of the image in chapter 3, in relation to the surrealist concept of the historical: "Historicism contents itself with establishing a causal connection between various moments in history. But no fact that is a cause is for that very reason historical. It became historical posthumously, as it were, through events that may be separated from it by thousands of years. A historian who takes this as his point of departure stops telling the sequence of events like the beads of a rosary. Instead, he grasps the constellation which his own era has formed with a definite earlier one. Thus he establishes a conception of the present as the 'time of the now' which is shot through with chips of Messianic time" (p. 263).

42

In *Entretiens* (Paris, 1952) Breton remarked of Lautréamont: "A great sign of the times seemed to us to reside in the fact that until that time his hour had not come, whereas for us it sounded with utmost clarity" (p. 48). Indeed, the discovery by Breton and Soupault of the last known copy of *Poésies* (1870) in the Biliothèque Nationale in 1918 (sometimes said to be 1919) is one of the foundational legends of surrealism.

43

"What is aura? A strange web of time and space: the unique appearance of a distance, however close at hand" (Benjamin, "A Short History of Photography" [1931], in Alan Trachtenberg, ed., *Classic Essays in Photography* [New Haven, 1980], p. 209. I develop this formulation further in chapter 7.

44

In *Late Capitalism* Mandel dates this wave from the crisis of 1847 to the beginning of the 1890s.

45

On this process see in particular T. J. Clark, *The Painting of Modern Life: Paris in the Art of Manet and His Followers* (New York, 1985), pp. 57–64.

46

Benjamin, PW 1002.

47

Giedion as cited by Benjamin, PW 494.

48

Ibid., p. 993.

49

Breton makes this allusion in his foreword to *La Femme 100 Têtes*. In this regard, just as Aragon paints the arcades as a "human aquarium" (P 28), so Ernst often depicts the interior as a feminine (sub)marine realm.

50

Dalí, "L'Ane pourri," *Le Surréalisme au service de la révolution* 1 (July 1930), translated by J. Bronowski as "The Stinking Ass" in *This Quarter* 5, no. 1 (September 1932), p. 54.

51

See Benjamin, "Paris—the Capital of the Nineteenth Century," p. 168.

52

Ibid., p. 159.

53

Dalí, "The Stinking Ass," p. 54.

54

As I have already alluded to Aragon in discussing the outmoded, I will focus on Ernst and Dalí here.

55

Aragon, *Je n'ai jamais appris à écrire,* quoted by Simon Watson Taylor in his introduction to *Paris Peasant,* p. 14. In *The Paintings of Modern Life* T. J. Clark uses a similar phrase, "the myth of modernity," in a different way: to demystify the political hegemony of the bourgeoisie that endures underneath the cultural surface of social mobility. I want to suggest that Aragon demystifies too—disenchants even as he reenchants.

56

For example, Aragon writes, "We are doubtless about to witness a complete upheaval of the established fashions in casual strolling and prostitution" (P 29). These transformations are minor but material (he also mentions the technique of shoeblacks, the look of stamps [P 82, 85]): they mark historical change in bodily memory.

57

Aragon, *La Peinture au défi* (Paris, 1930), translated by Lucy R. Lippard as "Challenge to Painting," in Lippard, ed., *Surrealists on Art* (Englewood Cliffs, N.J., 1970), p. 37.

58

Benjamin, "Surrealism," p. 179.

59

Sigfried Giedion, *Mechanization Takes Command: A Contribution to Anonymous History* (New York, 1948), pp. 361–362.

60

For the contextualization of psychoanalysis see (among others) Juliet Mitchell, *Psychoanalysis and Feminism* (London, 1974), pp. 419–435, and Stephen Toulmin and A. Janik, *Wittgenstein's Vienna* (New York, 1973).

61

See Werner Spies, "The Laws of Chance," in *Homage to Max Ernst* (New York, 1971), pp. 17–18. Also see Werner Hofmann, "Max Ernst and the Nineteenth Century," in the same volume.

62

Obvious enough, but not specific enough, as such desire is even more repressed in modernist architectures. See Anthony Vidler, "The Architecture of the Uncanny: The Unhomely Houses of the Romantic Sublime," *Assemblage* 3 (July 1987), p. 24.

63

I am indebted to Rosalind Krauss for this association.

———

64

Sometimes he makes this historical connection in his very materials. For example, his primal scene image in *La Femme 100 têtes* (see chapter 3 above) is constructed out of an 1883 illustration from the popular science magazine *La Nature* concerning the use of chronophotography in the capturing of hysterical symptoms at the Salpêtrière. See Albert Londe, "La Photographie en médecine," *La Nature* 522 (June 2, 1883), pp. 315–318. Londe was chief photographer at the Salpêtrière. (Thanks to Erica Wolf for her help on this source.) Appropriations of psychological illustrations are common in Ernst. See Werner Spies, *Max Ernst Collages,* trans. John William Gabriel (New York, 1991).

65

Letter of August 2, 1935 (to Benjamin), in *Aesthetics and Politics,* ed. Rodney Livingstone et al. (London, 1977), p. 112. Also see Adorno, *Kierkegaard: Construction of the Aesthetic* (1933), trans. Robert Hullot-Kentor (Minneapolis, 1989). Adorno relates this alienation to the social position of Kierkegaard as a *rentier* disconnected from the productive process.

66

Benjamin, "Paris—the Capital of the Nineteenth Century," pp. 167–168. This historicist eclecticism is no simple indication of decline; it can be read as a sign of mastery over both processes of signification and means of production. It also, of course, points to the expanded markets of imperialism.

67

Benjamin: "Since the days of Louis-Philippe the bourgeoisie has endeavored to compensate itself for the inconsequential nature of private life in the big city. It seeks such compensation within its four walls. Even if a bourgeois is unable to give his early being permanence, it seems to be a matter of honor with him to preserve the traces of his articles and requisites of daily use in perpetuity" ("The Paris of the Second Empire in Baudelaire," in *Charles Baudelaire: A Lyric Poet in the Era of High Capitalism,* p. 46). In *Mechanization Takes Command* (p. 365) Giedion notes that the stuffed interior, so marked in the Ernst collages, emerges with the new industrial bourgeoisie. In *The Railway Journey* (New York, 1977), p. 123, Wolfgang Schivelbusch in turn suggests that this stuffed interior served a psycho-physical function for the bourgeoisie: to soften the shocks of its own industrial order.

68

Giedion, *Mechanization Takes Command,* p. 8.

69

Ibid., p. 362.

70

Ibid., p. 361.

71

Letter of August 5, 1935 (to Benjamin), as cited by Benjamin in PW 582; "N [Theoretics of Knowledge]," p. 12.

72

Adorno: "Surrealism toppled the images of antiquity from their Platonic heaven. In Max Ernst's work they roam about like phantoms among the late 19th century middle class, for which art, neutralized in the form of a cultural heritage, had in fact become a ghost" (*Aesthetic Theory,* trans. C. Lenhardt [London, 1984], p. 415). I return to the feminization of these phantoms below.

73

Dalí, "The Stinking Ass," p. 54.

74

Dalí, "Objets surréalistes," *Le Surréalisme au service de la révolution* 3 (1931), translated by David Gascoyne as "The Object as Revealed in Surrealist Experiment," in *This Quarter* 5, no. 1 (September 1932), p. 198.

75

Benjamin, "Paris—the Capital of the Nineteenth Century," p. 168.

76

Dalí, "De la beauté terrifiante et comestible, de l'architecture modern'style" *Minotaure* 3–4 (1933), p. 71. He opposes "the ultra-decadent, civilized and European 'Modern Style'" to "savage objects," perhaps in part to scandalize the official taste for tribal art. See Dawn Ades, *Dalí and Surrealism* (New York, 1981), pp. 102–103.

77

In the article Dalí applies such terms directly to sculptural details in Gaudí buildings. Before him Charcot had suggested similar connections between hysteria and art nouveau. On this last point see Debora L. Silverman, *Art Nouveau in Fin-de-Siècle France* (Berkeley, 1990), pp. 91–106.

78

Dalí refers to art nouveau as "despised and neglected" in "The Stinking Ass" (p. 54). I return to this "repression" below.

79

Benjamin, "Paris—the Capital of the Nineteenth Century," p. 168.

80

Dalí, "De la beauté terrifiante," p. 76.

81

Dalí, "Derniers modes d'excitation intellectuelle pour l'été 1934," *Documents 34* (June 1934); significantly, this issue concludes with the *L'Amour fou* fragment "Equation de l'objet trouvé." Dalí sees anachronism in terms of trauma or "shocks" [*commotions*]: it marks us "in our flesh and in our memories"; it expresses "the terrifying white of the skinned bone of our own death."

82

Dalí, "De la beauté terrifiante," p. 73.

83

For an account of this part of his production see Ades, *Dalí and Surrealism,* pp. 168–169. "Avida Dollars" was the scornful nickname given Dalí by Breton.

84

In "Notes on Camp" (1964) Susan Sontag sees art nouveau as a favorite object of this sensibility, attracted as it is to the *démodé.* For Sontag camp is about aestheticization, androgynization, indeed any "theatricalization of experience" that hysterically disturbs distinctions of nature and culture, male and female, and so on. For this reason she refers it to gay culture, to the performance of gender, to "Being-as-Playing-a-Role." But this disturbance, she suggests, is finally more about dandyish duplicity than critical reversal: "Camp is the answer to the problem: how to be a dandy in the age of mass culture." See *Against Interpretation* (New York, 1968), pp. 275–292.

85

Robert Desnos, "Imagerie moderne," *Documents* 7 (December 1929), pp. 377–378.

86

Claude Lévi-Strauss, "New York in 1941" (1977), in *The View from Afar,* trans. Joachim Neugroschel and Phoebe Hoss (New York, 1985), pp. 258–267. Lévi-Strauss captures not only the aura but also the historicity of the outmoded: "As the relics and witnesses of an era that was already industrial, but in which economic pressures and the demands of mass production were not yet urgent and permitted a certain continuity of past forms and the existence of useless ornaments, these articles acquired an almost supernatural quality. They bear witness among us to the still real presence of a lost world. . . . Today all these objects [old kerosene lamps, outmoded old clothes, late nineteenth-century bric-à-brac] are avidly gathered in Parisian shops" (p. 263).

87

Several early surrealist associates (e.g., Drieu La Rochelle) became fascists or fascist sympathizers. On this connection see Alice Yaeger Kaplan, *Reproductions of Banality: Fascism, Literature, and French Intellectual Life* (Minneapolis, 1986).

88

Dalí, *Comment on devient Dalí,* as told to André Parinaud (Paris, 1973), translated as *The Unspeakable Confessions of Salvador Dalí* (London, 1976); and "Honneur à l'objet," *Cahiers d'Art* (Paris, 1936). In chapter 4 I pointed to a masochistic tendency, differently mediated, in fascism and surrealism alike.

89

The surrealist purging of Dalí on grounds of "counter-revolutionary actions involving the glorification of Hitlerian fascism" is recounted in Ades, *Dalí,* pp. 106–108.

90

In 1936, seven years after the surrealism essay, Benjamin wrote in "The Work of Art in the Age of Mechanical Reproduction" that "a number of outmoded concepts, such as creativity and genius, eternal value and mystery," must be "brush[ed] aside" (*Illuminations,* p. 218). Fascism had contaminated these values for him, and stronger measures than the surrealist outmoded were needed to resist it—though here too Benjamin was influenced by other practices, Brecht and productivism in particular. Together, these pressures drove him to overvalue the anti-auratic. He did so in order to advocate the emancipation of art from ritual. Ironically, this emancipation only delivered art to the stark alternative that Benjamin posed at the end of the essay: a politicization of art or an aestheticization of politics. In retrospect this was not much of an alternative by 1936. Even in the course of the essay Benjamin turns away from fascism in the position of ritual, only to confront it again in the position of spectacle.

91

Bloch, *Heritage of Our Times,* p. 97. The insight into the nonsynchronous, which Bloch might credit to surrealism too, is specific to its moment, which Gramsci

---

famously described as an interregnum full of morbid symptoms, and Bloch as a time "in decay and in labour at the same time" (p. 1).

92

Bloch, "Nonsynchronism," p. 31.

93

Ibid., p. 26.

94

Ibid., p. 36.

95

Ibid.

96

See, for example, Antonio Gramsci on "fossilization" in *Selections from the Prison Notebooks,* ed. and trans. Quintin Hoare and Geoffrey Nowell Smith (New York, 1971). His discussion of "Americanism and Fordism" (pp. 279–318) also thinks the dialectic of the mechanical-commodified and the outmoded but in ways very different from surrealism.

97

See Benjamin, "Surrealism," p. 189. Also Bloch in *Heritage of Our Times:* "Marxist *propaganda* lacks any *opposite land* to myth, any transformation of mythical beginnings into real ones, of Dionysian dreams into revolutionary ones. . . . The vulgar Marxists keep no watch over primitiveness and utopia, the National Socialists owe their seduction to them, it will not be the last. Both hell and heaven, berserkers and theology, have been surrendered without a fight to the forces of reaction" (p. 60). Shades of the present.

98

Bloch does precisely this in the short section "Hieroglyphs of the Nineteenth Century," in *Heritage of Our Times,* pp. 346–351.

99

Certain groups in the surrealist milieu attempted to address the same problems that fascism exploited—the nature of the sacred, the basis of the social in the sacrificial, the modern countertendency toward the atavistic—in an anthropological critique that, cognizant of the death drive, was not entirely bound to it: for example, the Collège de Sociologie formed around Bataille, Caillois, and Leiris. See *The College of Sociology,* ed. Denis Hollier, trans. Betsy Wing (Minneapolis, 1988).

100

In this sense, as Adorno (and others) remarked, fascism is indeed psychoanalysis in reverse.

101

Benjamin, PW 573; "N [Theoretics of Knowledge]," p. 4.

102

See Vidler, "The Architecture of the Uncanny," p. 24.

103

Once again Adorno is on target with his architectural allegory of this move: "The house has a tumor, its bay window. Surrealism paints this tumor: an excrescence of flesh grows from the house. Childhood images of the modern era are the quintessence of what the *Neue Sachlichkeit* makes taboo because it reminds it of its own object-like nature and its inability to cope with the fact that its rationality remains irrational" ("Looking Back on Surrealism," pp. 89–90).

104

See Griselda Pollock, "Modernity and the Spaces of Femininity," in *Vision and Difference* (London, 1988). As Pollock notes, some women (e.g., prostitutes) were allowed in public space, indeed were condemned to it; the public/private divide is also clearly a class divide. These other women, repressed from the interior, sometimes return to haunt it in Ernst.

105

As noted in chapter 2, Freud posed different conceptions of hysteria: among them, one in terms of the conversion of a repressed wish into a somatic sign through association, another in terms of the sexual confusion just described. As suggested in chapter 3, Ernst identifies with the hysteric precisely in this confusion—it is the essence of convulsive beauty for him.

7

———

AURATIC TRACES

1

"If psychoanalytic theory is correct in maintaining that every emotional affect, whatever its quality, is transformed by repression into a morbid anxiety, then among

———

such cases of anxiety there must be a class in which the anxiety can be shown to come from something repressed which *recurs*" (Freud, "The Uncanny," in *Studies in Parapsychology*, ed. Philip Rieff [New York, 1963], p. 47).

2

Walter Benjamin, "A Short History of Photography" (1931), trans. Phil Patton, in Alan Trachtenberg, ed., *Classic Essays on Photography* (New Haven, 1980), p. 209. Miriam Hansen develops the connection between aura and the uncanny brilliantly in "Benjamin, Cinema and Experience: 'The Blue Flower in the Land of Technology,'" *New German Critique* 40 (Winter 1987), pp. 179–224.

3

"Ego subjects itself to anxiety as a sort of innoculation" (Freud, *Inhibitions, Symptoms and Anxiety*, trans. Alix Strachey [New York, 1959], p. 88). For a helpful discussion of anxiety in Freud, see Samuel Weber, *The Legend of Freud* (Minneapolis, 1982), pp. 48–60.

4

Freud, *Inhibitions, Symptoms and Anxieties*, p. 81. For Freud the helplessness of the infant is *biological;* that of the immature subject confronted with sexuality *phylogenetic;* and that of the mature subject before an instinctual demand perceived as a danger *psychological.* By "phylogenetic" here Freud means to suggest that the period of latency in the sexual development of the subject recapitulates "the period of latency" experienced by the species in the ice age; the one interruption recalls the other. This "theory" was largely inspired by Sandor Ferenczi, *Thalassa: A Theory of Genitality* (1924). Incidentally, *The Trauma of Birth* was translated into French in 1928, and some surrealists had read it.

5

"Anxiety is the original reaction to helplessness in the trauma and is reproduced later on in the danger-situation as a signal for help. The ego, which experienced the trauma passively, now repeats it actively in a weakened version, in the hope of being able itself to direct its course" (ibid., pp. 92–93).

6

Benjamin also implies this in "The Work of Art in the Age of Mechanical Reproduction": "Man's need to expose himself to shock effects is his adjustment to the dangers threatening him" (*Illuminations*, ed. Hannah Arendt, trans. Harry Zohn [New York, 1977], p. 250). Again, any thorough theory of modernism must account for both registers of shock, the psychic and the social, as they are worked through in art—a project I intend to pursue.

7

The Freudian term for such signs is *Angstsignal,* and, as noted in chapter 2, Breton uses a similar term in *Nadja* (Paris, 1928; trans. Richard Howard [New York, 1960], p. 19; hereafter cited in the text as N). In a sense, *disponibilité* is a benign form of anxiety, since in anxiety as in *disponibilité* the object is not known but the danger is expected. Not incidentally, the surrealists retain the old trope of forest for feminine, and "forest of symbols" suggests again that this anxious array is feminized for the patriarchal subject.

8

Again, see Marleen Stoessel, *Aura, das vergessene Menschliche: Zu Sprache und Erfahrung bei Walter Benjamin* (Munich, 1983), as well as Hansen, "Benjamin, Cinema and Experience."

9

Benjamin, "A Short History of Photography," p. 209. This is not to say that this perception of the natural is not culturally coded and historically specific.

10

See Breton, "Langue des pierres," *Le Surréalisme, même* (Autumn 1957), pp. 12–14. Among the categories of the 1936 "Exposition surréaliste d'objets" were *objets naturels interpretés* and *objets naturels incorporés.* This concern with a sense inscribed in things seems indirectly posed against the (neo)classical grid of "words and things," as discussed by Michel Foucault in *Les Mots et les choses* (Paris, 1966).

11

Benjamin: "If we designate as aura the associations which, at home in the *mémoire involontaire,* tend to cluster around the object of a perception, then its analogue in the case of a utilitarian object is the experience which has left traces of the practiced hand" ("On Some Motifs in Baudelaire," in *Illuminations,* p. 186).

12

I use the parenthetical terms in order to suggest a possible correlation with the schema of anxiety mentioned in note 4.

13

Benjamin, "On Some Motifs in Baudelaire," p. 188.

14

Marx, *Capital,* vol. 1 (Harmondsworth, 1976), p. 165. Benjamin evokes the Marxist formulation more directly in another fragment of the *Passagen-Werk:* "Derivation of the aura as a projection of a social experience of people onto nature: the gaze is returned" ("Central Park," trans. Lloyd Spencer, *New German Critique* 34 [Winter 1985], p. 41). For a different inversion of the logic of the commodity also important to surrealism, see Marcel Mauss, *The Gift* (1925).

15

Brecht termed this aspect of Benjaminian aura "a rather ghastly mysticism" (*Arbeits-journal,* vol 1. [Frankfurt-am-Main, 1973], p. 16). Lukács was also less than convinced: "Allegorical personification has always concealed the fact that its function is not the personification of things, but rather to give the thing a more imposing form by getting it up as a person" ("On Walter Benjamin," *New Left Review* 110 [July–August 1978], p. 86).

16

Like the surrealists in this regard too, Benjamin projects this affect away from the psychic, as here when he refers to the prehistorical gaze of the stars rather than to the pre-Oedipal look of the mother: "Are not the stars with their distant gaze the *Urphänomen* of the aura?" (*Gesammelte Schriften,* ed. Rolf Tiedemann and Hermann Schweppenhauser [Frankfurt-am-Main, 1972] vol. 2, 3, 958). On this issue see Hansen, "Benjamin, Cinema and Experience," p. 214.

17

Hansen unpacks this uncanny paradox exactly: "Assimilated to an Oedipal economy, the memory of this imagined glance is likely to succumb to repression—and hence bound to return as distant and strange" (ibid., p. 215). The surrealists are even more ambivalent than Benjamin about this "patriarchal discourse on vision."

18

Benjamin, "On Some Motifs in Baudelaire," p. 188.

19

See *Totem and Taboo* (1913), trans. James Strachey (New York, 1950). For a reading of a modernist practice, that of David Smith, in terms of totemic "inapproachability," see Rosalind Krauss, *Passages in Modern Sculpture* (Cambridge, Mass., 1977), pp. 152–157, where she refers his interest in totemism to his surrealist beginnings.

20

A related set of affects is said to be produced by the evil eye, Medusa's head, Leonardo's *Mona Lisa,* etc.

21

Certainly the two concerns, surrealism and aura, are proximate in Benjamin: the essay on surrealism (1929) in which he develops the outmoded is not long followed by the essay on photography (1931) in which he develops the auratic.

22

Aragon, *Le Paysan de Paris* (Paris, 1926), translated by Simon Watson Taylor as *Paris Peasant* (London, 1971), pp. 128, 133; hereafter cited in the text as P. Aragon is close to Benjamin here: "The way I saw it, an object became transfigured: . . . it did not so much manifest an idea as constitute that very idea. Thus it extended deeply into the world's mass" (p. 128).

23

Dalí, "Objets surréalistes," *Le Surréalisme au service de la révolution* 3 (December 1931), translated in part as "The Object as Revealed in Surrealist Experiment," *This Quarter* (London), 5, no. 1 (September 1932), pp. 197–207. In this description we see again that the surrealist notion of the object is ambiguously connected to the Marxian concept of the commodity fetish.

24

Breton, *L'Amour fou* (Paris, 1937), translated by Mary Ann Caws as *Mad Love* (Lincoln, 1987), pp. 102–107; hereafter cited in the text as AF.

25

Benjamin, "On Some Motifs in Baudelaire," p. 190.

26

Paul Nougé, "Nouvelle Géographie élémentaire," *Variétés* (1929). Kraus is quoted by Benjamin in "On Some Motifs in Baudelaire," p. 200.

27

La Nature est un temple où de vivants piliers
Laissent parfois sortir de confuses paroles;
L'homme y passe à travers des forêts de symboles
Qui l'observent avec des regards familiers.

Comme de longs échos qui de loin se confondent
Dans une ténébreuse et profonde unité,

Vaste comme la nuit et comme la clarté,

Les parfums, les couleurs et les sons se répondent.

Baudelaire, "Correspondances," in *Les Fleurs du mal et autre poèmes* (Paris, 1964), pp. 39–40. I have used the translation that appears in Benjamin, "On Some Motifs in Baudelaire."

28

"Entretien avec Alberto Giacometti," in Georges Charbonnier, *Le Monologue du peintre* (Paris, 1959), p. 166.

29

Claude Lévi-Strauss, *The Way of the Masks,* trans. Sylvia Modelski (Seattle, 1982), pp. 5–7 (translation modified to conform to the above translation of "Correspondances"). This passage derives from a text on Northwest Coast art published in the *Gazette des Beaux-Arts* in 1943. As regards surrealist collections of tribal work see Philippe Peltier, "From Oceania," in William Rubin, ed., *"Primitivism" in 20th-Century Art: Affinity of the Tribal and the Modern* (New York, 1984), vol. 1, pp. 110–115.

30

Benjamin, "On Some Motifs in Baudelaire," p. 182.

31

In this regard, too, aura functions very much like anxiety.

32

Breton, *Signe ascendant* (Paris, 1947).

33

For Breton this was the importance of analogical thought. "The primordial ties are cut—ties that only *le ressort analogique* succeeds fleetingly in reestablishing." "I have experienced intellectual pleasure only in *le plan analogique*" (ibid.).

34

Freud, "The Uncanny," p. 51.

35

These two conceptions share a phenomenological base, but, as Miriam Hansen has stressed, they are fundamentally different: the gaze in Benjamin is temporalized, in Lacan spatialized, and the same is true of the two groups of surrealists. See Hansen, "Benjamin, Cinema and Experience," p. 216.

36

This is the term used by de Chirico in "Meditations of a Painter"; see chapter 3.

37

As I implied in chapter 3, perspectival space, repressed in high modernism, returns in surrealism in uncanny—distorted—form. Should we not see the breakdown of this system in high modernism as a crisis in patriarchal subjectivity rather than simply as a heroic breakthrough in pictorial convention?

38

Caillois, "Mimicry and Legendary Psychasthenia," *October* 31 (Winter 1984), p. 30. For Lacan see *The Four Fundamental Concepts of Psychoanalysis,* trans. Alan Sheridan (New York, 1977), pp. 67–119. Concerning the paranoid aspect of the Lacanian gaze, see Norman Bryson, "The Gaze in the Expanded Field," in Hal Foster, ed., *Vision and Visuality* (Seattle, 1988). For Bryson the subject of the Lacanian gaze is not dispossessed so much as remaindered: its very tenaciousness as a subject renders it "paranoid." In "Pynchon, Paranoia, and Literature" Leo Bersani argues somewhat differently that paranoia is a last guarantee of the subject (in *The Culture of Redemption* [Cambridge, 1990]).

39

As in the fascination with the veiled-erotic in Breton and the fantasy of the cave in Giacometti.

40

As suggested in chapter 6, this submarine trope concerns a surrealist association between repressing and submerging. Several Ernst interiors, for example, are submarine realms that are further associated with the feminine (the phrase "morass of dreams" is from his *Femme 100 Têtes*). Full of deluges and rescues as these interiors are, they beg to be read through the maternal redemption discussed by Freud in "A Special Type of Object Choice Made by Men" (1910). (Of course, a related association is active in Freud, most famously here: "Where id was, there ego shall be. It is a work of culture—not unlike the draining of the Zuider Zee." See *New Introductory Lectures on Psychoanalysis,* trans. James Strachey [New York, 1965], p. 71.) For the Baudelairean use of the subterranean trope, see Benjamin, "Paris—the Capital of the Nineteenth Century," in *Charles Baudelaire: A Lyric Poet in the Era of High Capitalism,* trans. Harry Zohn (London, 1973), p. 171.

41

Unlike Aragon, Breton would have the city be free of all signs of the historical—a repression that may partly produce its uncanniness. The subject of the surrealist city is too broad to be adequately treated here. For an introduction see Marie-Claire Bancquart, *Le Paris des surréalistes* (Paris, 1972).

42

Breton, *La Clé des champs* (Paris, 1953), pp. 282–283.

43

Hélène Cixous, "Fiction and Its Phantoms: A Reading of Freud's 'Das Unheimliche,'" *New Literary History* (Spring 1976), p. 543.

44

In this regard both the Palais idéal and *Les Vases communicants* are suggestive titles.

45

Tristan Tzara, "D'un certain automatisme du goût," *Minotaure* 3–4 (December 14, 1933).

46

Ibid. Note how the (self)destructive term is again projected away from surrealism—here to its modernist other. In a text published five years later in the same journal, Matta, who worked in the Le Corbusier office (of all places), rendered this program of an intrauterine architecture both more literal and more fantastic: "Man regrets the dark thrusts of his origins, which wrapped him in wet walls where blood was beating near the eye with the sound of the mother. . . . We must have walls like wet sheets that get out of shape and fit our psychological fears" ("Mathématique sensible, architecture du temps," *Minotaure* 11 [May 1938], p. 43). On these matters now see Anthony Vidler, "Homes for Cyborgs," in *The Architectural Uncanny* (Cambridge, 1992).

47

In *Dada, Surrealism, and Their Heritage* (New York, 1968), William Rubin sees the Minotaur as the "symbol of irrational impulses" and Theseus as the surrealist who probes the unconscious consciously (p. 127), a reading that reestablishes the very dichotomies that surrealism sought to overcome.

48

It is the prostitute who mediates these terms; this may be why she is such a fixated image in the surrealist unconscious.

49

Denis Hollier has grasped the surrealist function of the labyrinth exactly: "Neither father's work not maternal womb (neither human nor natural), the labyrinth is basically the space where oppositions disintegrate and grow complicated, where diacritical couples are unbalanced and perverted, etc., where the system upon which linguistic function is based disintegrates, but somehow disintegrates by itself, having jammed its own works. . . . Distance like proximity, separation like adhesion remain undecidable there. In this sense one is never either inside or outside the labyrinth— a space (perhaps that is already too much to say) that would be constituted by none other than this very anxiety, which is, however, incurably undecidable: am I inside or outside?" (*La Prise de la Concorde* [Paris, 1974], translated by Betsy Wing as *Against Architecture: The Writings of Georges Bataille* [Cambridge, 1989], p. 58).

50

This trope was also cherished by Benjamin. One of his legends concerns a revelatory map of his life doodled on a napkin at the Deux Magots—in the form of a labyrinth. Fatidically, this labyrinth was lost.

8

BEYOND THE SURREALISM PRINCIPLE?

1

This is not to suggest that desublimatory strategies are no longer effective—as many different feminist, gay and lesbian, and AIDS activists and artists can attest. It is to suggest that old associations of the instinctual with the feminine, the homosexual, the primitive, etc., be broken.

2

See my "Armor Fou," *October* 56 (Spring 1991). For a critique of this use of the psyche as a metaphor of the social, see Jacqueline Rose, "Sexuality and Vision: Some Questions," in Hal Foster, ed., *Vision and Visuality* (Seattle, 1988).

3

André Breton, *Entretiens* (Paris, 1952), p. 218; my italics.

4

J. G. Ballard, "Coming of the Unconscious," *New Worlds,* 164 (July 1966), reprinted in *Re/Search* 8/9 (1984), pp. 102–105. Also see Jonathan Crary, "Ballard and the Promiscuity of Forms," *Zone* 1/2 (1985).

5

Fredric Jameson, *Postmodernism, or the Cultural Logic of Late Capitalism* (Durham, 1991), p. 309. In fairness to Jameson, he elsewhere advances the critical possibilities of the nonsynchronous and the utopian.

6

Jean Baudrillard, *For a Critique of the Political Economy of the Sign,* trans. Charles Levin (St. Louis, 1981), p. 194. On this account surrealism may be the only outmoded thing left!

7

Breton, foreword to Max Ernst, *La Femme 100 têtes* (Paris, 1929).

8

Walter Benjamin, "Surrealism: The Last Snapshot of the European Intelligentsia" (1929), in *Reflections,* ed. Peter Demetz, trans. Edmund Jephcott (New York, 1978), p. 192.

Max Ernst, *La Femme 100 têtes,* 1929: "The might-have-been Immaculate Conception." © 1992 ARS, New York/SPADEM, Paris. *Page 77.*

Max Ernst, *The Master's Bedroom,* 1920. Overpainting. Werner Schindler Collection, Zurich. © 1992 ARS, New York/SPADEM, Paris. *Page 82.*

Max Ernst, *La Femme 100 têtes,* 1929: "Germinal, my sister, the hundred headless woman. (In the background, in the cage, the Eternal Father.)" © 1992 ARS, New York/SPADEM, Paris. *Page 85.*

Alberto Giacometti, *The Palace at 4 A.M.,* 1932–1933. Construction in wood, glass, wire, and string. The Museum of Modern Art, New York. © 1992 ARS, New York/ADAGP, Paris. *Page 86.*

Alberto Giacometti, "Objets mobiles et muets." Drawings in *Le Surréalisme au service de la révolution* 3 (December 1931). © 1992 ARS, New York/ADAGP, Paris. *Page 88.*

Alberto Giacometti, *Woman with Her Throat Cut,* 1932. Bronze. The Museum of Modern Art, New York. © 1992 ARS, New York/ADAGP, Paris. *Page 94.*

Hans Bellmer, *Doll,* 1935. Photograph. Manoukian Collection, Paris. © 1992 ARS, New York/ADAGP, Paris. *Page 100.*

Hans Bellmer, "Variations sur le montage d'une mineure articulée." Photographs of first *Doll* in *Minotaure* 6 (Winter 1934–1935). © 1992 ARS, New York/ADAGP, Paris. *Page 104.*

Hans Bellmer, illustration of mechanism of first *Doll* in *Die Puppe,* 1934. © 1992 ARS, New York/ADAGP, Paris. *Page 108.*

Hans Bellmer with first *Doll,* 1934. © 1992 ARS, New York/ADAGP, Paris. *Page 116.*

Arno Breker, *Readiness,* 1939. Bronze. *Page 117.*

Hans Bellmer, *Machine-Gunneress in a State of Grace,* 1937. Construction in wood and metal. The Museum of Modern Art, New York. © 1992 ARS, New York/ADAGP, Paris. *Page 121.*

Protection of Men. Suite of photographs in "Aboutissements de la mécanique," *Variétés* (January 15, 1930). *Page 124.*

Photographs of automatons and mannequins in Benjamin Péret, "Au paradis des fantômes," *Minotaure* 3–4 (December 14, 1933). *Page 132.*

Juxtaposition of photographs in *Variétés* (March 15, 1929). *Page 138.*

Juxtaposition of photographs in *Variétés* (October 15, 1929). *Page 139.*

Juxtaposition of photographs by Herbert Bayer and E. L. T. Mesens in *Variétés* (October 15, 1929). *Page 141.*

Anonymous photograph in *Variétés* (December 15, 1929). *Page 142.*

Juxtaposition of photographs in *Variétés* (January 15, 1930), with figures by Man Ray, Brancusi, and Sophie Taeuber-Arp. *Page 143.*

Suite of photographs titled "Aboutissements de la mécanique," *Variétés* (January 15, 1930). *Page 146.*

Max Ernst, *Self-Constructed Small Machine,* 1919. Pencil and rubbing from printer plates. Bergman Collection, Chicago. © 1992 ARS, New York/SPADEM, Paris. *Page 154.*

Raoul Ubac, *Fossil of the Eiffel Tower,* 1939. Photograph in *Minotaure* 12–13 (September 1939). *Page 156.*

Flea market at Saint-Ouen, Paris. Photograph in *Nadja*, 1928. *Page 160.*

Photograph of the Passage de l'Opéra, 1822–1935. From Johann Friedrich Geist, *Arcades: The History of a Building Type*. *Page 171.*

Max Ernst, *Une Semaine de bonté*, 1934. Collage. © 1992 ARS, New York/SPADEM, Paris. *Page 175.*

Max Ernst, *Une Semaine de bonté*, 1934. Collage. © 1992 ARS, New York/SPADEM, Paris. *Page 180.*

Max Ernst, *La Femme 100 têtes*, 1929: "The monkey who will be a policeman, a catholic, or a broker." © 1992 ARS, New York/SPADEM, Paris. *Page 181.*

Brassaï, photographs of Paris Métro details by Hector Guimard, commissioned by Salvador Dalí, in *Minotaure* 3–4 (December 14, 1933). *Page 184.*

Brassaï and Salvador Dalí, *Involuntary Sculptures*, 1933. Photo-text in *Minotaure* 3–4 (December 14, 1933). © 1992 DEMART PRO ARTE/ARS, New York. *Page 185.*

Brassaï, *The Statue of Marshal Ney in the Fog*, 1935. Photograph. © 1992 DEMART PRO ARTE/ARS, New York. *Page 192.*

Man Ray, Untitled, 1933. Photograph. © 1992 ARS, New York/ADAGP, Paris. *Page 205.*

Max Ernst, *Health through Sports*, c. 1920. Menil Collection, Houston. © 1992 ARS, New York/SPADEM, Paris. *Page 208.*

INDEX